S0-BAH-308

Sasanian Persia

INTERNATIONAL LIBRARY OF IRANIAN STUDIES

1. *Converting Persia: Religion and Power in the Safavid Empire*
Rula Abisaab
978 1 86064 9707

2. *Iran and the World in the Safavid Age*
Willem Floor and Edmund Herzig (eds)
978 1 85043 930 1

3. *Religion and Politics in Modern Iran: A Reader*
Lloyd Ridgeon
978 1 84511 073 4

4. *The Qajar Pact: Bargaining, Protest and the State in Nineteenth-Century Persia*
Vanessa Martin
978 1 85043 763 5

5. *The Fire, the Star and the Cross: Minority Religions in Medieval and Early Modern Iran*
Aptin Khanbaghi
978 1 84511 056 7

6. *Allopathy Goes Native: Traditional Versus Modern Medicine in Iran*
Agnes Loeffler
978 1 85043 942 4

7. *Iranian Cinema: A Political History*
Hamid Reza Sadr
978 1 84511 146 5

8. *Sasanian Persia: The Rise and Fall of an Empire*
Touraj Daryaee
978 1 85043 898 4

9. *In the Shadow of the King: Zill al-Sultan and Isfahan under the Qajars*
Heidi A. Walcher
978 1 85043 434 4

10. *Decline and Fall of the Sasanian Empire: The Sasanian-Parthian Confederacy and the Arab Conquest of Iran*
Parvaneh Pourshariati
978 1 84511 645 3

11. *The Forgotten Schools: The Baha'is and Modern Education in Iran, 1899–1934*
Soli Shahvar
978 1 84511 683 5

12. *Khatami's Iran: The Islamic Republic and the Turbulent Path to Reform*
Ghoncheh Tazmini
978 1 84511 594 4

13. *Revolutionary Ideology and Islamic Militancy: The Iranian Revolution and Interpretations of the Quran*
Najibullah Lafraie
978 1 84511 063 5

14. *Becoming Visible in Iran: Women in Contemporary Iranian Society*
Mehri Honarbin-Holliday
978 1 84511 878 5

15. *Tribeswomen of Iran: Weaving Memories among Qashqa'i Nomads*
Julia Huang
978 1 84511 832 7

16. *Islam and Dissent in Post-revolutionary Iran: Abdolkarim Soroush, Religious Politics and Democratic Reform*
Behrooz Ghamari-Tabrizi
978 1 84511 879 2

17. *Persia in Crisis: Safavid Decline and the Fall of Isfahan*
Rudi Matthee
978 1 84511 745 0

18. *Blogistan: The Internet and Politics in Iran*
A. Srebeny and G. Khiabany
978 1 84511 606 4

19. *Christian Encounters with Iran: Engaging Muslim Thinkers after the Revolution*
Sasan Tavassoli
978 1 84511 761 0

Touraj Daryaee is Howard C. Baskerville Professor in the history of Iran and the Persianate World and Associate Director of the Dr. Samuel M. Jordan Center for Persian Studies and Culture at the University of California, Irvine. He works on the history of ancient and early medieval Iran and is the editor of the International Journal of Ancient Iranian Studies.

'Touraj Daryaee synthesizes a new generation of Sasanian scholarship to present the first single volume study of such important history – important not only for understanding Iranian, but Roman and early Islamic histories as well. The author's erudition is very impressive and he masters complex sources with exemplary clarity.'

Gene Garthwaite, Professor of History, Dartmouth College, New Hampshire and Jane and Raphael Bernstein Professor of Asian Studies, Dartmouth College, New Hampshire

'Touraj Daryaee is a well-known scholar of Sasanian history and religious texts who knows the subject well and has published widely in his field. This will be a useful publication for scholars and those interested in Sasanian history.'

Vesta Sarkhosh Curtis, Curator, The British Museum

'Touraj Daryaee's *Sasanian Persia* is far more detailed than all previous work on the subject, with a multitude of new materials and sources. It is a masterpiece of research and will be the last word on Sasanian Iran in all of its aspects – from political history to religion, society and commerce.'

– *Richard N. Frye, Emeritus Professor of Iranian Studies, Harvard University*

'Touraj Daryaee, one of the most outstanding young scholars dealing with Sasanian history today, uses the utmost skill in order to shed light not only on the historical plot, but also on the administration and the economy of the Sasanian kingdom. His treatment of such subjects may be set as an example; this is a panoramic survey, concise, clear and "reader friendly" throughout.'

Ze'ev Rubin, Professor of Ancient History, University of Tel Aviv

Sasanian Persia

The Rise and Fall of an Empire

Touraj Daryaee

Published by I.B.Tauris & Co. Ltd in association with
the Iran Heritage Foundation

Reprinted twice in 2010 by I.B.Tauris & Co Ltd
6 Salem Road, London W2 4BU
175 Fifth Avenue, New York NY 10010
www.ibtauris.com

Distributed in the United States and Canada
Exclusively by Palgrave Macmillan
175 Fifth Avenue, New York NY 10010

First published in 2009 by. I.B.Tauris & Co Ltd

International Library of Iranian Studies, Vol. 8

ISBN: 978 1 85043 898 4

A full CIP record for this book is available from the British Library
A full CIP record is available from the Library of Congress

Library of Congress Catalog Card Number: available

Typeset in Baskerville by
Swales & Willis Ltd, Exeter, Devon

Printed and bound in Great Britain by
CPI Antony Rowe, Chippenham, Wiltshire

Contents

The author wishes to thank Mrs. Nastaran Akhavan
for her support in publication of this book,
made in memory of Jafar Akhavan

Acknowledgments

I owe much of what is contained in this book to my mentors and teachers, H.-P. Schmidt, M.G. Morony, C. Rapp, and M. Bates. I would like to thank friends and colleagues who have discussed the material with me or have guided me or given me material for the book. They include K. Abdi, S. Adhami, I. Afshar, D. Akbarzadeh, M. Alram, P. Andami, R.N. Frye, A. Gariboldi, R. Gyselen, K. Kamali-Sarvestani, A. Khatibi, A. Mousavi, M. Omidsalar, Z. Rubin, R. Shayegan, S. Solyemani, M. Stausberg, J.T. Walker and D. Whitcomb. I also have benefited from my students and teaching assistants, Katherine Martinez, Haleh Emrani, Khodadad Rezakhani and Warren Soward, as well as the constant support and discussions of the following people in my endeavor, M. Amanat, M. Behrooz, H.E. Chehabi, A. Matin-Asgari, and above all my mother, Mina Naraghi, to whom I dedicate this book.

My research for this book was supported by grants from California State University, Fullerton; American Institute of Iranian Studies; University of California, Irvine and through the generosity of my friend N. Rastegar.

Touraj Daryaee
University of California, Irvine

List of Plates

Located between Page 106 and 107

Prolegomena

The impetus for writing a history of the Sasanian Empire arose from the fact that there currently are no books on this period of Persian/Iranian history in the English language. The two parts of the third volume of *The Cambridge History of Iran*, edited by Ehsan Yarshater, not only deal with the Sasanians, but also with the Parthians. Richard Nelson Frye's two important books, the *Heritage of Persia*, and *The History of Ancient Iran* deal with the entire period of ancient Persian/Iranian history, where the Sasanians are covered in a chapter or two. Most recently, Josef Wiesehöfer's admirable book, *Ancient Persia* has again provided a complete review of the ancient Persian/Iranian history. Students of late antique history in the United States and Britain and other English speaking countries who deal with the Sasanian history are thus forced to consult either the classic work of Arthur Christensen *L'Iran sous le Sassanides* (1944) in French or Klaus Schippmann's *Grundzüge der Geschichte des sasanidischen Reiches* (1990) in German. This book was written to fill this gap.

As a graduate student at the University of California, Los Angeles, it was a mystery to me as to why no historian had attempted to provide a useful handbook covering Sasanian history, while it was one of the most important civilizations in late antiquity and the most powerful neighbor and nemesis of the Roman Empire. There are of course several obstacles to presenting a history of the Persian Empire in late antiquity. The linguistic challenge maybe one reason for why historians of this period do not deal with the Sasanians. Not only are documents and sources pertaining to this period of a varied nature, but they are also in different languages, making the mastery of all of them a daunting if not impossible task. One should also mention that those who deal with Iranian languages and archaeology have had a monopoly over ancient Persian history and only a few historians dedicate themselves to this field. This is clear from the meager number of positions occupied by historians of ancient Persia/Iran in universities across the world. Lastly, for historians who deal with antiquity, especially in the West, ancient Persia/Iran becomes only significant when they have to make a tangential reference to the enemies of the Greeks and Romans. One only has to look at the map of the ancient world to see this uneven and at times warped view of ancient historians. I believe that in order to understand the ancient world in the context of world history one has to not only know the Mediterranean world, but have a wider perspective and see how the different civilizations developed on their own as well as in interaction with one another. The center of the ancient world was not exclusively at Rome, unless historians of antiquity make it so. There were many centers, one being Ctesiphon, the capital of the Sasanian Empire rivaling Rome and Constantinople.

What I have done here is to provide the basic outlines of the history of the Sasanian civilization, where its history, society, religion, economy, administration, languages and literature are reviewed with an updated bibliography. Much of our perception in regard to the Sasanians has changed since the time of Christensen's book and it is time to take the first step and provide a history of late antique Persia/Iran. This would be of use not only for the students of Persian/Iranian history but also those of Rome, India and Central Asia. There will certainly be more books on this subject and period, but until then, it is hoped that this book guides those who are interested in the history of the Near East in late antiquity, a period which usually appears to draw a blank in many text books and historical horizons of not only lay but also professional historians.

Of course one must ask why the Sasanians are important. Briefly put, the Persian Empire which came to being in the third century CE to the seventh century CE established the first post-Hellenic civilization on an imperial scale in the Near East. This empire then interacted and influenced India and Central Asia to the East and the Levant and the Eastern Mediterranean to the West. It was also an influence on the Arabian Peninsula in the south as well as the Caspian region to the north. Sasanian cultural and economic influence was felt from the Persian Gulf to the Yellow Sea and on the Silk Road. Its values and traditions, such as ethical dualism, an imperial vision in the unity of the world, came to exercise an important influence in world history. Regionally, the Sasanian Empire was a unification of the Iranian and Mesopotamian core civilizations which was so potent that when Islam entered the picture, it had no other choice but to follow the Sasanian model in many respects. Scholars suggest that the Abbasid caliphate was in many ways a revival of the Sasanian Empire. I too hold to this belief. As for Iranian history, the Sasanians were the dynasty which shaped some of the important ideas and mores of the Persianate society from Tajikistan to modern-day Iraq. In a way the Sasanians made the Persian worldview and civilization take hold over what later Marshal G. Hodgson termed the Perso-Islamicate world. As much as Islam may have shaped the Persiante world in the later period, the Sasanians first established the foundations of an Islamicate civilization. For Iran, the very idea of Iran and the name given to the territory is a Sasanian invention which lasts in the minds of people and in the Persian literary tradition till today.

Chapter 1 presents an overview of Sasanian political history on its own, rather than a political history of Iran from the perspective of Rome, from 200–700 CE. As it will become apparent, different sets of sources make themselves useful for the beginning, middle and later Sasanian periods. In fact this is a historiographical issue with which scholars still grapple: the matter of the effectiveness of a late literary source for the early Sasanian history. For example, Tabarī provides a nice narrative of Sasanian history based on one or a series of older sources which go back to the Sasanian royal chronicle, the *Xwadāy-nāmag* "Book of Lords," or "Book of Kings." The problem with using such a source for early or perhaps even middle Sasanian history is that the work that we hold in hand is a ninth-century work in Arabic, by a Muslim, in a different cultural setting. Tabrī's sources were mostly in Arabic which was then based on Middle Persian sources written some two or three centuries earlier. These Middle Persian sources, especially the *Xwadāy-nāmag*, were put in their complete form during the time of Xusrō I, also known as *anūšag-ruwān* "Immortal Soul", in the sixth century CE. Because of the political and social problems just before and during his early reign, Xusrō I very much manipulated the past to justify his reforms. Thus, a reformulation of early and middle Sasanian history took place at the Sasanian court to fit the world-view and aims and aspirations of this great monarch. Consequently, older accounts were re-written to fit the new Sasanian ideology that had formed in the sixth century CE.

Then how useful would Tabarī be for us in studying the third, fourth or even fifth century CE Sasanian Empire? The obvious answer at first would be: not much. How could we trust such a source? But the issue is much more complicated than that. For one thing, while we have more and divergent sources for the third century, such as the Middle Persian royal inscriptions, Roman sources, and Armenian historical tradition, for the fourth and especially fifth century there is little evidence and few sources. Do we stay silent for the fifth century and make do with what we have, which is very little, or try, according to historians, to do a reading against the grain? At this point, material culture, specifically coins and seals and bullae (seal impression on clay) become important as alternative sources. But each of these sources provides us with only specific information on aspects of Sasanian civilization. Thus, again we have to go back to Tabarī and by comparing the existing alternative sources (Roman, Armenian, and Syriac accounts, Sasanian inscriptions, coins, archaeological reports and even later Persian sources) come to a better use of Tabarī's very important text. This is why Tabarī and sources like his can not be used throughout the text, but appear more important in the second half of the chapter on political history. The same could be said for the other Arabic and Persian histories, in that they are very important for post fifth-century Iran.

In the same vein, Middle Persian inscriptions which provide us with Sasanian and Iranian mores, values and outlook, albeit it from an imperial world-view, become essential for the third century and partly for the fourth century. Then suddenly for the fifth century, numismatics or the study of coins, along with Armenian, Roman, Syriac sources gain in importance. However, there is another kind of problem with these sources. Armenians who shared much, both culturally and religiously, with Iran before the fourth century suddenly turn to Christianity and the struggle between the Zoroastrian Armenians and Iranians with those of the newly adopted Christian faith plays out in much of late antique history. The Armenian historiographical tradition thereafter is very much colored by a Christian world-view, where anything before is considered pagan. Those Armenians or Armenian noble houses who conspired with the Sasanians and their co-religionists are naturally deemed evil, while those who fought for Christ against the Zoroastrians are the beneficent ones. One then could not be surprised that most of the Sasanian kings and their ministers or the Zoroastrian magi are seen as aggressive pagan figures coming to destroy the religion and way of life of the Armenian people. Still, the Armenian texts betray the realities of the third century and onwards (again reading against the grain), in that they display the Armeno-Iranian world-view and the importance of Zoroastrianism in the region and the important institutions and offices that existed in both kingdoms. The Armenian sources also give us a different perspective on the Iranian–Roman conflict and movement in Mesopotamia and the Caucuses and the effect of such dealings on the region. The Syriac sources are also similar in outlook with the exception that there is no Syriac nation or kingdom and so it is religion and language that makes its imprint. Notices on political, social and religious history of Sasanian Empire are gleaned from these Syriac sources, albeit from a Christian perspective. In some of these sources the king is good, the magi bad and the Zoroastrian turned Christian, or the pious virgin becomes martyred for the faith. If one is able to get through these literary topoi, one can find useful details about life in late antiquity Iran.

The Roman sources, in both Greek and Latin are also important, but they are generally hostile. In the third century, the conflict is political. The Romans from Rome have ended up in Mesopotamia (from one continent to another), but raise the alarm of the "Persian or Iranian threat," something that we see also in the contemporary American empire, half way around the world. These sources supposed that the Iranians should fold and just give in on their own sovereignty and leave the workings of their region to the other "empire," because might makes right! From the mid fourth-century CE, things become even more complicated and some of the sources even more hostile, as the Roman Empire gravitates towards Christianity. Fourth century sources such as Ammianus Marcellinus who has much to say about the Sasanians, still use old stereotypes of the Persians from other sources. Still Ammianus lived in a time where he saw Persians in action and was privy to their manner and war capabilities. His observations on the Sasanian army perhaps are most useful. With the coming of Christianity there is then both political and religious tension between the two empires. Take, for example, Agathias, an important sixth-century historian. He was able to go to Ctesiphon and had access to the Sasanian royal archive through a friend. But Agathias is wholly hostile to the Iranians and the Sasanian Empire and he rarely has anything nice to say about them. It is as if we are reading Procopius' *Secret History*, but the title is changed and has become Agathias' *Secret History*, and not about Justinian and Theodora, but about Ardaxšīr I, Xusrō I and their ancestors and practices. Still such sources are of importance and by brushing aside the usual topoi, the anti-Persian bias, self-aggrandizement and sense of superiority, we gain some detailed information on the Sasanians and their relations with the Romans. These are some of the problems encountered when dealing with the political and textual history of the Sasanian Empire.

Chapter 2 surveys the religions of the Sasanian Empire. I intentionally use the plural in that we are conditioned to view ancient Iran as only Zoroastrian. It is true that the basis of Iranian psyche and world-view was and is shaped by Zoroastrianism, but other religions were also in existence and had an impact upon Sasanian policies and religious view. The Sasanians were certainly Mazda worshippers and created a view of Zoroastrianism that was to be the foundation of the Zoroastrian tradition until recent times. But others, such as Jewish Persians also were part of this society and were recognized and usually honored by the King of Kings. The Reš-galūt, the leader of the Jewish community in exile interacted with the government and represented his community. Jews participated in government and owned land and slaves, just like non-Jewish Iranian subjects of the king. The Jewish leadership made alliances with the Zoroastrian nobility and kings through marriage, thus creating Jewish-Persian kings in Sasanian Iran. Of course this depends on from which community one views such an alliance, Jewish or Zoroastrian. How this affected the Christian community is a difficult question to answer, but by the fifth century CE a Christian Persian church was also established, with the Catholicos residing at Ctesiphon as well. Unlike the Jews, the Christian proselytes ran into more trouble with the Zoroastrian Magi, the government, and the king who tried to keep peace and order in the empire. Social and religious strife was detrimental to the well-being of the empire. By the fifth century, however it had become apparent that Christianity was an important and growing religion, whether the king wished it or not, and so it was decided to co-opt it into the religious world of Sasanian Iran. By creating a Persian-Christian church under the control of the King of Kings, the growing number of Christians came under the control of the empire. This also served to diffuse the Christian Roman propaganda which had caused religious strife and tension in the Sasanian Empire. From then on, the Roman Emperor was not the only leader of the Christians in the *oikumene*; rather there were two, the second being the King of Kings at Ctesiphon.

Manichaeism is the other important religious tradition whose similar universalistic tendencies, like all universalistic religions, ran into trouble after an initial success. The religion of Mani and the Gnostic tradition, I believe, is of great importance in the history of Iranian tradition. It has impacted upon Iran in ways that we are still trying to identify, even in the Islamic period. But there are no Manicheans here today to push their case and cause. Manichaeism died out in the fourteenth century in Central Asia. Still, Manichaeans lived in and around the Sasanian Empire and influenced the religious tradition of the empire.

What are our sources? As for Zoroastrianism, the most important of the traditions for the Sasanian period, we are blessed with inscriptions of the third century Zoroastrian priest Kerdīr who pushed for an "orthodoxy" in the third century CE. Zoroastrian Middle Persian texts, mainly from the late Sasanian and early Islamic period are our most important sources, along with non-Zoroastrian observations on Sasanian Zoroastrianism. Interestingly, seals and bullae also provide evidence of Zoroastrian and other religious traditions as well. The slogans and depiction of religious devices all tell us about dress, gestures, slogans, beliefs, reliefs and onomastic issues. Other devices such as magic bowls and prayer amulets provide us with another view of religion in the Sasanian empire, in that they demonstrate a less isolated and a more interactive and popular religious tradition in Sasanian Empire.

Chapter 3 deals with the much neglected economic history of the Sasanian Empire. When historians of the ancient world discuss "ancient" economy, they only think of Greece and Rome, in similar ways to which ancient Persian/Iranian history is omitted from most history departments and is placed in department of Near Eastern Languages and Cultures or Civilization. This is a tacit statement in the North American academic setting that beside the Greeks and the Romans, other people do not have history, that Iranians/Persians are another group of "people without history," but they do possess languages and culture (which for the Greeks and the Romans obviously is done in the "Classics" department). We have ample sources for Sasanian economic history, but they are not textual, rather more material. Again coins, seals, archaeological excavations along with disparate textual references, both foreign and in Iranian languages provide us with information on the Iranian economy. The recent finds of Middle Persian documents from the central Iranian Plateau and the Bactrian documents from the eastern Iranian world which are now published by N. Sims-Williams will provide us with a new view of the economic history of the period. The Middle Persian parchments still await translation and are not accessible to scholars. But horde (coins found in jars) finds within and outside of the Sasanian Empire tell us about Sasanian monetary circulation and the importance of the Sasanian coins in the international economy of Asia.

Chapter 4 is concerned with Sasanian society, another difficult subject to tackle. The reason for this is that our sources are usually late and tend to reflect on the past. The other issue is how to construct or imagine Persian/Iranian Society in the Sasanian period? I have given a standard class-structured division of the society as the Sasanians themselves wished it to be presented. That is, I let the Sasanian Middle Persian texts themselves tell us how the society was. Once this idyllic view is presented, then the more difficult task of deconstructing it and providing a closer picture to social reality is attempted. As texts and histories need to deal with both genders, I have provided a section on women. We must remember that the texts are male-centric, religious and provide a man's ideal view of women. This is of course not the reality and one has to seek avenues of providing alternative sources to challenge such a scheme. Also, the poor and the downtrodden did not sit idle, but and rose up, protested and were put down. One has to remember that for the Sasanians as most empires, order was the most important thing, because in their minds it brought prosperity for all.

The final chapter deals with texts and languages of the Sasanian Empire. I hope that the reader understands that the Sasanian society, as in today's Iran, was an empire with multiple groups of people speaking different languages, some of them related, who have left us diverse literary accounts. The chapter may read like a menu of languages and texts, but even so we lack such a menu in its entirety. My lack of sophistication in literary theory also may be the main culprit. However, I have tried to be more imaginative and inquisitive than the existing menus on Middle Persian in existence.

Still, this book is a prolegomena, like this chapter, for Sasanian history and civilization and I intend to deal with the various aspects of what I discuss in this work in the near future. The study of the Sasanian Empire is so neglected that I believe any work on any aspect of this civilization is useful. For the critics of this view, I use Shapur I's statement in the Hājjiābad inscription, about his shooting skill and that of others, as an analogy: "Now whoever may be strong of arm, let them put their foot in this cleft on this rock and let them shoot an arrow towards that cairn. Then whoever cast an arrow as far as that cairn, they are indeed strong of arm."

Touraj Daryaee
University of California, Irvine

Chapter 1

The Political History of *Iran* and *an-Iran*[1]

IRAN BEFORE THE SASANIANS

The Achaemenid Empire had made the Persians the dominant power in the known world from the sixth to the fourth centuries BCE. This fact usually escapes us, as we in the West have been so infatuated with Greece and the cluster of islands which surround it in antiquity. This Persian dominance in a sense meant the unification of the three major river civilizations, those of Egypt, Mesopotamia and India. This interaction brought various religious, technological and political ideas together and brought the world into a new phase of its existence under Persian rule. For examples those who worshipped Humban, the great Elamite deity, learned about Ahuramazda, the Zoroastrian deity par excellence, and the followers of Ahuramazda learned about Marduk, who sat at the head of the Mesopotamian deities. The Hebrews, the ethical monotheists, came into contact with the Zoroastrians and a fruitful period of interaction began which left its mark on beliefs of all sides. This interaction no doubt took place in an atmosphere of tolerance which the world had rarely seen and was to be a lesson for the succeeding Greco-Macedonian armies and the period known as the Hellenistic Age.

In the fourth century BCE, Alexander was able to conquer the Satrapies of the Persian Empire. Even in this Greco-Macedonian venture, one can see Alexander not as a foreign conqueror, but as someone who attempted to justify his conquest by claiming to be the rightful heir to the Persian throne. As his conquests took him to the heart of Persia, he began to adopt Persian customs, partake in the ceremonies of the Magi and marry Persian princesses to symbolically continue the royal Acahemenid line. For Persia, to follow P. Briant's view, Alexander was only the last of the Achaemenid rulers. Now the

Greco-Macedonians had become part of an already existing world order whose new masters they had become.

Alexander did not live to see the fruits of his conquests and died in Babylonia, leaving his generals squabbling over the spoils. One of his generals, Seleucus (312–308 BCE), was able to establish the Seleucid Dynasty in Persia. This dynasty only nominally controlled the Iranian Plateau and by 250 BCE there already were signs of weakness and fragmentation. At this time Greco-Macedonian colonies had been established on the Iranian Plateau, but soon these conquerors were subsumed by Persian culture and only a few held out in garrisons. We are not sure of the local population's reaction to these political events, but if the Zoroastrian literature is of any measure, Alexander and his motley group of conquerors were seen as wicked, coming from the seed of the demon of Wrath who had ravaged the earth, killed the Magi, and destroyed the Mazda-worshiping religion. Only then, Alexander ran off to that dark, stinky place which the Zoroastrians knew as the House of Worst Existence, i.e., Hell.

By 238 BCE the Arsacids had invaded the eastern Iranian Plateau and a new dynasty, mindful of both the Persian and Greco-Macedonian heritage, was established. The Arsacids in time gravitated more and more towards Persian culture and adopted the ideas and ideals of the old Persian rulers. We are ill informed about the province of Persis (Fars), the heartland of the Persians, but based on the meager evidence, it can be said that they were semi-autonomous and remembered much of their old tradition. The local rulers, the *frataraka*,[2] whose coinage demonstrate their respect for the past, ruled the area. They were followed by other local rulers who also minted coins in their own name and came to be known as the kings of Persis. By the beginning of the third century CE, for reasons unknown, there was an effort by a local Persian family known as *Sasan* to expand their power far beyond its locality of the city of Istakhr. Then a favorite son of Persis, named Ardashir (reminding us of the Achaemenid throne name Artaxerxes and of course the more recent Persis king Ardashir/Ardaxšahr) changed the course of history again.

ARDASHIR I AND THE ESTABLISHMENT OF THE SASANIAN EMPIRE

Ardashir I was able to defeat Ardawan (Artabanus IV) at the plain of Hormozgan in 224 CE and established the Sasanian Empire.[3] From then on, Ardashir took the title of *šāhān šāh* "King of Kings" and began the conquest of a territory which would be called *Iranshahr* (*Ērānšahr*). But before this fateful battle between the last Arsacid king and the institutor of the Sasanian dynasty, much had happened internally and externally in order for this new dynasty to come to power. To the west, the Roman Empire was going through one of its worst centuries, an anxious period, when its future seemed unsure. Roman armies whose allegiance lay with their generals brought chaos to the empire and one "Barrack Emperor" followed another, with some ruling for a very short time. During Caracalla's rule the empire was ruled by religious fanatics and imbued with civil strife. Ardawan IV had held his own fighting Caracalla and the Romans close to Nisibis in 217 CE. A treaty in 218 CE brought a monetary settlement and kept most of Mesopotamia in the hands of the Arsacids. The next two emperors, Elagabalus (218–222 CE) and Alexander Severus (222–235 CE) were faced with their own internal problems, preventing them from making the Arsacids and then the Sasanians their sole priority.

While Ardawan was able to repel the Romans, internally he had been challenged by Balash (Vologases VI) who minted coins in his own name until 221–222 CE, demonstrating the fact that the issue of an all-powerful King of Kings had not been settled in the Arsacid Empire.[4] So it would not seem amazing that a local warrior and his family in the province of Persis was able to rise and begin conquering the surrounding territories in a short time. Ardawan had bigger problems and could not turn his attention to a minor upstart in Persis.

The Sasanian campaign in controlling the province of Persis began in 205–206 CE, when the father of Ardashir I, Pabag[5] dethroned the local ruler of Istakhr, by the name of Gozihr, from the Bazrangid family. According to the sources, Pabag was a priest of the fire-temple of Anahid at the city of Istakhr and this must have been a stage for the rallying of the local Persian warriors who were devoted to the cult of this deity.[6] Anahid is important, since she is an object of devotion in the Zoroastrian sacred text, the *Avesta*, (see Yasht V or the *Aban Yasht*) by heroes, warriors and kings. During the Achaemenid period, in the beginning of the fifth century BCE, Artaxerxes II also worshipped Anahid (Anahita) along with Mihr (Mithra) and Ohrmazd (Ahura Mazda). Thus, her cult must have been an old one in Persis and the temple may have served as a location where the Persian tradition was kept alive. Anahita's warlike character was the symbiosis of ancient Near Eastern (Ishtar), Hellenic (Athena/Anaitis) and Iranian tradition which provided legitimacy for kingship in the Sasanian period.[7]

Pabag had envisaged his eldest son, Shabuhr, as his heir since we have coins representing both Shabuhr and his father. Nevertheless,

Shabuhr died under mysterious circumstances. On these coins the obverse has the legend *bgy šhpwhly MLK'* "(His) Majesty, king Shabuhr" and the reverse *BRH bgy p'pky MLK'* "son of (His) Majesty, king Pabag."[8] Ardashir and his followers seem to be the culprits who benefited the most out of this "accidental death," but that cannot be proved for certain. If the graffiti at Persepolis is an accurate portrayal of Pabag and his son Shabuhr, one can make several assumptions. One is that the Sasanians were becoming or had become a family that held both secular and religious power in Persis. Second, the cult of fire, which is very much an idea connected with Zoroastrianism, was alive before Ardashir came to power.[9] Third, the proximity of the graffiti of Pabag and Shabuhr to the Achaemenid structures suggests that these monuments were important for the Sasanians. We may assume that after the death of Shabuhr, Ardashir became the next heir and began to complete the conquest of Persis and beyond. By this time Ardawan IV had become alarmed, but neither the forces sent nor the army under his direct command were able to defeat Ardashir. Walakhash/Balash, the Parthian challenger to Ardawan IV in Mesopotamia, outlived the Parthian king, but he was the next victim of Ardashir in 229 CE. By this time most of the Iranian Plateau[10] and the Arab[11] side of the Persian Gulf had become part of his empire.[12]

In his invasion of Armenia,[13] Syria and Cappadocia, Ardashir came into conflict with Rome and Emperor Alexander Severus (222–235 CE).[14] In a letter to Ardashir, Alexander Severus had made it clear that his invasion of the Roman Empire would not be as successful as his conquest of his other neighbors.[15] While Severus was alive, neither Ardashir nor the Romans were able to defeat one another (wars of 231–233 CE).[16] However, once Severus died in 235 CE, Mesopotamia, Dura, Carrhae, Nisbis and finally Hatra were invaded by the Sasanians.[17] Ardashir then retired and spent the last years of his life in Persis while his son, Shabuhr I who had taken part in the 240 CE campaign, continued his conquests and the expansion of the empire. One might ask why Ardashir had taken on these campaigns against the Romans? This was probably due to the fact that the stable borders between the two empires of Rome and Parthia had previously been Oshroene, Hatra, and Armenia, but Severus had conquered Oshroene which put the heartland of the Arsacid and later Sasanian dynasty in danger.[18]

We should say more about Ardashir, since he is an important personage in the development of the Sasanian outlook and imperial ideology. The material remains of his rule are especially rich in providing us with his world-view. In commemoration of his victory, he commissioned several rock-reliefs at Firouzabad, Naqsh-i Rajab and Naqsh-i Rustam. At Naqsh-i Rustam, he is shown on his horse standing over the dead body of Ardawan. Ohrmazd faces him on a horse as well, standing over the body of the evil spirit Ahreman, and is handing the symbol of sovereignty to Ardashir I.[19] This relief demonstrates that Ardashir believed or wanted others to believe that he was appointed by God to rule over a territory which the inscriptions call *Iranshahr* (realm of the Iranians/Ayrans) and the people *Ērān* (Iranians). The name used for this territory had precedence in the *Avesta* and designated the mythical homeland of the Aryans, now transposed onto the region where the Sasanians were ruling.[20] This idea was to be accepted by the Zoroastrian and non-Zoroastrian population of the empire and lived on in the collective memory of Persians in various stages and among the various strata of Iranian society and governments till modern times.[21] This idea should not be mistaken for the Classical historian's testimonies, relaying that Ardashir was attempting to regain the Achaemenid Persian territory.[22] What is clear is that a notion of what *Iranshahr* meant was present in the religious sphere, which may have given rise to political concepts of a set territory. This is gained from the third century inscription(s) of the Zoroastrian priest Kerdir who tells us what was considered to be *Iranshahr* and what was considered to be *an-Ērān* or "non-Iranian" lands. Kerdir tells us that he established many fires and priests in *Iranshahr,* which according to him were the following provinces: Persis, Parthia, Babylonia, Mesene, Adiabene, Azerbaijan, Isfahan, Ray, Kerman, Sistan, and Gurgan, to Peshavar. Kerdir tells us that Syria, Cilicia, Armenia, Georgia, Albania and Balasgan which were under Sasanian control were deemed as *an-Ērān.*[23] This term is also used in an adjectival form, giving *Ērīh* "Iranianess," and an antonym, *an-Ērīh* which may be equivalent to the ancient Greek concept of *barbaroi* along with all its cultural trappings.

Ardashir's coins[24] also bear a standard formula which the succeeding kings in the third and the fourth centuries adopted: *mazdysn bgy ... MLK'n MLK' 'yl'n MNW ctry MN yzd'n* "Mazdaean Majesty, [name of the king], King of Kings of *Ērān,* whose lineage (is) from the gods."[25] According to this legend, Ardashir considered himself a worshiper of Mazda (Ohrmazd) "*mazdysn*" first and above all.[26] Second, he saw himself of divine descent: "*MNW ctry MN yzd'n.*" This of course brings us to the question of from whom did he believe he was descended? Which "gods" were his forefathers? The eponym of the dynasty, i.e., *Sasan* is clearly important to this question. It was thought that the epigraphic form *ssn*, which appeared on certain Parthian ostraca and other documents, designated *Sasan* as a Zoroastrian deity, although he was not mentioned in the *Avesta* or the Old Persian material.[27] Recently, Martin Schwartz has suggested that the deity mentioned on the ostraca has nothing to do with *Sasan*, but represented *Sesen*, an old Semitic god which is found in Ugaraitic as early as the second millennium BCE.[28] Be that as it may, in the first century CE, in Taxila we find coins with the name of *Sasa* which may be connected with *Sasan* because the emblem on the coin matches those on the coat-of-arms for Shabuhr I.[29] The Persian epic, the *Shahnameh* of Ferdowsi, also mentions an eastern connection for *Sasan* which leads us to believe that this family may have come from the east. Still, despite this difficulty and confusion, we can state that Ardashir saw himself as the descendent of the gods, "*yazdān*," and the Sasanians may have elevated *Sasan* to divine status.[30] It is altogether possible that this idea was part of the Hellenic past of Iran. Alexander the Great and the Seleucids considered themselves descendants of *theos* "god" and more importantly *epiphanies*, "god-made-manifests," which matches that of *MNW ctry MN yzd'n* of the early Sasanian inscriptions.[31] The artistic elements in early Sasanian period may also corroborate this suggestion, as the image of Ohrmzad and Ardashir I are similar in Naqsh-i Rustam and other early rock-reliefs.[32]

SHABUHR I AND WAR WITH ROME

Ardashir's son, Shabuhr I had become his co-regent in 240 CE. This is apparent from a coinage which portrays both men together, and was probably ordered by Ardashir to ensure a safe succession. This was because there were other sons of his who had been given governorship of other provinces, and they might have wanted to assume the throne, just as he had done in his youth. This system is characteristic of the Sasanians, under whom sons were sent to rule different provinces and when the ruler died, one of the heirs would assume the throne. In this manner, there was always a danger of dynastic squabbling, of which the Sasanians had their fair share. The method of succession was initially based on the choice of the preceding king, but later the nobility and the Zoroastrian priests assumed the decision.[33] Shabuhr I did accompany his father in battle, which made him battle ready and in fact ensured his success in wars against Rome. In 243 CE, Gordian invaded Mesopotamia to retrieve what had been taken by Ardashir and his son after Alexander Severus' death. But Shabuhr tells us (according to ŠKZ) that he was able to kill him at Misikhe in 244 CE, close to the Euphrates river which he later called Peroz-Shabuhr (Victorious is Shabuhr).[34] It is now known that Gordian had died in Zaitha in northern Mesopotamia in 244 CE at a time when warfare between the two sides seemed unlikely.[35] Thus, it is suggested by some that after the defeat, the Roman forces murdered Gordian in retreat at Zaitha.[36] According to Shabuhr I's Ka'be-ye Zardosht inscription, Gordian had come with a force composed of "Goths and Germans" (ŠKZ Pa4/37 *gwt w grm'ny*), and they were defeated in a headlong battle. Consequently, Philip the Arab was forced to sign a treaty which ceded much territory and a large sum of gold as war reparations, amounting to 500,000 denarii.[37] The territories that the Sasanians were able to take from the Romans were large parts of Mesopotamia and Armenia.[38] We should not lose sight of the fact that the newly established Sasanian dynasty was also confronting a branch of the Arsacid family in Armenia and so it needed to flush out any such resistance to secure its northern flank while fighting the Romans. For this reason the great kingdom of Armenia was to have a turbulent history during the Sasanian period.

Shabuhr I commemorated his victory in a rock-relief at Naqsh-i Rustam showing him subjugating the two Roman emperors to his will. He also left us a long resume of his deeds at Ka'be-ye Zardosht in Persis, which is the first long testament from the Sasanians themselves and demonstrates their outlook in an epic narrative. In his *res gestae* he provides information on his religious conviction, lineage, the areas that he ruled over, and also the fate of the Romans. It is interesting to note that Shabuhr I tells us that the Caeser (*Gordian*) lied, putting the matters in a Zoroastrian doctrinal context where the Romans represented the concept of Lie/Disorder, against the Persian representatives of Truth/Order.[39] In any case, the second campaign of Shabuhr began in 252 CE against a Roman force of 60,000 at Barbalissus. It ended in total defeat of the Romans, and if we are to believe the ŠKZ narrative, some 37 towns in Mesopotamia and Syria were taken.[40] The reason for this campaign is again given in a phrase in the ŠKZ: *W kysr TWB MKDBW-t W 'L 'rmn-y wyns 'BD-t* "and Caesar again lied and did wrong to Armenia."[41] What was this lie? In effect, although Philip had promised to give Iranians control over Armenia, he did not cede Armenia to the Sasanians. Instead, Philip only agreed to go back to the old treaty from the time of Augustus and the Arsacids where the Roman emperor crowned the Armenian ruler who was picked by the Arsacid King of Kings.[42] At the time of the Sasanians, of course the Arsacid family of Armenia would not have agreed with such tradition, nor would have the Sasanians who saw their nemesis to the north being crowned by the Romans.

In 260 CE Shabuhr I begun his third campaign and took eastern Mesopotamia and Syria[43] and the coast of eastern Mediterranean. At this battle the emperor Valerian along with senators and soldiers were captured and deported to the Sasanian territory.[44] Now Goths, Romans, Slavs and other people from the Near East were incorporated into the Sasanian Empire. Before this, no other person could have claimed that he was able to kill a Roman emperor, make one tributary, and capture and imprison the third. Shabuhr was very much aware of his feat and did not hesitate to mention his heroism in his inscription.[45] At a rock-relief in Persis, Valerian is shown kneeling before him and today at the city of Bishabuhr, among the ruins of the city, a place is marked as *zendan-e valerian* "Valerian's prison." This victory by Shabuhr I did not escape the attention of Roman sources either, although the reason for Valerian's defeat, as many now wrote as Christians was his paganism and tormenting of Christians, while others gave a more sober view of the captured emperor.[46]

Although the borders between Rome and Persia fluctuated between the Tigris and the Euphrates, depending on the military success on either side, this did not mean that travel was restricted. In fact people from both sides traveled from one side to another, engaged in trade, and intermarried. This openness and ease of movement from one side of the border to another made spies useful, and supplying information on the enemy was seen as a great betrayal by both sides.[47] For now, Mesopotamia was in Persian hands, but Armenia needed to be dealt with as it had resisted Ardashir and defeated his army.

Armenia would be the focal point between the Sasanians and the Romans and remained so until the end of the Sasanian period. The Armenian situation was quite complex and important for both sides, because of the strategic and economic interests, and the fact that Armenia served as a buffer between Persia and Rome. Considering that a branch of the Parthian royal family remained in Armenia, it is quite easy to imagine why Shabuhr wanted to put an end to the problem of Armenia. He planned the assassination of king Xosrov and installed a king loyal to him by the name of Tirdates (Tirdād) who ruled from 252–262 CE. Armenia's importance in the eyes of the Persians is well manifested, as in the case of several of the heirs to the Sasanian throne who were stationed in Armenia and were called *wuzurg-Arman-šāh* "The Great King of Armenia."[48] No other province of the Sasanian Empire had such an important title attached to it.

SHABUHR I AND MANI

During Shabuhr's reign his religious outlook became a matter of importance. The Zoroastrian "church" was being formed by Kerdir, who was trying to establish a body of laws, canonize the *Avesta*, create a common doctrine, unify the belief system, and establish a Zoroastrian religious hierarchy tied to the State. At the same time Mani emerged from Mesopotamia, professing a religion which by all accounts was universal. Manichaean sources state that during the last years of Ardashir's reign Mani had crossed the empire and had gone to India. During Shabuhr I's reign he had come back to the Sasanian Empire, appeared before the king and was honored, stayed with the king for sometime and was given permission to preach throughout the empire.[49]

At this time it would be wrong to see Zoroastrianism as an exclusive religion, since Zoroastrianism was a religion that could be adopted by the conquered people. Shabuhr's tolerance of Mani, and at the same time his commitment to Ohrmazd and Zoroastrianism has caused problems for historians. But if Shabuhr saw the growing power and structure of the Zoroastrian priesthood, might he not have attempted to show them that the King of Kings was still the one who has the last say? Were it not the Sasanians who were the caretakers and priests of the Anahid fire-temple and were schooled in the rites and ceremonies? Sasanian concern with politics should not have diminished their religious authority, at least until the time of Wahram I. Mani was able to propagate his religion during Shabuhr I's rule and that of his son. Still, Shabuhr I mentions in his *res gestae* that many Wahram fires were established and that lamb, wine, and bread were offered to the gods for the soul of the kings and queens of the family of Sasan. All of these, to a Zoroastrian priest may have seemed "pagan," and the king's cult may just have been that.

SASANIAN COURT AND BUREAUCRACY

If one compares the retinue, the bureaucracy and the size of the court, between Ardashir I and Shabuhr I, one begins to see that there was an increase in the administrative apparatus and the size of the court. This would be natural, since if an empire was to be centralized and to be functioning, it needed to have not only a king, but also governors (*šahrābs*), viceroys (*bidaxš*), a steward of royal property (*framādār*) a commander of the royal guard (*hazārbad*), scribes (*dibīrs*), treasurers (*ganzwars*), judges (*dādwars*), and a market inspector (*wāzārbed*), along with the local kings (*šahrdārān*), princes of royal blood (*wāspuhragān*), grandees (*wuzurgān*), minor nobility (*āzādān*), and other officials as mentioned in the *res gestae*. The nobility (*wuzurgān*), whose loyalty to their clan was paramount, now submitted to the Sasanians.[50] Such families as Waraz, Suren, Andigan, Karen, and others were given various honors and positions, such as being master of ceremonies or crown bestower. They also displayed their clan emblem or coat-of-arms on their caps (*kulāfs*) as is apparent on the rock-reliefs at Naqsh-i Rajab and Naqsh-i Rustam. We do not know which symbol belonged to which clan and what the symbols exactly meant, whether they were insignias or names of the clans made into designs.

JOUSTING FOR KINGSHIP: WAHRAMS AND NARSEH

The next king, Hormizd I (270–271 CE), probably the youngest son of Shabuhr I came to the throne and ruled for only a short time,[51] but he is associated with good rule and the building of the city of Ram-Hormizd in Khuzistan. Tabarī states that Hormizd had been appointed as the ruler of Khurasan and because of his fearlessness and extreme loyalty to Shabuhr was chosen as heir to the throne. He may have shown a military talent, like his father, during Shabuhr's campaign in the 260s which gave reasons for the king to appoint him as heir. He was chosen over his elder brother Narseh, who in the Shabuhr Ka'be-ye Zardosht inscription was called king of Sistan (*Sagān-šāh*). Religiously, again it is not clear why Hormizd I allowed Mani to preach his message freely and also let Kerdir continue his activity, giving him new ranks and titles. This may have been part of his campaign of dual containment, controlling both religions that were attempting to dominate the region. Wahram I (271–274 CE) also had a relatively short rule, but we have more information about him and his eventful career. He was the eldest son of Shabuhr I, but had been bypassed by Hormizd. He had been appointed as the king of Gilan by his father. Initially, Kerdir appears to have backed his succession and consequently the Zoroastrian priesthood and the person of Kerdir benefited from his enthronement. In 274 CE Mani was sent from the east to present himself to Wahram, and we have a Manichaean text which describes the harsh treatment of the prophet. He was scolded as not being a good doctor nor having any benefit, and Wahram ordered his arrest and imprisonment.

Wahram II came to the throne in 274 CE and may have needed Kerdir's support in bypassing Narseh, who was now the Great King of Armenia, and it is in this period that Kerdir begins his real ascent to power. Kerdir also began the persecution of the non-Zoroastrians in the empire, such as the Jews, Christians, Manichaeans, Mandeans and Buddhists.

During the rule of Wahram II (274–293 CE) Kerdir achieved higher rank and status, and it is during this period that the Sasanian kings lost much of their religious power as caretakers of the Anahid fire temple to Kerdir, making him the judge of the whole empire. This meant that from now on, the priests acted as judges throughout the empire and probably court cases were now based on Zoroastrian law except when members of other religious minorities had disputes with each other.[52] More will be said of these developments in the chapter on religion. Wahram II is the first ruler to have a family portrait struck on his coins. On the *drahms* (silver coins), he is shown with his queen Shabuhrdukhtag who was his cousin, and his son, Wahram III.[53] He also had several rock-reliefs carved as memorial with his family. This is an interesting feature of Wahram II in that he was very much concerned to leave a portrait of his family[54] which incidentally gives us information about the court and the Persian concept of the royal banquet (*bazm*).[55]

This included wine drinking, feasting, music and games being played before the king and the courtiers as evidenced not only from the rock reliefs, but also the silver dishes from the Sasanian period. While the term *bazm* means "feast," the Armenian sources give us its true use during the Sasanian period. (Armenian) *bazmoc'k'* "to recline," meant a banqueting-couch which the nobility and the king used during feasting at the court. The courtiers would recline on cushions (*barj*), where the number of the cushions signified their importance in the court. Some of these banqueting couches had room for two people, referred to as *taxt* or *gāh* where one's proximity to the King of Kings showed his/her honor and closeness to him.[56] Naturally, those whose *taxt* or *gāh* was further from the king, signified their lesser rank, and if moved further, was a sign of demotion and disgrace. These portraits may also have been a means of justifying Wahram II's succession over Narseh who by now must have been quite dissatisfied from being bypassed several times, although he was the Great King of Armenia, a title reserved for the heir to the throne. Wahram II's precarious situation is also clear because of the revolt of his brother Hormizd in Sistan in 283 CE. Although the chronology of the events are not clear, we are told that Hormizd was supported by the Sistanis, Gilanis and the Kushans (Rufii)[57] in his campaign against Wahram II.[58] This was not the only problem that Wahram II had as we hear of religious strife as well, namely in the province of Khuzistan led by a certain mowbed who held power there for some time.[59]

Plans had already been made by Emperor Probus to invaded the Sasanian territory, but he died and so Carus begun the war and invaded Mesopotamia, laying siege to the capital Ctesiphon while Wahram II was in the East, but he died in Mesopotamia in 283 CE.[60] The next emperor, Diocletian, who had to deal with the internal problems of Rome, made a treaty with Wahram II which demarcated the Perso-Roman borders. Now Wahram II could deal with his brother, Hormizd, and Diocletian was able to focus his attention on the reforms in his empire, bringing order to an otherwise chaotic Roman realm. This treaty divided Armenia among the two powers and left western Armenia in the hands of Tirdat (Tirdates IV) while Narseh ruled over greater Armenian (thereafter called Persarmenia). By 293 CE, when Wahram II died, his rival Hormizd had been pacified in the east, but dynastic squabbling continued. Wahram's son, Wahram III who was known as King of the Sakas (*sagān-šāh*),[61] was brought to the throne by one faction, perhaps with the backing of Kerdir, Adur-Farrobay, king of Meshan, and Wahnām, son of Tartus. But Narseh was not going to be bypassed again. He left for Mesopotamia and was greeted by a group of the nobility and men who had given their allegiance to him. We do not know what happened to Wahram III, but Wahnām was captured and executed and Narseh finally became the King of Kings.

Again Narseh has blessed us by leaving his personal attestation at Paikuli in northern Mesopotamia. It is a biography and a narrative justifying his succession to the throne, in which it is related that the nobility and courtiers asked him to take the throne when he met them.[62] There are similarities between this inscription and others in the Near East, such as the Behistun inscription of Darius I and other pre-Achaemenid ones which has given cause to some to believe that it is less reliable source. In fact, recently it has been claimed that the Paikuli inscription may be devoid of much historical information because it belongs to the genre of epic literature composed since time immemorial in the ancient Near East. One cannot accept this assumption certainly, and while it can be agreed that the story is told in an epic setting (formula), I do not know in how many ways a king could relate his story and his campaign. Relating a story or historical event in a specific form or formula should not necessarily deplete the story of its historical significance.[63] After all, kings made war, defeated their enemies, and ruled over their kingdom. These issues in themselves are the genre that gives cause to a king to commission an inscription.

It should be said also that again a constant feature of the Persian civilization represents itself, as is evident in the Behistun and the Naqsh-i Rustam inscriptions. In the Paikuli inscription we come across the notion that the enemies of the rightful king (Narseh, follower of Truth/Order) were followers of Lie (Demon/Disorder).[64] This binary opposition which is a hallmark of Sasanian Zoroastrianism worked well for demonizing the king's enemies. Narseh's rock-relief at Naqsh-i Rustam is also important in that it shows him receiving the symbol of sovereignty from the deity, Anahid.[65] Leaving the religious implications aside, could this mean that politically Narseh was able to regain the control of the fire-temple of Anahid at Istakhr and was re-orienting his devotion to this deity at the cost of Kerdir's power? Of course it is possible that devotion to Lady Anahid was never forsaken, but I think the mere representation of Narseh along with Anahid may hint at a religio-political shake-up in the Sasanian Empire. This perhaps reaffirmed the tradition of Narseh's father and grandfather, Shabuhr I and Ardashir I, and his own as the original and legitimate rulers who began their campaign around the cult of this deity.

On the foreign front Narseh was less successful. He declared war on Rome in 296 CE because of Roman meddling in Armenia. While initially he was able to withstand the Roman forces under Galerius, in the second battle the Sasanian army was defeated and he lost his wife and family.[66] In 298 he negotiated a peace treaty (Treaty of Nisbis) in which in exchange for his family's return and peace, he ceded parts of Mesopotamia, restoring Armenia to Tirdat, and the King of Iberia was now to be chosen by the Romans.[67] This Roman influence in Iberia (Georgia) was to be detrimental to Sasanian influence in the region, since in 330 CE the Georgian king and nobility adopted Christianity. Narseh's rule announced a new balance of power among the Romans and the Persians. This weakness in imperial aspiration may be apparent from the omission of *an-Ērān* from his titles on some of the coin legends.

THE THIRD CENTURY: AN OVERVIEW

It can be said that in the third century CE the first two rulers of *Iranshahr* established and organized a Persian Empire from the province of Persis. Persis in the third century appears to have had a centrality, not only because it is the first province that all of the early Sasanian rock reliefs mention, but also because it is the location from where the family of Sasan rose. From the later sources we also learn that, just like

Constantine in the fourth century, Ardashir I also attempted to establish a blueprint for a religion, but a religion that he and his ancestors worshipped, what they called *mazdēsn* or Mazda-worshipping religion, *i.e.*, Zoroastrianism. This is the first word that appears on the coins and inscription of Ardashir and Shabuhr, suggesting their deep devotion and proclamation for Ohrmazd. Ardashir along with his wise priest, Tosar, sifted through the existing oral and written tradition kept throughout the empire and especially in Persis, and began the canonization of the doctrines of what we today call Zoroastrianism. By the time of Shabuhr I the Romans had realized that a new power existed in the East which could defeat any Roman army and even kill its generals and hold captive its emperor. Shabuhr I's inscription also demonstrates the fact that the administrative apparatus of the Sasanian Empire had grown and became more sophisticated. This is to be expected if an organized and vibrant empire was to exist. Shabuhr I, however, also tried to use Manichaeism, a religion which seems to have attracted many from different regions in Asia and the Mediterranean world as an alternative to Zoroastrianism. While Zoroastrianism was the religion of his father and forefathers, Shabuhr I understood that in order to have a universal empire, a universal religion which could cement loyalty to the king and state was much desired. To be the ruler of Iranians was one matter, but to rule over *an-ērān*, needed a more universal religion.

The growing number of Zoroastrian priests, however, would not allow this to happen and after Shabuhr's death, under king Wahram I, Kerdir and company made sure that Mani was stopped and later met an early death and that the King of Kings remained *mazdēsn* and that the Zoroastrian religion was spread at any cost to the empire. In a way Kerdir is responsible for the preservation of the Zoroastrian tradition until its full development under later Sasanians. Shabuhr I may have begun to imagine that the concept of *Iranshahr* would not necessarily be tied to Zoroastrianism, although it had its origin in that tradition, and that any citizen, i.e., *mard ī šahr* "male citizen"/*zan ī šahr* "female citizen," would be able to be considered as *Ērānagān* "Iranians." This idea would take place in another century or so, but it was too early for it to take hold in a new empire. The Zoroastrian priests not only made themselves an important part of the imperial government, but also would become ever more involved in the day-to-day workings of society. They also reduced the religious power of the King of Kings, especially after Shabuhr I's "ungodly" meddling with Mani. If Zoroastrianism was to survive, it needed to have a hierarchy, a religious tradition in the name of the *Avesta*, and its traditions needed to be zealously maintained. While the Wahrams caved into these demands, Narseh struck back and attempted to make the family of Sasan the ultimate decision maker. By the end of the third century CE, an equilibrium had been reached between the church and the state and none was able to really exist without the other or to overtake the other.

Internationally, Rome now had to face a new and more centralized empire which had specific geo-political agendas and it did not fear coming into conflict with the Mediterranean empire. The presence of this Mediterranean empire, centered in Rome, in Syria and more importantly in Mesopotamia created the notion that it is certainly an imperialistic empire. As Mesopotamia served as the heartland of the empire with its capital Ctesiphon, and an agricultural center along with Khuzistan, the presence of the Roman forts only a short distance to the west made the Sasanians wary. This may be a prime reason for which early on Ardashir and Shabuhr I waged war on the Roman holdings in those regions. We are not so clear on the eastern campaigns of the Sasanians, but it is sure that they were able to establish a strong foothold there and secure their border against the Kushans.

SHABUHR, ARMENIA, AND THE WARS IN THE WEST AND THE EAST

Hormizd II (302–309 CE) succeeded his father, but did not do much militarily, and, even worse for the Sasanians, during his reign Armenia under king Tirdates IV adopted Christianity. He had tried to consolidate Persian-Armenian relations by marrying his daughter Hormizdduxtag to the Armenian prince Wahan Mamikonian,[68] and such an alliance must have affected the loyalties of some of the Armenian noble families. Consequently some of the Armenian feudal clans (*naxarars*) converted as well and supported Tirdat against those *naxarars* who were loyal to the Sasanians and more specifically those who honored the ancient Mazdean/Zoroastrian tradition of Armenia. It has usually been the case that Armenians have seen this momentous event as a break from the old "pagan" past, when the Armenian nation and identity was established through the medium of Christianity. But one can look at the event in another way as well, namely through the eyes of the Armenians who did not convert to the new religion. Those Armenians who chose to stay faithful to their ancient heritage went down into Armenian historiography as either villains or worshiping *Ormizd*, *Anahit*, and *Vahagn* and Christian historians attempted to erase them from the Armenian historical memory, except a few as the evil-doers.[69]

For many Armenian *naxarars* and especially those of the noble clans, their past history and religion must have meant something important and the adoption of new ways and religion (Christianity) must have not been accepted very easily. After all, according to these Armenian nobles, it was King Tirdat who was the heretic who adopted a religion from the West, supplanting the Armenian Mazdeans who had been worshipping Ohrmazd since the sixth century BCE. James Russell has put an end to the modern Armenian notions of a pagan past vs. Christianity. According to Armenian historiography which is Christian and hostile to Zoroastrianism, Armenia was pagan, illiterate and disunited, but when in the early fourth century Christianity was adopted, there was a united vision and a united people or "nation." Russell has shown that the Armenians from ancient times were a people who, although their culture was under Persian and Zoroastrian influence, had their own view of what Zoroastrianism meant and gave it an Armenian outlook.[70] So the few "evil" *naxarars* mentioned in the Armenian historical narratives who supported the Sasanians were those who in fact chose to keep their ancient Armenian tradition at the expense of the newcomers. The issue of the future of Armenia was not to be decided at this time and the adoption of Christianity further caused problems and divided Armenian society for some time to come.

When Hormizd II died, his son Adur-Narseh was chosen to rule, but he ruled only briefly and was deposed by the nobility and the priests. Then the infant son of Hormizd II, named Shabuhr II (309–379 CE) was put on the throne. In regard to this king we have the legend that the courtiers and the clergy placed the crown on the womb of his mother when she was pregnant. We may assume that during the early years of his reign, the court and the Zoroastrian priests ran the empire and the empire was secure and stable structurally and administratively to survive without a strong monarch. This scenario also signaled to the courtiers and the nobility that the empire could be managed without a powerful king which would benefit them. The Arabs in eastern Arabia raided the southwestern provinces of the Sasanian Empire, while Constantine and the other emperors battled for the soul of the Roman Empire which made the Persians safe from the Western front. When Shabuhr II came of age (325 CE), he took revenge on the Arabs and hence received the title "Shoulder Piercer" (Arabic *Dhū al-Aktāf*), referring to the punishment inflicted on the Arab tribes. As a result of his campaigns some of the Arabs were pushed into the heartland of Arabia and the Persian Gulf region remained in the hands of the Sasanian Empire. This was part of the overall strategy of the Sasanians to secure the Persian Gulf. Some Arab tribes were forcibly displaced and relocated into the Sasanian Empire. The Taghlib tribe was settled in Darayn (a port in Bahrayn) and al-Khaṭṭ; the Abd al-Qays and Tamim were settled in Hajar, and the tribe of Bakr b. Wa'il was settled in Kerman and the Hanazila in Ramila (vicinity of Ahwaz).[71] To keep the Arabs from mounting further attacks Shabuhr II constructed a defensive system which was called *war ī tāzīgān* "wall of the Arabs."[72] This wall appears to have been close to the city of Hira which came to be known as *Khandaq i Shapur* (Ditch of Shabuhr).[73]

It is again here that we hear of Arab forced immigration into the Sasanian Empire by Shabuhr II, namely Bakr b. Wā'il and Banu Hanzalah in Kerman and Khuzistan.[74] Thus the relation between the Arabs and Persians was just not on the frontiers, but also within the Sasanian Empire.[75] Also for the first time we hear of the Chionites (*Xyōn*) tribes encroaching onto the empire from Central Asia, but Shabuhr II was able to contain them and make peace with them.[76] Shabuhr II placed his son, who now took the title of "King of Kushan" (*kūšan-šāh*), on the throne in the east as is apparent from the coins and a few inscriptions in Kushan territory.

On the western front, the Roman rulers' backing of Armenia caused Shabuhr II to begin a campaign against them. When Constantius came to the throne (337–338 CE), war began and Shabuhr II laid siege to Nisibis three times, and there was constant warfare which did not go in favor of either side. The defensive system of fortresses and *limes* hindered Shabuhr's campaign in the region, but some forts such as Vitra fell to him.[77] The encroachment of the nomadic tribes in the Central Asia forced Shabuhr II to turn his attention to the east,[78] and the war with Rome ended in stalemate by 350 CE. Around this time we first hear of the Hunnic tribes, who were probably the Kidarites (Chinese *Jiduolo*), encroaching onto the Sasanian Empire and were also menacing the Gupta Empire (320–500 CE) in India. Shabuhr II, who had just returned from the Syrian front, was able to contain his eastern foes by making an alliance with their king, Grumbates, against the Romans. By such action, he foresaw an ally to attack against the Romans.[79]

It is quite possible that Shabuhr II defeated his eastern foes and established Sasanian domination over the Kushans.[80] This theory can be substantiated from the two Middle Persian inscriptions which mention that the eastern boundary of the Sasanian Empire under Shabuhr II included Sind, Sistan, and Turan.[81] Also Ammianus Marcellinus lists the provinces of the Sasanian Empire in that period as Assyria, Susiana, Media, Persis, Parthia, Greater Carmania,

Hyrcania, Margiana, the Bactriani, the Sogdiani, the Sacae, and Scythia at the foot of Imaus (Himalayas), and beyond the same mountain, Serica, Aria, the Paropanisadae, Drangiana, Arachosia, and Gedrosia.[82] Al-Tabarī, additionally mentions that, among his city building projects, Shapur II established cities in Sind and Sijistān,[83] which confirms his rule over that region. Finally, most of the gold coins minted by Shabuhr II are from eastern mints such as Marw where the Kushans also minted gold coins. Also, a large amount of copper coins from the mints of Sakastān and Kabul exist.[84] This may mean that Shabuhr II was able to extract a large amount of gold and other precious metals from his defeated eastern enemies.

In 359 CE Shabuhr II, with the backing of king Grumbates, attacked Syria, laid siege to Amida, entered it after 73 days,[85] and deported its population to Khuzistan. The city of Amida was sacked and its population deported as punishment because the son of the Kidirite king was killed. In 361 CE, the new Roman emperor, Julian, counter-attacked and won against Shabuhr II with victories in 363 CE, and even laid siege to Ctesiphon. The capital, however, was not taken because of disorder and pillaging among the Roman forces.[86] In anticipation of Julian's victory against the Persians an inscription was placed in upper Jordan valley, with the premature title of BARORVM EXTINCTORI, probably because at his initial success in Antioch in March of 363.[87] We are told that among the Roman generals there was a Persian renegade by the name of Hormizd who commanded the cavalry. Julian had destroyed his own naval ships, so that his forces would not retreat,[88] and Shabuhr II responded by adopting a scorched-earth policy in Mesopotamia which resulted in hunger among the Roman forces. In June of 363 Persian forces equipped with elephants defeated the Romans, and Julian was badly wounded in battle, probably by a *kontophoroi* "cavalry spearmen," and died in his tent.[89] Eutropius, who was an eyewitness to this campaign, affirms that Julian was killed by the hand of the enemy.[90]

Jovian was elected emperor and had to make peace with Shabuhr II, which the Romans called *ignobili decreto* "shameful treaty,"[91] ceding eastern Mesopotamia, Armenia and the adjoining regions, 15 fortresses as well as Nisibis.[92] Persian terms and conditions were conveyed by Surenas (Sūren) who agreed to have the mainly Christian population of Nisibis moved to Roman territory while the Persian standard was raised over the city.[93] Jovian left Mesopotamia and the Romans would not engage the Sasanians further as Emperor Valens had to deal with Germanic tribes in the Balkans.

On the Armenian front, during the early years of Shabuhr II's life Armenia under king Tirdates IV (298–330) adopted Christianity (314 CE). Consequently some of the Armenian feudal clans (*naxarars*) converted as well and supported Tirdat IV against those *naxarars* who were loyal to the Sasanians, and more specifically, those who honored the ancient Zoroastrian tradition of Armenia, still worshiping *Ormizd, Anāhit*, and *Vahagn*. The precarious internal struggle and the wavering loyalties of the *naxarars*, the king, and the clergy ushered in a turbulent period in Armenian history, and the sources for this period are confused. King Tiran, who had attempted to keep Armenia independent by playing both the Romans and the Persians, lost his life to Shabuhr II. He was replaced by his son, Aršak II (350–367 CE) who initially also tried to appease both the Romans and the Persians, but who finally joined Julian's expedition against the Sasanians.[94] As part of the peace treaty between Shabuhr II and Jovian, Armenia and Georgia were to come under Sasanian control and the Romans were not to get involved in Armenian affairs.[95] The Armenian king was captured by the Persians and imprisoned in the Castle of Oblivion (in Armenian sources known as Fortress of Andmaš or Castle of Anyuš in Khuzistan), where he is said to have committed suicide while being visited by his eunuch Drastamat.[96] The cities of Artashat, Vałaršapat, Eruandashat, Zarehawan, Zarishat, Van and Naxchvan were taken and their populations deported, among whom there were many Jewish families.[97] The pro-Persian *naxarars*, namely Vahan Mamikonean and Meružan Arcruni accompanied Shapur II and were rewarded for their help, and two Persians, Zik and Karēn with a large army were placed over Armenian affairs.[98] Georgia was also placed under Persian control where Shapur II installed Aspacures in eastern Georgia, but eventually the Roman emperor Valens succeeded in installing Sauromaces in western Georgia.[99]

Pap (367–374 CE), who was the son of the Armenian ruler Aršak who had fled to the Romans, was placed on the throne in 367 with Roman backing. The Armenians were able to withstand Shabuhr II's attack near Bagawan in 371 CE.[100] Pap, however, was not popular with many of the *naxarars* or the Armenian church because of his pro-Arian policy, which caused him to be slandered by the Armenian sources as devoted to the *dēwān* "demons" due his mother's religious beliefs (Queen P'aranjem of Siwnik').[101] Pap became a victim of internal divisions and fighting among *naxarars* and the *sparapet* Mušeł Mamikonean and was eventually killed at the instigation of Emperor Valens.[102] Armenia, however, was divided between Shabuhr II and Valens in 377 CE and a state of relative peace reigned in the Caucuses.

Internally, the Zoroastrian priest named Adurbad i Mahrspandan was to canonize the *Avesta* and the Zoroastrian tradition. As Richard Frye has stated, the semblance of the Ottoman *millet* system was first begun during this period, where the Christian bishop resided at Ctesiphon and, along with the Jewish *exilarch*, paid his poll tax in return for peace and security. By this time religious communities were being established and the foundation of a Late Antique society in Persia was being laid by the Zoroastrian priests, the Jewish rabbis, and the Christian clergy.[103] We do not know how far Shabuhr II was able to cut the power of the grandees and the clergy, but since he was a strong ruler he was able to hold his own. The only hint which may suggest that the Zoroastrian clergy were able to impose themselves on the monarchy is that Shabuhr II is one of the last kings to call himself "whose lineage (is) from the Gods." It may be that finally the King of Kings had become a secular ruler, whose religious authority had become minimal.

It is exactly at this juncture in history that the Sasanian monuments disappear in Persis and appear in the north, in Media. We may consider that the Zoroastrian priests in Persis had become too powerful and the king decided to shift their focus not only away from their traditional stronghold where they were from, but to another place where a new image was to be presented. It is not clear what motivated this move by the king, or the adoption of the new titles. The artistic style is essentially different from those in Persis. Mithra's image becomes prominent, along with Ohrmazd. Ardashir II and Shabuhr III are presented motionless and standing frontally, flanked by two small Middle Persian inscriptions, bearing the traditional formula which Ardashir I had first adopted on his coins and inscriptions.[104] They are not receiving a diadem from the gods, nor victorious over any enemies, rather posing for a personal portrait. At Taq-ī Bustan, the monuments of Ardashir II (379–383 CE) and his son, Shabuhr III (383–388 CE) are present. These kings along with Wahram IV (388–399 CE)[105] all met a violent end which suggests the growing power of the nobility and the priests since the time of Shabuhr II.[106] This growing power of the nobility is also reflected in the brief description of Ardashir II's rule who is said to have killed a number of the great men and holders of authority in order to reduce their power.[107] During Wahram IV's reign, Armenia lost any semblance of independence, and the western part become part of the Roman empire and the east was put under the rule of the King of Kings' brother, Wahram Shabuhr (Armenian *Vramshapuh*) as king of Persarmenia in 394 CE. But Wahram IV's greatest achievement was the stopping of the Huns who had entered Syria and northern Mesopotamia.[108]

FOURTH CENTURY: AN OVERVIEW

For the fourth century CE it can be said that Christianity was seen as a major threat to Zoroastrianism and a break from the ancient tradition by the Armenians. By adopting Christianity, Armenia and then Georgia began to come closer to the Eastern Roman Empire. This is because Constantine and his successors first allowed Christianity to thrive, and then it was tied to the institution of the emperor and the empire. The Roman Emperors saw themselves as the leaders of all Christians in the world, and hence the Christians in the Sasanian Empire had become suspect. A strong king such as Shabuhr II and a Zoroastrian priest like Adurbad i Mahrspandan reacted to the expansion of Christianity. This tactic was not to be fruitful, and in the fifth century CE another way was found to appease the situation. A strong and long-lived king like Shabuhr II brought security to the Sasanian Empire and secured its borders in the west and the south. In the east it appears that Shabuhr II had been able to control the encroachment of the various nomadic tribes from the East such as the Huns and Kidarites. Shabuhr II was able to create an alliance and a semblance of allegiance with the Huns and later the Kidarites. Shabuhr II's raids into the Arabian Peninsula and the coast was not only to punish the Arab tribes, but perhaps to secure the Persian Gulf region. The Sasanians could now call the Persian Gulf their *mare nostrum*. The institution of kingship, however, was to be redefined as the Zoroastrian ecclesiastical hierarchy strengthened. From now on the King of Kings was not known to be from the lineage of the gods (*yazdān*) any more, but rather a secular ruler who continued to be a Mazda worshipper.

YAZDGERD I AND PEACE WITH CHRISTIANITY

With the reign of Yazdgerd I (399–420 CE) we begin to get a new ideological outlook and treatment of the minorities in the empire. His coins add the slogan "who maintains peace in his dominion" (*Ramšahr*) while the Sasanian sources called him "sinner" (Arabic *al-Athīm*; Persian *bazehkar*). This is purely a priestly propaganda, because he not only killed some Zoroastrian priests who had looked down upon his good treatment of the religious minorities, but also treated the Jews and the Christians favorably.[109] In fact Christianity became a recognized religion, when the first synod of the "Nestorian Church" was convened in 410 CE, during the rule of Yazdgerd I.[110] Agathis calls Yazdgerd I a pro-Christian monarch, but, what is more important, a "friendly and peaceable," ruler who never once made war on the Romans.[111] So his title would be fitting for the period, but we can connect this to Kayanid ideology as well. In the Middle Persian epic *Ayādgār ī Zarērān* (The Testament of Zarer) the last Kayanid ruler, Kay Wištāsp, is given the title *Ramšahr* which appears in the *Dēnkard* as well.[112] This title suggests gravitation towards an Avestan/Kayanid ideology even before seeing such titles and terminology as *kay* "Kayanid" and *xwarrah* "Glory." How much of this new ideological framework is due to the contacts with the East is difficult to say, but the attention increasingly given to the eastern boundaries of the empire must have had an impact upon the view of the king.

By all accounts, the rule of Yazdgerd I was peaceful and with mutual respect with the Roman Empire. In fact the emperor Arcadius (383–408 CE) asked the Persian ruler to become the guardian of his son Theodosius II[113] and this tradition would live on, sometimes the Romans and sometimes the Persians asking the other side for guardianship of the heirs to the throne of the respective empires. This action indicates that by the fifth century both empires saw each other as equals and worthy to have their heirs at the court of the other, or simply securing succession and being more fearful of internal opposition than each other's forces. We should not forget before Yazdgerd I, the three kings who followed one another had met violent deaths at the hands of the nobility and so Yazdgerd I had to react and that he did, by killing many of them, hence being called the "sinner" in the official Sasanian record. This title of Yazdgerd I may be as much for his tolerance of other religions and opening a new chapter in the history of Christianity in Persia as for establishing a balance of power between the institution of kingship and the noble families and the Zoroastrian priests.

WAHRAM GUR, PROBLEMS IN THE EAST AND CHRISTIAN PERSECUTION

In 414 CE, when Yazdgerd I died, his eldest son, Shabuhr left Armenia (Wahram Shabuhr/Armenian *Vramshapuh*) to take the throne but he was murdered by the nobility who placed Khusro, who was not related directly to Yazdgerd I, on the throne. This action suggests the nobility and priestly class' distaste for what Yazdgerd I had done which ultimately put his own sons in danger. Another son of Yazdgerd I, Wahram who had been sent to the Arab court at al-Hira, returned with an army of mainly Arabs and forced Khusro to abdicate in

421 CE. By all accounts Wahram (421–438 CE) was a successful ruler; in 422 CE in the west a peace treaty was signed giving religious freedom to the Christians in the Sasanian Empire and to the Zoroastrians in the Roman Empire. This was in the face of persecution of Christians which seems to have begun at the end of Yazdgerd I's reign,[114] or more probably in the beginning of Wahram's reign, instigated by the Zoroastrian priests.[115] He defeated the Hephthalites, another tribe in the east, killing their king and stopping their encroachment on the eastern borders of the empire. While on his campaign it appears that he had left his brother Narseh who was the youngest of his brothers in charge and when Wahram returned, Narseh was appointed as the ruler of Khurasan. We also hear of the office of *Wuzurg-framadār* which was given to Mihr-Narseh.[116] At this time Armenia's status also changed when the Armenian *naxarars* once again sought the aid of the Sasanians in the deposing of their king, Artashes, the son of Vramshapuh. In 428 CE, Wahram V removed him and placed a margrave (*marzbān*) in Armenia, ushering in what is known in Armenian history as the *marzpanate* period.

There are many romantic accounts about Wahram V, such as the importation of Indian minstrels as entertainers (*lurs*), and his penchant for drinking and especially hunting, receiving the epithet of *Gur* "onogur." The composition of the first Persian poem is also attributed to him in early Persian compendia, which is a stretch of the imagination. But it was this imagination that he captured even by his mysterious death, where it is said that one day while hunting in Media (Māh) he fell into some marshes or a well and disappeared, and his body was never found. He was also remembered by the composers of the Zoroastrian apocalyptic texts as the one who brought about an age when there was peace and that evil and the demons went into hiding.[117]

In the early years of the rule of Yazdgerd II (438–457 CE), the focus shifted to the east and battling what the sources call the Kushans, probably the Huns. Yazdgerd was stationed in Khurasan for some time until he was able to secure the eastern flank of the empire, and Bactria came under the control of the Sasanians. He then moved towards Armenia and Albania, as the defense of the Caucasus from the Huns moving westward was imperative, a campaign which also involved the Romans.[118] There were further problems in Armenia, probably at the instigation of Mihr-Narse (*Wuzurg-framādār*/Armenian *Vzurk hramatar*), who issued an edict in which Zoroastrianism was re-imposed as the official religion in Armenia.[119] This edict provides us with an interesting glimpse into the Zurvanite tendency of Mihr-Narseh and the reasons why the Armenians should convert to Zoroastrianism.[120] This caused an uprising by some of the Armenian *naxarar*s who had become Christian. We can tell that the Armenians were not united for this cause and as a result at the battle of Avarair in 451 CE the Armenian forces, led by Vardan of the Mamikonian's family, were annihilated, and many were deported to Persia.[121] This calamity was not to be forgotten by the Armenian (Christian) people and became a symbol of resistance and remembrance against their Zoroastrian neighbors.

This anti-Christian measure did not only befall the Armenian Christians, since there are also Syriac martyrologies from this period which mention Christian and Jewish persecutions. Consequently Yazdgerd II is remembered well by the Zoroastrian priests and the Sasanian chronicle as someone who defeated his enemies (non-Zoroastrians) but who behaved with benevolence towards the Zoroastrians and the army. In terms of imperial ideology, he is the first to use the new title of "Mazdaean Majesty Kay" (*mzdysn bgy kdy*). This means the Sasanian kings were no longer seen as in the image of gods, at least in the empire where these coins were circulated, but were connected with the Avestan dynasty of the Kayanids. However, we should remember that this trend had begun with Yazdgerd I and the title of *Ramšahr*, and that *kay* was the second manifestation of this Kayanid ideology. It is especially interesting that this Avestan orientation takes place at the exact time when a Sasanian king is again concerned with the east and when the king resided in that region for several years. We cannot say that his stay in Khurasan or contact with Bactria would have brought about this fascination with the Kayanids, since we have the *Ramšahr* title appearing before. This Kayanid identity, which was now to be adopted wholesale by the Sasanians was to manifest itself in several titles which will be dealt with below. By a Kayanid ideology it is meant that rather than looking to the Achaemenids as their ancestors (for all we know they might have seen the Achaemenid monuments as the work of the kings of Persis), they connected themselves to the primordial kings, especially the Kayanid kings in the *Avesta*.[122]

The two sons of Yazdgerd II, Hormizd III (457–459 CE) and Peroz (459–484 CE) ruled consecutively, although the latter deposed the former in a power struggle. Peroz fled to the east to Khurasan and with an army probably consisting of Kidarites or Hephthalites regained the throne. Meantime, while Hormizd III may have crowned himself, we hear that their mother, Denag was governing the capital or parts of the capital. During this confusion Albania gained independence and the eastern boarders of the empire were laid open to Hephthalite attack.

When Peroz came to the throne, he pacified Albania, but allowed the Armenians to practice Christianity and made an agreement with the eastern Roman Empire to cooperate in defending the Caucus passes. The Sasanians met their match against the Hepthalites in Khurasan and in 469 CE Peroz and his harem and retinue were captured by Khwashnawaz. This calamity took place during the third major battle, while during the first two, his war was partly financed by the Romans.[123] This was the low point of Sasanian rule, where they in fact became tributaries to the Hephthalites and ceded territory to them for returning the king and his entourage to Sasanian territory. The chief priest (*mowbed*), Peroz's son, Kavad, and his daughter were held by the Hephthalites as assurance hostages.[124] The only reason that the Romans did not attack Persia at this time was because emperor Zeno was facing internal problems and could not turn his attention to the east.[125]

We know there were religious persecutions, especially against the Jews, at this time and drought and famine were rampant in the empire, as well as a revolt in Armenia in 482 CE.[126] But Peroz took it upon himself to revenge his loss in the east. This time in 484 CE, his actions cost him his life, seven of his sons, and his entire army.[127] It is here that we hear of the famous legend of the "pearl earring" of Peroz which was so precious that before dying he threw it to the ground so that no one would wear it.[128] The short rule of Balash (Walāxš) (484–488 CE) was uneventful and since the empire was weak, the king kept peaceful relations with Armenia and the Hephthalites by giving tribute to the latter. Balash appears to have been dominated by the noble families and it is interesting that we see the creeping influence of the Parthian noble families at this time. One such person is Zarmihr Sokhra of the Karen clan, who saved the rest of the Sasanian army after Peroz's death, and the other Shabuhr of the Mehran clan.[129] Balash was deposed by the nobility and the priests in 499 CE, when Kavad I (488–496, 499–531 CE) was brought to the throne.

FIFTH CENTURY: AN OVERVIEW

The fifth century kings were generally weak and the nobility and the Zoroastrian priests were able to exert their influence at the cost of the court. Some kings like Yazdgerd I did punish some Zoroastrian priests and the nobility to reduce their power, but this only hampered their eventual take-over of the Sasanian state for a short time. This, however, did not mean that the empire was ineffective or not centralized. The bureaucratic apparatus, under the control of the priests, had reached such a level of sophistication that the death of a king would not bring the empire down, something that worked to the advantage of the priests and the nobility. This centralization is also apparent with the growing number of titles as they appear on administrative seals,[130] as well as the appearance of mint-marks on the coins. Economically, the empire was not faring well, because of the drought, famine and the incisive wars which had resulted in giving huge sums of tribute to the Hephthalite, nor had there been any victories in the west to enable the collection of gold from the Romans.

KAVAD, MAZDAK AND DISORDER

Thus Kavad I had to face economic and political problems which confronted the empire at the end of the fifth century. It is at this time that we have some information on Zoroastrian sectarianism in the Sasanian Empire. In the first period of Kavad's rule a Zoroastrian priest by the name of Mazdak was able to capture the attention of Kavad I, enabling both to make reforms which went beyond the accepted religious dogma and the established social order. Mazdak brought a social reform which caused much resentment during and especially after its success in the minds of the Zoroastrian priests. Sources tell us that Mazdak preached an egalitarian social system, one in which equality in sharing wealth, women and property was propagated. Byzantine sources state that it was Kavad who introduced to Persians the idea that they should "have communal intercourse with their women."[131] Mazdak's outlook had theological and cosmological dimensions which will be discussed in some detail in the chapter on religion, but it also had political and social ramifications.[132] Here, however, one needs to see the Mazdakite movement in terms of its function as a political tool for Kavad. Kavad was able to use Mazdak's ideas to weaken the power of the nobility and the grandees, the large land owners and the priests who now were involved in every aspect of the state and were not always honest.[133] Mazdak's teaching went against the social division which was enforced by the *Avesta*, or perhaps how the Zoroastrian priests had interpreted the *Avesta*. Now Mazdak had a new and perhaps novel interpretation of the Zoroastrian tradition. Kavad may or may not have believed in his message, but he certainly used it to his advantage, in leveling the upper classes and making the king more appealing and accessible to the masses by adopting Mazdakite ideas. Imperial granaries were given away and land was redistributed among the peasants. In the Zoroastrian texts composed by the very priests who were against this reform, this period is seen as a time of chaos where women were shared by all, and no one knew one's lineage anymore.

The remaining dissatisfied nobility and the priests had Kavad arrested and imprisoned in the "Prison of Oblivion," in 496 CE and they put his brother Zamasp on the throne for several years. Zamasp is noted for his gentleness and sense of justice which may be anti-Mazdakite propaganda,[134] and he probably attempted to undo Kavad's reforms. Kavad, with the help of his sister was able to escape to the Hephthalites. He raised a force there and was able to come back to the throne in 499 CE, when Zamasp abdicated in his favor. This action also demonstrated the beleaguered situation of the empire, where in a time of chaos a small force was able to overrun the nobility-priest alliance. Kavad forced the Mazdakite religion not only upon the population of the empire where many must have been happy, especially the lower classes, but also upon the clients of the Sasanians, such as the Arabs in Najd and Hijaz in the first quarter of the sixth century.[135]

Once the economic, political and social situation was under control, Kavad began to institute reforms that were fundamental to the empire in the sixth century and were usually credited to Khusro I. The office of the "protector of the poor and judge" *(drīyōšān jādaggōw ud dādwar)* was created from the ranks of the *mowbeds* (chief priests) to help the poor and the downtrodden which was not only a reaction to the Mazdakite movement, but a general trend in Christianity, Zoroastrianism, and later Islam.[136] Administratively, four chanceries (*diwān*) were created for the empire which probably corresponded with the military division of the empire under the rule of four generals (*spāhbeds*).[137] Prior to this an *Ērān-spāhbed* led the army, but now it had become exceedingly difficult to be on several fronts at once. The survey of agricultural lands and reorganization of the tax system was also begun during his rule as was the creation of new districts in the empire.[138]

Religiously, Christian Nestorianism became the officially tolerated church in Persia and by the time of Khusro I we are told that the leader of the Christians had the title of *Ērān Cathollicos.*[139] Luckily for the Sasanians, the Hephthalites were in demise and division by 515 CE. In the West, however, things were different and there was a protracted war beginning in 502 CE, ending a long period of pence. Procopius informs us that Kavad owed money to the Hephthalites,[140] while another source suggests that the Persians were unhappy because the Romans had been unwilling to help in the defense against the Huns.[141] Kavad successfully invaded Armenia and took Theodosiopolis.

Then from Armenia he moved westward and laid siege to Amida in Mesopotamia and was able to take it.[142] Kavad made further incursions westward, but was only partially successful in his predatory invasion in search of booty. The negotiations, however, paid off for the Persians and in 506 CE the war was concluded. In 524 the Iberian king Gourgenes sided with the Romans, because Kavad was trying to impose Zoroastrianism. This act threatened the Persian control over that kingdom but the Persians were able to hold the area under firm control by 528 CE. Mesopotamia bore the brunt of further battles, beginning in 527 CE, and the Arab tribes and the Huns also became involved. By 529 CE there were negotiations which broke down and Kavad invaded Dara in 530 CE, coinciding with Justinian's reign. His capable general, Belisarius, was sent to defend the city against the Persian general, Mehran.[143] There were further campaigns on the Mesopotamian-Syrian border as well as in Armenia in 531 CE, but none of these wars had a clear winner.

KHUSRO I, REFORMS AND THE SASANIAN REVIVAL

The Sasanian revival was taking place at this time and its effect was that Georgia as well as parts of inner Arabia and Oman were now controlled by the Persians.[144] Persians had already settled in Central Asia and traders had gone to India, China and as far away as Indonesia.[145] They were more interested in business and wanted to control the trade in spices and silk, motivated by economic gain, rather than as a state sponsored activity. When Kavad died in 531 CE, the Mazdakites supported one of his sons by the name of Kawus who was the eldest and also the heir (another Kayanid name along with his father). Here we have information that the court and the religious hierarchy decided in favor of Khusro I, who was younger, but also an anti-Mazdakite. Kawus was ruling in the north in Tabarestan and battled Khusro I, but was ultimately defeated.[146] By this time Khusro I became instrumental in the murder of Mazdak and a large number of his followers who had felt secure enough to proclaim their allegiance to Mazdak openly. Although the *Shahnameh* may be exaggerating the end of the Mazdakites, it has captured the mind of the Persians to this day in describing his end: "Kasra (Khusro) owned an estate with high walls. He ordered holes to be dug there and had the followers of Mazdak implanted, heads in the ground and feet upwards."[147] He then is said to have told Mazdak to enter the garden of the estate to view the seeds that he had sown and had borne fruit, and when the *mowbed* saw his followers in such a state he cried aloud and fell to the ground. He was then hung alive and killed by volleys of arrows. At the end of the story, Ferdowsi proclaims: "If you are wise, do not follow the path of Mazdak."[148]

Khusro I (531–579 CE) represents the epitome of the philosopher-king in Sasanian and Near Eastern history. There is so much that has been attributed to him that it is quite difficult to discern fact from fiction. But certainly he was able to capture the imagination of the people of that region even after the fall of the Sasanians and the coming of Islam. Khusro I's reforms and changes to the empire were to become a blue-print for Kings and Caliphs and Sultans alike. Before undertaking major changes, however, he needed to secure his power on the throne. His power was initially contested by his brother, Kawus, whose stronghold was the north, in Mazandarān. Historical sources have it that the nobles who did not favor Mazdak and his followers sided with Khusro I. But in effect Khusro I followed his father's vision of administrative and economic reforms and in order to achieve this, the power of the great noble houses needed to be reduced. Once this had happened it appears that Khusro I presented himself as the anti-Mazdakite candidate, aspiring to a time when there was stability and social order, while in reality he was creating a new order after the defeat and the destruction of the old order.

When Khusro I came to power as an anti-Mazdakite, he did not restore the power of the great noble houses and the large landed aristocracy, instead he favored the small landholding gentry known in the Middle Persian sources and the Perso-Arabic sources as *dehgān*s/*dehghān*s.[149] The *dehgān*s would not only become the backbone of the Sasanian military, but more importantly the economic foundation of the state as tax collectors. They would also remain as the repository of the Persian culture and history in time to come, up to the eleventh century, when one of them in his poor economic state completed the *Shahnameh* or the *Book of Kings*.

To secure the borders of the Persian Empire, Khusro built as a defensive measure a series of walls (*war*), in a similar fashion to Hadrian's Wall in northern Britain and the Great Wall of China. The Persian walls, however, were built on the borders of the four sides of the empire. One was built in the northeast, along the Gurgan plain to defend against the Hephthalites, one in the northwest at the Caucasus passes, one in the southeast, and one in the southwest called the "wall of the Arabs" (*war ī tāzīgān*), in southwestern Persia.[150]

Intellectually, there seems to have been an opening of relations and ideas with other people, especially India and Rome. Works on medicine, astronomy, mirrors for princes, fables and stories, and manuals for games such as chess were brought and translated from India.[151] From Rome, musical instruments, various scientific works, medical treatises, and philosophical texts were translated. Some philosophers came to the court of Khusro I from Athens, especially after the closing down of the school of neo-Platonists by Justinian. Khusro I's interest in philosophy is indicated by noting that he was called "Plato's Philosopher King."[152] More will be said about the cultural development in the Sasanian empire in a separate chapter. Khusro I and the Roman Emperor, Justinian, however, represented the enlightened monarchs and memorable rulers of Late Antiquity. Their sense of being just (*ādel*), as Persian texts refer to Khusro I, their campaign in the codification of laws (probably begun in the time of Khusro I and last compiled under Khusro II, the *Madyān ī Hazār Dādestān*), and administrative and military reforms took place almost simultaneously in both empires. Scholars argue whether one king influenced the other, but rather than trying to see the process one way, one can view the relations as reciprocal, where each encouraged and perhaps wanted to outdo the other.

Khusro I made new administrative and military innovations as well and completed Kawad's reforms. He divided the empire into four regions, placing a general (*spāhbed*) in each quadrant. Now instead of the great General of the Iranians (*Ērān Spāhbed*) there were four *spāhbed*s in the northeast, northwest, southeast and southwest. He created a registry or *dīwān* for the military. He also drew on different tribal people such as the Daylamites to enforce the military which in time led to a different military composition whose loyalty lay with the king. There were also tax reforms, where taxes were excised not only based on the amount of land, but based on the type of product or produce.

WAR IN THE EAST AND IN THE WEST

With these reforms Khusro I was able to reinvigorate the Sasanian Empire. The success of these reforms can be gleaned from his military successes. In the east in 557–558 CE, Khusro I defeated the Hephthalites and between 572 to 577 CE, checked Turkic incursions into the Near East.[153] In the west, Khusro I concluded negotiations with Justinian which came to be known as The Eternal Peace in 532 CE, and it was favorable to the Persians. The Persians would receive gold to protect Caucasus pass, kept control over most of Armenia and Iberia and the Romans relinquished their bases in Mesopotamia.[154] In 540 CE, however, Khusro I began a campaign in the west, being informed by the Gothic king, Vitiges, of Justinian's campaigning in North Africa and Italy, and Armenian pleas for help from the Persians.[155] He began his campaign in Mesopotamia and Syria, where the city of Antioch was taken.[156] There was another campaign in 542 CE by Khusro I, but a plague dissuaded the king from going further. Warfare continued in 543 CE where the Romans were defeated in Armenia, and in 544 the Persians laid siege to Edessa, exacting a large amount of gold from its inhabitants. In 540 CE at the instigation of the Armenians and the Lazics, Khusro I again invaded Armenia to reduce Roman harassment in the region. This war proved to be a long one, beginning in 541 and lasting until 557 CE when a truce was agreed upon. Then Khusro I took to the eastern borders of his empire, waging war on the Hepthtalites and defeating them, thereafter controlling the lands all the way to the Oxus.

This truce lasted until 565 CE when Justinian died. When Justin II became the new emperor, he demanded control over Suania.[157] This became a cause for war and war proved disastrous for the Romans and by 573 CE the Persians had made substantial gains in the Caucuses, Mesopotamia and Syria. Dara was again taken by Khusro I, which was a blow to the already ill Justin.[158] With the new emperor, Tiberius, there were negotiations over Mesopotamia but the fighting continued in the Caucuses in 574–575 CE and then in Mesopotamia. This phase of the war continued during the reign of Emperor Maurice and beyond till the seventh century.[159] Khusro I was able to gain a foothold in the Arabian Peninsula, all the way to Yemen. Because of his spectacular victories and achievements, Khusro I minted such legends on his especial issue coinage as "Iranians has become fearless" (*ērān abē-bēm kard*), and "Iranians became strong" (*ērān abzōnhēnēd*).[160] This is the Sasanian Empire at the apex of its glory and power, headed by a philosopher-king.

Khusro's son, Hormizd IV (579–590 CE), did not match his father's grandeur, nor his political outlook. He is noted for his arrogance, tyranny and he made many enemies at the court.[161] Sebeos tells us that Hormizd IV was responsible for the killing of many of the nobility, which must have made him much hated.[162] He continued his support of the landed gentry *dehgans* who probably grew in strength at the cost of the nobility (*āzādān*) and dealt harshly with the Zoroastrian priests as well. In the east in 589 CE, the Turks were met by the Sasanian General Wahram Chubin, whose victory over them made the general famous within the empire. He was from the noble Arsacid family of Mehran, which could trace its genealogy further back than the Sasanians. When

Wahram Chubin had a minor defeat in Armenia against the Romans, Hormizd IV slandered him and made false accusations against him, which caused the general to rebel and move towards Ctesiphon.[163] With the help of the nobility, led by Wistahm and Windoe, they deposed the king and brought his son, Khusro II to power.

These events took place in 589–590 CE and it was quite important that it was the first time someone outside the family of Sasan had attempted to take over the empire, which probably was a shock to the Sasanian family. This may characterize the strength of the centralized system and the problems with Sasanian imperial propaganda, especially when a weak or hated king was on the throne. The institutions which were reformed and strengthened during the time of Kavad I and Khusro I were so powerful and entrenched by this time that they functioned regardless of the political chaos. The same may be said of the local affairs, where the *dehgans* became the important officials and local matters became more important for the local population than the political affairs of the empire. One can suggest that when further damage was done to the Sasanian imperial image in the seventh century, during the Arab Muslim conquest, it did not really shake up the institutions and officials of the empire, in that the "system" continued to function under Muslim governors. This is evidenced by the adoption of the Persian administrative system and its employees by the Caliphate.

KHUSRO II AND THE EMPIRE AT ITS GREATEST EXTENT

Turning to the late sixth century CE, Khusro II (590–628 CE) was not able to withstand the forces of Wahram Chubin[164] and did not feel safe within the empire, so he fled to the Eastern Roman Empire in 590 CE, taking refuge in the city of Hierapolis and seeking the aid of emperor Maurice.[165] The Roman emperor supplied Roman and mainly Armenian forces to Khusro II, enabling him to come back to the empire that same year and defeat Wahram. The now renegade general took to the east and was eventually assassinated at the instigation of Khusro by the Turks. We know that Wahram considered himself a legitimate king, since he minted coins for two years (590–591 CE), in the first year in the southwest, primarily in Iraq and Media and then in the second year in the northeast to where he had fled. Even after his death, Wahram captured the imagination of the people who composed songs and stories about him that survived in Arabic and Persian.

When Khusro II came to the throne, he began to take revenge on those who had had a hand in the murder of his father, although we are not sure if he himself was innocent of the crime. His uncle Wistahm, who had been Khusro's supporter, was targeted by his enemies and as a result he took himself to Media, minted coins in his own name and probably lived there until 600 CE.[166] So in the last decade of the sixth century, two people who were not deemed to be the legitimate rulers by the Sasanians minted coins. This is significant, since in 366 years, no one except the Sasanian king was allowed or was able to mint coins in his own name. It is with this damage to the Sasanian prestige that we may turn to Khusro II's conquests.

Khusro II consolidated his power around the Persian Gulf and sent envoys to Arabia, as far as Mecca, to inquire about the situation. The last king of al-Hira, al-Nu'man III ibn al-Mundir was killed and the Lakhmid state put under other Persian loyalists in 602 CE. When the Roman emperor Maurice was murdered and Phokas came to the throne, Khusro II used this event as a pretext for the conquest of Syria and beyond. First Roman Armenia was captured by Khusro II,[167] and in 604 CE with blazing speed, his two generals Shahin and Shahrwaraz conquered Syria.[168] Palestine and then Egypt were taken in 619 CE, and the Persians even went as far as Libya,[169] while Anatolia was conquered between 619–622 CE. We have vivid descriptions by Antiochus Strategos of the conquest of the city of Jerusalem in 614 CE and the taking of the holy cross which resonated negatively in the Roman Empire and was much lamented.[170] This shocked the Eastern Roman empire which in 610 CE had made Heraclius its emperor.[171] Heraclius was intent on leaving for North Africa, but it is said that he was persuaded by the clergy to stay and with the aid of church funds, he mounted a counterattack. From the Black Sea he entered Armenia and went into the heart of the Persian Empire in 624 CE, sacking the sacred Adur Farrobay temple at Ganzak[172] in retaliation for the taking of the "True Cross" by the Sasanains from Jerusalem. The first real crusade between the Christian world and the East thus had taken place, even before the Arab Muslims began their conquest. Along with the retreating Persian army, the Persian nobility and those attached to the Persians also retreated from Syria and Iraq.[173] In a matter of years, Khusro II went from a world conqueror, emulating the Achaemenid territorial integrity to a humiliated king who was unable to protect the sacred Zoroastrian fire-temples and his subjects. Khusro II was removed in 628 CE by the nobility and the priests, and all the conquered territories were returned to the Romans by 630 CE.[174]

IMPERIAL IDEOLOGY, KINGSHIP AND POWER IN THE SEVENTH CENTURY

In terms of imperial ideology we may say that while the early Sasanians considered themselves to be from the lineage of the Gods, they also used Persian Achaemenid and Parthian titles, such as "King of Kings" on their coins and inscriptions. This heritage was set aside by the adoption of the Kayanid ideology from the fourth to the sixth century CE. However, Khusro II proclaimed a return to the dual heritage of the Achaemenid and Kayanid ideology by minting coins in his name with the title of "King of Kings" and also inscribing for the first time the slogan, "increased in glory" (*xwarrah abazūd*). *Xwarrah* is central to the ancient Persian royal ideology as demonstrated in the *Avesta*, and is a prerequisite for rulership in the Iranian world. In Persian art this glory is shown usually with a halo around the king's head.[175]

Khusro II was a warrior-king similar to the kings of the early Sasanian period. His grotto at Taq-ī Bustan shows him in full body-armor, characteristic of the Sasanian heavy cavalry, and shows the deity, Anahid, the lady of the waters, above him. In many ways Khusro II represents the culmination of Sasanian absolutism and a return to the past glories for one last time. While Ohrmazd was held to be supreme, at Taq-ī Bustan one also encounters two other deities, namely Mihr and Anahid. These are the triple deities that were worshiped by Artaxerxes II in the fifth century BCE, thus, there is a full return to devotion to these deities. The opulence of the court of Khusro II is clearly demonstrated by the Taq-ī Bustan rock-relief, where the king is shown on a boat, hunting, and musicians playing their harps, along with the retinue. Khusro II has gone down in Persian history as an opulent[176] king who brought ruin to the Persian Empire. But perhaps his religious policy, specifically his interest in Christianity was a source of his condemnation by the Zoroastrian sources.[177] His favorite wife, Shirin is well known in the epic and romance literature, and is also said to have propagated Christianity in the empire,[178] along his other Christian wife Maryam who was an Eastern Roman princess.

FRATRICIDE AND THE DISINTEGRATION OF THE SASANIAN EMPIRE

After Khusro II, Kavad II (Šērōe) came to the throne in 628 CE. He committed fratricide, killing almost every eligible or capable male heir in the Sasanian family. This again maybe due to the fact that his father Khusro II had crowned a younger brother of his, named Mardānšāh, as his heir. Nonetheless, Kavad II's action would have a devastating effect on the future of the empire. He did not want to be associated with his father's memory, a fact apparent from his coinage which reverted to the style of Khusro I.[179] In 629 CE however, Kavad II made a peace treaty with Heraclius in which he returned all the lands that were held by the Sasanians,[180] and the Persian general Shahrwaraz met the emperor at Arabissus Tripotamus, where the Eupharates became the permanent boundary between the Sasanian Persian and the Roman empires.[181] Kavad II was himself assassinated, like his brothers, which further demonstrates the beleaguered state of royal affairs at Ctesiphon.

In 630 CE, Kavad's young son, Ardashir III came to the throne and it was during his reign that for a third time the Sasanian family was challenged by an outsider. This was the Sasanian general who had fought and led the armies of Khusro II, Shahrwaraz. He soon entered the capital, Cetsiphon, and put an end to the rule of the young king and proclaimed himself the new King of Kings. His actions may have been partly the result of his respect for Khusro II, since he punished and killed all those who had had a hand in the murder of the fallen king. His peace with Heraclius in 629 CE and probably the latter's backing, according to one Armenian source, gave Shahrwaraz the impetus to conquer and take over the throne.[182] This again was a serious setback to the Sasanian imperial ideology. However, he was not able to secure his throne and in a matter of months he, too, was killed.[183]

QUEEN BURAN AND THE DECLINE OF SASANIAN LEGITIMACY

One of the daughters of Khusro II, named Buran, came to the throne in 630 CE and ruled for two years.[184] Her rule was a period of consolidation of the imperial power and the rebuilding of the empire. She attempted to consolidate the empire and relieve the population of heavy taxes, as the Islamic sources report. Her notions of the past and respect for her father are also clear, since she reverted her coinage type to that of her father. She also minted gold coins which were ceremonial in nature and were not meant for wide circulation which, however, stated that she was the restorer of her lineage, i.e., the race of gods which was emphasized in the early Sasanian period. The legend on her coin reads: "Buran, restorer of the race of Gods" (*Bōrān ī yazdān tōhm winārdār*).[185] Of course something should be said of a woman assuming the throne in the Sasanain Empire. She was probably brought to the throne because of the fact that she was the only legitimate heir, along with her sister, who could rule, as Kavad II had murdered all of her brothers.[186] Buran also attempted to keep good relations with the Romans and sent the *Catholicos* Mar Isho-Yab to Heraclius and so she had the opportunity to reorganize the empire.[187]

Buran was also deposed by another Sasanian general and here we see that the military generals are assuming power in the face of the shaken institution of kingship, the competing nobility and the Zoroastrian priests. Following her, Queen Azarmigduxt ruled for a brief period, and her coins have the bust of a man, probably a reuse of the older coins, not having enough time to mint new coins. Between 630 CE when Buran died to 632 CE when Yazdgerd III assumed the throne, there were a number of "contender-kings" who assumed the throne and were either removed or were challenged by other distant members of the family of Sasan. This period may be called a period of factionalism and division within the empire. We have a list of kings who struck coins and others who are known only from the literary sources, but this era is confusing in terms of succession and only a tentative sequence of rulers can be supplied. The list is as follows: Jošnasbandah, Azarmigduxt, Hormizd V, Khusro III, Peroz II, and Khusro IV.[188] The late Sasanian Empire was beginning to resemble the Parthian feudal system before the fall of the Arsacids. This system left the local officials and *dehgans* as the most powerful elite, since the rulers and governors were not able to hold power.[189] From the numismatic evidence it appears that Hormizd V, Khusro III, Peroz II and Khusro IV ruled different areas of the empire simultaneously from the end of 631 CE to 637 CE, when Yazdgerd III had already been on the throne for some years.[190]

Thus we can say that during this period, some power resided at the capital at Cetisphon where the king was crowned, and in the provinces the deposed kings moved from province to province, and the *dehgans* who were probably the most numerous, working with the local Zoroastrian priests, ruled the different regions of the empire. It is ominous that Yazdgerd III was crowned at the Anhāhīd fire-temple at Istakhr in 632 CE, the old center of power for the family of Sasan. This may be not just a symbolic act, but also a reflection of the region's loyalty to the Sasanian family, making Yazdgerd feel secure in Fars. His rule, however, coincided with the Arab Muslim invasion of the Near East and the Eastern Mediterranean.

YAZDGERD III: THE WANDERING KING OF THE IRANIANS

Yazdgerd III was forced to move from province to province demanding loyalty, money and support. During this monarch's rule, Persia looked like the medieval Germanic system of rule, i.e., a Wandering Kingship. From 633 CE, the Arabs were able to enter Iraq but were defeated at the battle of the Bridge in 634 CE. In 636 CE at the battle of Qadisiyya the Sasanians under the leadership of Rustam were defeated and the capital, Ctesiphon, fell to the Arab Muslims who entered it unopposed, with the nobility and the courtiers fleeing before them to the heart of Persia.[191] Under Caliph Umar's direction, Khuzistan fell in 642 CE and in the same year Media was taken at the battle of Nīhāvand. This laid the heart of Persia open to conquest without any major resistance. We should remember that during the reforms of Kavad I and Khusro I the army was divided into four contingents, each placed at a bordering region. Thus when one army was defeated, the heart of the empire was laid open. The in-fighting between factions must have also depleted the unity and power of the standing army. The Arab Muslim victory was successful for a series of reasons. In addition to the internal problems, the heavy Sasanian cavalry was no match for the Arab light cavalry which was much more maneuverable. The Islamic texts usually report the number of the Persian soldiers to have been in the hundreds or tens of thousands and several times larger than the Arab armies. This is pure fiction and it is boastful literature which aims to aggrandize Arab Muslim achievement, which may be compared to the Greek accounts of the Greco-Persian wars. The Sasanian army would not have been able to muster such a large force against the Arabs, since many had been killed or were not present because of the long wars with the Roman Empire and the internal strife. In any case, Yazdgerd III fled to Persis, but the Arabs were able to conquer that region by 650 CE and he was forced to flee to the east. There he was faced with local officials who were unwilling to help him and he was defeated by a confederation of local officials, the margrave of Merv and the Hephthalite ruler of Bāghdīs. Tradition has it that he was killed in 651 CE in Merv by a miller who did not recognize that Yazdgerd was the King of Kings.

The sons of Yazdgerd III fled to the east asking the T'ang emperor, Gaozong, to aid them in their battle against the Arab Muslims. Peroz, the elder son of Yazdgerd III established a kingdom called the "Persian Area Command" (*Bosi dudufu*) at Sistan, stationed at Zarang between 658 and 663 CE. He was recognized as the legitimate king of Persia by the Chinese,[192] but by 674–675 CE we hear that he went to the Chinese capital, probably because of further Arab Muslim victories.[193] He died in around 679 CE and his son Narseh was placed on the throne of Persia in exile. Peroz has been remembered by a stone statue of him which is still in existence at the entrance of the mausoleum of Gaozong with the inscription: "Peroz, King of Persia, Grand General of the Right Courageous Guard and Commander-in-chief of Persia."[194] There the family of Sasan kept their royal status, became military generals, and had temples built at Tun-huang (sha-chou), Wu-wei (Liang-chou), Ch'ang-an (founded in 631 CE) and at Loyang and lived along with the other Persians who had been there for commercial activity or had fled as a result of the Arab Muslim conquest.[195] The other son of Yazdgerd III, Wahram (Aluohan in Chinese sources) attempted to recapture the lost territories from the Arab Muslims. Although he was ultimately unsuccessful and died in 710 CE,[196] the Middle Persian texts especially a small Middle Persian poem called *Abar Madan ī Wahram ī Warzāwand* (On the Coming of the Miraculous Wahram) may have a kernel of truth in regard to his campaigns. Wahram's son, Khusro (*Juluo* in Chinese sources) with the aid of the Turks invaded Persia, but was not able to defeat the Arabs either and this is the last time we hear of someone from the family of Sasan trying to capture the throne of Persia.[197] The Arab Muslims conquerors met stiff resistance in parts of the empire from some of the *dehgāns* and the Zoroastrian priests as well, while others agreed to pay a poll-tax and remain in charge of their territory and submit to the Arab governors. Part of the Sasanian military also joined the Arab forces and as a result kept their status and continued the conquest of the region and Central Asia. The conquest brought Asia closer together and now Arabs, Persians, Indians and the Chinese met each other on the Silk Road again, and with less strife. After Wahram's death the Persians had to wait only 40 years to topple the Arab rulers at Damascus, and by the ninth century, they would establish their own independent dynasties in Persia. Even then the Muslims rulers, be it Persian, Arab, or Turkish, remembered the Sasanians and claimed to be the descendants of Sasan in one way or another.[198] The family of Sasan was never forgotten.

Chapter 2

The Society of *Iranshahr*

A constant feature of Iranian history is the symbiotic relationship between the settled population and the nomadic tribes. However, because of the lack of sources we only have a glimpse of this relationship, and it is only when the nomadic tribes aid or disrupt the imperial order that they come to light in our sources. There are different ways of approaching the study of Persian society in late antiquity, and the traditional view has been to look at the class divisions established by the Sasanian monarchy using the archaic religious tradition of the Avestan period. The Sasanians with the establishment of *Iranshahr* transposed Avestan norms and also its class structure onto the society in the Iranian plateau. The existing society, however, was not the same society of antiquity and had its own characteristics which had developed in the Achaemenid and the Parthian period. For our purpose here it is important to look at the society of *Iranshahr* through the prism of Sasanian world-view and that is class organization. Still, one should have the nomadic traditions in sight when discussing the urban history of Sasanian Iran. Alessandro Bausani in his brilliant book *I Persiani*[1] has outlined the main features of the interaction between the urban and the nomadic population in Islamic Iran and some of its tenets may be applicable to Sasanian Iran as well.

ORGANIZATION OF THE SOCIETY: NOMADISM VS. URBANISM

Sasanian empire aimed to be an urban empire. It appears that more people settled in the old and new cities which were part of the Sasanians' urbanization plan. For example, by the end of the Sasanian period, Mesopotamia had the largest population density in the pre-modern period. This was not an accident, rather it was part of a plan of urbanization, road and dam building project of the Sasanian empire in its heartland. The establishment of cities is the main feature of the Sasanian state-building program which had political, social and economic repercussions for late antique Persian society. Middle Persian texts such as the *Šahrestānīhā ī Iranšahr* (The Provincial Capitals of Iranshahr) demonstrate the vigor with which the Sasanian kings established and re-established cities under their own names. Ardashir I himself is credited with having established many cities, the most important being *Ardashir-xwarrah* in Persis, and Shabuhr I established even more cities, again the most notable being *Iran-xwarrah- Shabuhr*.[2] The insertion of the word *Iran* as part of city names as has been suggested was purposeful and was based on Avestan ideas and linked archaic "myth" and "epos" of Persia in the third century CE.[3] The appearance of *Iran-xwarrah* as part of city names is part of the revival of the Avestan ideology of "glory of the Aryans" which demonstrates Sasanian ideological beliefs.[4] Many of the cities were also populated by Romans, Goths, and people of different religious persuasions such as Christians, and probably pagans from the Fertile Crescent and other captives seized during the wars with Rome. These deportations resulted in the influx of a non-Persian population into the empire. Many of these captives were skilled workers, such as engineers, who were put to use in the building of royal cities, and of the infrastructure such as bridges and dams while the Persian population became acquainted with Roman technology. The economic impact of this deportation and settlement was very important and will be dealt with in the chapter on economy. Still it appears that in part the reason why Shabuhr I undertook military campaigns in the west was to collect booty and payment from the Romans, the bolstering of Sasanian power in the Caucuses, Mesopotamia and the Fertile Crescent, and the importation of skilled workers to populate newly built or re-established cities in the empire. This is especially true for the establishment of the royal cities and their workshops which were populated by foreign workers. This action also had another implication which eventually caused an influx of Christians and the spread of Christianity in the empire.[5]

As opposed to the settled population we have little evidence of the nomadic tribes which inhabited the Iranian plateau. The most prominent group of nomads are designated by the word (Middle Persian) *kurd*. While the word may have stood for the Kurdish people who were nomadic, in the Middle Persian literature it was used for nomads in a larger sense who may have had an uneasy relationship with the urban minded Sasanians. Their co-option into the Sasanian military, if we are to believe Ibn Balkhi's account, would suggest that they were ultimately utilized by the state.[6] The same would hold true for the Daylamite and Gilani tribes who are much better known and who were also used in the military in the Sasanian and the Islamic period as well. The other group worth mentioning is the Kermani who also appear to have been a nomadic tribe and are said to have lived in the province of Persis, according to Istakhri. Both the Kurds and the Kermanis appear in Middle Persian texts as part of an army which corroborates their usage in the Sasanian/early Islamic military.[7] Between the city dwelling population and the nomads the landed gentry (*dehgāns*) played an important role, and their prominence was to come to the fore from the sixth century CE onward due to the reforms of Kavad I and Khusro I.

ŠĀHĀN ŠĀH: THE KING OF KINGS AND THE ORDER OF THINGS

At the head of the Sasanian Empire stood the King of Kings (*Šāhān Šāh*). His well-being and health was always prayed for and the slogan "May you be immortal" (*anōšag bawēd*) was used to respond to him. On the Sasanian coins, from the sixth century one finds the sun and moon on the four quadrants which suggest that the king was at the center of the world and the sun and moon revolved around him. In effect he was the "king of the four corners of the world," which was an old Mesopotamian idea. All other rulers were his subordinates, since there were three other minor thrones present at the court for Roman, Turkic and Chinese rulers. The awe inspiring court and throne room is given detailed treatment in Sasanian sources. The king's dress was colorful and he wore makeup and his beard was adorned with gold, with a crown which was so heavy that it was suspended from the ceiling.[8]

When one had the chance of coming before the king, he/she saw the King of Kings behind a curtain, hidden from the eyes of the common person. The idea of distance between the ruler and the masses was something which can also be found in the Roman and the Chinese world. These rulers must have been conscious of each other's court protocols and tried to copy and outdo one another. When coming before the Persian king one prostrated oneself (*pad rōy obast*) which was known as *Prosykenisis* in the Eastern Roman and *Kowtow* in the Chinese world. He was only to be in contact with the "Keeper of the Curtain" (*xorram-bāš*) and it was through him that the desires of the king were made known. This was the private side of Persian kingship. He, however, gave audience to the people on two major occasions, the New Year (*Nowruz*) and the *Mihragan*. As de Jong has suggested, these two festivals brought the different classes, or at least their leaders together and bound the society under the rulership of the king. By the exchange of gifts, this solidarity between the institution of kingship and the different classes was emphasized and maintained symbolically.[9] It is also noteworthy to mention that these two festivals fell exactly six months apart from one another which meant that this connection could be maintained on a regular and steady basis through the year. Early Sasanian kings were considered divine, as they themselves mentioned in their royal inscriptions. They were known as *bay* "divine," which can also be translated as "majesty," whose lineage was tied to the deities. Thus, the king was not an ordinary human being and was to be respected and conveyed an air of holiness. In time when Zoroastrian theology and imperial propaganda had developed further, the kings emphasized their sacred duty even more. As Ohrmazd had established order out of chaos and battled chaos in the cosmos, so the king battled and fought chaos to bring back order on earth. Through order the well-being of the people was secured and this well-being was only feasible through the dispensation of justice by the king. This title is very much associated with one of the most famous Sasanian kings, Khusro I who ruled in the sixth century CE. If the king was unjust, then the society could be thrown into chaos. On the other hand if society and its order fell into disorder, it was incumbent upon the king to bring back order in society. By order here one means an orderly class division which according to our sources was upheld vehemently.

PĒŠAG: CLASS DIVISION

With the urban-minded Sasanians we must turn to the city and urban social organizations in order to understand the social history of Persia. In was in this milieu that the Sasanians were best able to control and expand their socio-political patterns. It must be emphasized that we are unsure at which time class ordering and divisions reached their ultimate rigidity or even how rigid they really were, since it is only the eighth and ninth century Middle Persian texts written from a religious perspective that supply detailed information in this regard. These texts may suggest an ideal social ordering, thus they represent Sasanian aspirations which were certainly at work. One may state that by the end of the third century CE this rigidity may have begun to take shape. The various sources suggest that there were four estates or classes (*pēšag*) which were recognized by the state and propagated by the religious apparatus.

The priests (*āsrōnān*) composed a class which was further divided in rank and function: the chief priests (*mowbedān*), priests attending the fires (*hērbedān*), expert theologians *(dastūrān)*, judges *(dādwarān)*, and learned priests (*radān*) were chosen from the ranks of the religious body. If one looks at such texts as the *Hērbedestān* one comes across more priestly titles, which attest to their importance and specialty in their religious activity.[10] They functioned in various capacities within the state apparatus and the court as well. As mentioned, the judges were from this estate because they were the ones who had knowledge about those religious matters which regulated the laws and norms of the empire. They also acted as councilors (*andarzbed*) and, based on the epigraphic remains, we know of councilor-priests (*mowān andarzbed*) who were also important functionaries. Other important priestly offices included the Priest of Ohrmazd (*ohrmazd mowbed*).[11] We must remind ourselves that these titles were not all created at one time or the beginning of the Sasanian dynasty, but rather there was a proliferation of ranks and titles as the administrative and religious apparatus of the state grew. By the fifth century CE each class of priests had their own chief and we have evidence for two of them, the chief of the *mowbeds* known as *mowbedān mowbed*, and for the teacher-priests attending the fires, the *hērbedān hērbed*.

The priests were trained in seminaries where religious scripture and the prayers were learned and memorized and theological matters were discussed under supervision. These religious schools included the *mowestāns* and *hērbedestāns*. In certain sources we also come across a title which appears to have been the highest position among the priests which may be translated as "Zoroaster-like" (*zarduxšttom*).[12] The *zarduxšttom*'s residence is not clear but he certainly had to remain in the empire and not venture out if we are to accept the Middle Persian texts.[13] The term which covered the religious body as a whole was *dēnbarān* who were concerned with learning and culture (*frahang*).[14] The performance of correct ritual ceremonies brought about the success of the warriors against the enemy and of the farmers for better cultivation of the land and salvation for the masses.[15] Thus not only their guidance, but also their actions, made certain the well being of the society. The Middle Persian text the *Dādestān ī Mēnōg ī Xrad* spells out the functions of the priest and those activities in which they should not partake. These include the usual expectations from a priest of any religion: "to uphold the religion, worshipping the deities, passing judgments in religious and ritual matters based on past testaments, directing people to do well, and to show the way to heaven and to invoke the fear of hell."[16]

Not all priests were of course working in the state apparatus or were part of the Zoroastrian state church; some were either denounced or simply seen as heretic. The priests not only functioned in the religious and the legal apparatus, but also in the economic sphere as well. They were in charge of overlooking the taxes which were to be collected for the state as evidenced by the appearance of their signature in the form of signet rings on bullae "or the ostraca evidence". In one instance a priest is condemned for cheating or lying over which the religious courts had jurisdiction.[17] The *hērbed*s also functioned as teachers of the religious hymns and rituals for the people, and their religious focal point was probably the fire-temples (*ātaxš kadag*). A Middle Persian text supplies a list of the sections of the *Avesta* which may have been memorized by the *hērbedān* which were the *Yašt*, *Hādōxt*, *Baɣān*, and the *Wīdēwdād*. They must have also learned the meaning or its translation, i.e., the *zand*.[18] Christian martyrologies of the sixth century also attest to the memorization and chanting of the sacred hymns. A large number of structures which have come to be known as *Chahar Taq* were probably these centers (fire-temples), which the Zoroastrian population frequented. Not only those who wanted to say their prayer before the fire or listen to the *hērbed*, but also in time of hunger and thirst people would seek the fire-temples for relief.[19]

By the late Sasanian period there were probably wide gaps in terms of priestly functions and outlook which parallel Christianity in Medieval Europe. This means that the *mowbedān mowbed* and other groups of priests lived in luxury and opulence and functioned in the administrative apparatus as apparent from their signet rings, while others lived a simple life and toiled and worked the land. The sixth book of the *Dēnkard* has preserved for us an important passage in which two priests till the land and pull water from the well and recite their religious mantras.[20] A priest of high rank passes by and sees their activity which impresses him and consequently he sends them thousands of silver coins (*drahms*) along with the sign of nobility (*wandag ī āzādīh*).[21] They, however, only take two *drahm*s and send the rest back, stating that they will only take what is needed. This story, however, dogmatic in nature, demonstrates using Christian terminology, an ascetic lifestyle. It may have gained prominence for a group of priests (in our text these being *hērbeds*) which portrays a very different picture of Sasanian Zoroastrianism.[22] The most important fire-temple in the empire belonged to the priestly estate known as *Adur Farrobay* and it was their ceremonial center.

The warriors (*artēštārān*) composed the second estate of the society and their function was to protect the empire and its subjects, the armies were initially headed by an *Iran-spahbed* "General of the Empire." Later during the time of Kavad and his son, Khusro I, this office was abolished and four *spahbed* "generals" were assigned to the four quarters (*kusts*) of the empire. By then another office, the (*artēštārān sālār*) "Generalissimo," had assumed the highest rank in the Sasanian army. The army included and gained the support of the local kings (*šahrdārān*); princes related to the king (*wispuhrān*); the grandees (*wuzurgān*); and the gentry (*āzādān*). The function of the warriors who were in effect the largest part the nobility was to protect the empire, and to deal with people with gentility and keep their oath.[23] By the late Sasanian period, however, the enlisting of nomadic mercenary forces weakened the position of the upper classes in the military.

There were divisions within the military including the cavalry (*aswārān*) and the foot soldiers (*paygān*). Just as the clergy had to attend seminaries, the soldiers were also to be trained in the military sciences and manuals of military warfare which were in existence and whose remnants are present in the *artēštārestān* in the *Dēnkard*.[24] The alliance between the priests and the warriors was of paramount importance since the idea of *Iranshahr*, which had manifested itself under the Sasanians as a set territory and ruled by the warrior aristocracy, conceptually had been developed and revived by the priests. This alliance was very important in the survival of the state at the beginning of the Sasanian Empire, and it became part of the idyllic axiom of the Zoroastrian religion, where religion and the state were seen as two pillars which were inseparable from each other. It was believed that one would not be able to survive without the other. In reality, both groups attempted to impose their will on the other and this long battle caused the final fragmentation and the weakening of the empire.

The army was known as (*spāh*) and was divided into further divisions. The cavalry (*aswārān*) was the most important part of the army, which usually consisted of the *wuzurgān* and the *āzādān* and those who showed exceptional talent in the art of war. In the fourth century CE Ammianus Marcellinus describes the Persian cavalry. It was clad in body armor, with helmets which only had holes for the eyes. Their horses were also covered with armor; the groto of Khusro II at Taq-ī Bustan represents the culmination of the advancement in Sasanian armor, but still reminds us of the description by Ammianus Marcelinus. Their weapons, based on al-Tabarī's description of the reforms under

Khusro I, included: horse mail, soldier's mailed coat, breastplate, leg armor plates, sword, lance, shield, mace, and fastened at his waist, a girdle, battle ax, or club, bow case containing two bows with their strings, thirty arrows, and two plaited cords.[25] By the sixth century the chancery of Warriors (Arabic *dīwān al-muqātilah*) set a stable stipend for cavalry.[26] It was from among these soldiers that the elite corps called "the Immortals," was chosen[27] and whose leader was probably the *puštigbān-sālār* "Commander of the Royal Guard."

There was also a light cavalry which was composed of mercenaries or tribal people in the empire which included the Dailamites, Gilanis, Georgians, Armenians, Turks, Arabs, Kushans, Khazars and Hephtalites who were feared by the Romans. The other form of cavalry which was used in wars was the elephant corps (*pīl-bānān*). These animals could be considered the tanks of the ancient world and the Persian proximity to India ensured a steady supply of these animals. Ammianus Marcelinus describes the elephants as having an awful figure and savage, gaping mouths, they could scarcely be endured by the faint-hearted, and looked like walking towers.[28] Based on Tabarī we can see that elephants were used as early as the third century CE in the reign of Shabuhr I who used war elephants to raze the city of Hatra.[29] Piruz used 50 elephants in his campaign against the Hephthalites in the fifth century CE;[30] a relief at Taq-ī Bustan depict elephant corps during the time of Khusro II; and according to Islamic sources they were used against the Arabs in the seventh century.

The infantry (*paygān*) was headed by the *paygān-sālār* "commander of the infantry." They were fitted with shields and lances; behind them in the battle line were the archers. Maurice's *Strategicon* gives us detailed information on the strategies, as well as the intricacies and differences between the weapons and their uses between the Persian and the Roman soldiers.[31] Naturally the cavalry and the infantry forces required a huge logistical apparatus which was sustained by the conscripts among the population, to feed, repair weapons, tend to the wounded, establish tents, etc. The Sasanians also utilized Roman know-how when it came to the use of siege weapons which included scorpions, balistae, battering rams, moving towers, catapults, and moles.

Something should be said of the Sasanian navy, since it was instrumental from the beginning when Ardashir I conquered the Arab side of the Persian Gulf.[32] The control of the Persian Gulf was a necessity militarily as well as economically, making it safe from piracy, Roman encroachment, and controlling the Arab tribes. Again based on al-Tabarī it appears that the Persian ships (*kaštīg*) held 100 men and eight of them were sent to Yemen during the rule of Khusro I in the sixth century.[33] Another early Islamic source corroborates that Khusro I had sent 100 men each on eight ships, which suggests the Persian naval vessels carried up to 100 men. The interesting point of the story is that the men were those who were confined to his prison. Thus it could not have been a very effective naval force. As the story goes, six of the ships arrived safely to the shores of Aden under the command of Wahriz.[34] The leader of the navy would have had the title of **nāvbed*.[35]

The other titles and classifications that we have are again from late sources where we are told that there were several other military positions which included Commander of the forts (*argbed*), warden of marches (*marzbāns*), the hereditary title of the general of Tūs in the east *kanārang*, and the army General (*gund-sālār*).[36] The warrior estate also had a designated fire-temple, *Adur Gushnasp* which was only second to *Adur Farrobay*. This fire-temple was at Shiz, near Ganzak at the south-east direction of Lake Urmiya, where the king and the warriors went to worship. Wahram Gur (V) sent booty of jewelry to be hung in the fire-temple after defeating the Turks in his campaign against them.[37] What we should remember is that Ardashir I made similar offerings to the fire-temple of Anahid at Istakhr in the third century CE. His offerings were the heads of the rebels, but this fact may suggest that while the Zoroastrian priests dominated the Anāhid fire-temple, *Adur Gushnasp* may have taken some specific cultic function.

The third estate consisted of the husbandmen (*wāstaryōšān*), and farmers (*dahigān*), whose function was to till the land and keep the empire prosperous, and were represented by a chief of husbandmen (*wāstaryōšān sālār*). They were producers of the foodstuffs as well as the tax base for the empire and as a result the land under cultivation was surveyed by the government and taxes exacted from it. During the reforms of the Kavad and Khusro I, land and the different types of yield and taxes were estimated based on its production. Cultivation of the land was a beneficent act in the Zoroastrian religion and letting it sit idle a sin. The function of the farmers was "farming and bringing cultivation and as much as possible, bringing ease and prosperity."[38] *Adur Burzenmihr* was the third major fire-temple which existed in the empire and it was the place where the husbandmen went during certain ceremonial occasions.

The fourth estate was much more numerous than the other three and treated somewhat separately by Zoroastrian law. They were the artisans (*hutuxšān*).[39] Based on the structure and the differentiating language in our Middle Persian texts, one understands an uneasiness of the priests with the artisans/merchants. The text, the *Dādestān ī Mēnōg ī Xrad* (Chapter 30), discusses the function of first three estates, and while the priests, warriors, and the husbandmen are treated under this chapter the artisans are treated in a separate section (Chapter 31). The language and the length employed in specifying the function of this estate demonstrates the negative view of the Zoroastrians in regard to the artisan class: "(They) should not undertake a task with which they are not familiar, and perform well and with concentration those tasks which they know. Ask for fair wages, because if someone does not know a task and performs that task, it is possible for him to ruin it or leave it unfinished, and that man himself is satisfied it would be a sin for him."[40]

The negative tone of this passage as compared with that of the previous passage dealing with the first three estates demonstrates that when the Zoroastrian priests began to codify laws in regard to social matters, the artisans/merchants were placed at the very bottom.[41] This dim view of the artisans or the merchant class is especially important in the face of the large number of artisans/merchants in Persia in Late Antiquity. This negative view somewhat contributed to the reduction of the Zoroastrian involvement towards these tasks and the movement of religious minorities toward artisanship and commerce. It appears the government was never involved in opening economic markets or actively engaged in business, but rather private corporations were to be the major proponents of trade. The government was only to assure the upkeep and safety of the roads and to exact toll road taxes. It was the individual who contributed most to the flourishing economy.

The Sogdian "Merchants" who lived in the northeastern territory of the Sasanian Persian empire were not necessarily Zoroastrian and were open to religious ideas of different traditions.[42] When we hear of Persian colonies established in the Far East for commerce and trade in such things as silk, the Christian Persians become more prominent. The Christians would have used this anti-Zoroastrian stance in regard to artisanship and commerce to their advantage, filled this gap in society, and through patronage enlarged their numbers. Christian attitudes were much more positive than those of the Zoroastrians towards commerce and artisanship, and this may be a reason for the strength of Christianity in the aftermath of the Islamic conquest of the Near East. While the Manichaean Hearers were artisans and merchants, the Manichaean Elect, much like Zoroastrianism priests, did not concern themselves with commerce. This is especially interesting in light of the fact that the Elect were dependent on the Hearers for their basic needs. This may be a reason why Islam spread rapidly when it was introduced to the Iranian plateau, because it was business-friendly.

From the seventh century the Sogdian merchants, the Manichaean artisans, and the Zoroastrian businessmen saw Islam as a religion that was pro-commerce and supported this estate.[43] After all the Prophet Muhammad, a merchant himself, lived in Mecca, an important commercial city, and he was well aware of the importance of the merchant class in society. The same reason may be given for the disappearance of Buddhism in eastern Persia (including Afghanistan), where economic matters enforced religious gravitations toward Islam. There is an irony in such a scenario in which the state was aware of the fact that the artisan/merchant class was a great source of income, wealthy and powerful, but it still focused on agriculture which was the dominant mode of production, and kept the artisans and merchants as the lowest strata of the society. Perhaps the religious foundations of Persian society also enforced this negative view to the rise and acceptance of the artisan/merchant class as an important group, and consequently artisan/merchant gravitation towards Manichaeism and Christianity first, and then to Islam became natural.

The royal workshops were controlled by the state to hold up the standards in the making of such commodities as the silver dishes used as propaganda instruments and production of glass and other goods for the nobility. Roman, Goths and Mesopotamian skilled workers were among this group which used Roman techniques in artistic production. Then the cities where these foreign laborers were established and those who functioned in the royal workshops were kept under close watch. A guild Master *(Kārragbed)* was in charge of the production and the workers. The absence of a fourth major fire-temple for this artisan/merchant estate also signifies their lowly status and/or the number of non-Zoroastrian members of the estate. All four estates were overseen by a *pēšag sālār* which according to legal texts was the chief of the estates.[44]

This is a general division of the society according to the Middle Persian and Islamic sources, but we may look at the society in terms of two groups as well: the haves and have not, or the nobility and the masses. In this division one can make distinctions between court life, and the life of the others, and finally the poor, slaves and the mob. Women were not to be treated separately but as part of the society, where the class that a woman was born into dictated her rights and privileges, governed by the Zoroastrian law which covered all of the society. The metics were also an important part of the society, especially since many were forcibly settled in the empire during the kings' campaigning in the west, for the repopulation of the empire and the introduction of new skilled workers. This group, which was mainly composed of Romans, Goths and the Christian population of Syria, were again used as farmers and slaves, depending on their skills.

COURTLY LIFE AND FOOD BASED ON MIDDLE PERSIAN SOURCES

From the textual and the material evidence the court life and the life of the nobility was extravagant and pleasurable. In the Middle Persian text *Khusro and the Page* (*Xusrō ud Redag*), the various foods, drinks, desserts and games in which the nobility engaged are spelled out. We have already mentioned the important court activity of feasting (*bazm*), in which the courtiers gathered, ate, drank, and made merry. These courtly events are depicted on silver plates showing the king seated, while dancing girls perform to the musicians. A variety of musical instruments and musicians existed which included the harp-player (*čang-srāy*), vina-player (*win-srāy*), the long-necked-lute-player (*win-kannār-srāy*), the Pandean flute-player (*sūr-pīk-srāy*), the cither-player (*tambūr-srāy*), the lyre-player (*barbut-srāy*) the flute-player (*nāy-srāy*), and hand-drum-player (*dumbalag-srāy*).[45]

Juggling and other performances such as rope-dancing (*rasan wāzīg*), chain-playing (*zanjīr-wāzīg*), pole-climbing (*dār-wāzīg*), snake-charming (*mār-wāzīg*), hoop-springing (*čambar-wāzīg*), arrow-playing (*tīr-wāzīg*), cup-juggling (*tās-wāzīg*), rope-walking (*wandag-wāzīg*), air-playing (*andarwāy-wāzīg*), pole-and-shield-playing (*mēx ud spar-wāzīg*), armor-playing (*zēn-wāzīg*), ball-playing (*gōy-wāzīg*), javelin-playing (*sil-wāzīg*), dagger-playing (*šamšēr-wāzīg*), club-playing (*warz-wāzīg*), bottle-juggling (*šīšag-wāzīg*), and monkey-playing (*kabīg-wāzīg*)[46] performed before the court, while the cook (*xwahlīgar*)[47] stood attentively beside the fire and the food, covering his mouth so as not to contaminate the royal feast. Maidens of good voice (*xwaš āwāz*) also sang along while playing their harps (*čang-srāy-kanīg*) along with a vina-player (*win-srāy*),[48] while the dancing girls poured wine in the cups and courtesans kept them warm. The musician/minstrel (*huniyāgar*) who was known under other names such as *rāmišgar*, or *gosān* and later *chamagu* of course did not necessarily need to be a female. In fact the most famous is the legendary Bārbad at the court of Khusro II who sang along with the other legendary female counterpart, Nakisā and sang about the story of the king and his favorite wife, Shirin.[49] In fact there exists a categorization of "voices" (*wāng*), in the Zoroastrian tradition where "vina-voice" (*win wāng*) is described as singing by the righteous and the *Avesta* was read in the same manner which was accompanied by a kind of string (*zīh*) instrument.[50] This is reminiscent of the Manichaean tradition, where hymn-singers (*mahrsarāyān*) sang the sacred words accompanied by string and other instruments.[51] This oppulance and atmosphere of entertainment at the court, especially at the time of Khusro I in the sixth century CE signaled the idea that not only all is well in the Sasanian Empire, but that Persia is prosperous.[52]

The nobles engaged in riding (*aswārīh*), archery (*kamānwarīh*), and jousting with spears (*nēzagwarīh*) which burnt off the extravagant food which was consumed. Some of these dishes are mentioned which included a young sheep (*mēšag*) rubbed with a kind of sour and bitter gruel (*āb-kāmag*) and thickened butter-milk (*kāmag*); peacock (*frašmurw*) and pheasant (*titar*), and duck (*murw ī ābīg*) were served. Already the sense that well-fed animals and free-range chickens supplied the best meat is mentioned in a text, where a chicken fed on hemp-seed (*šādānag*), barley flour (*ard ī kaškēn*), and olive-oil (*rōgn ī zayt*), and made to run (*tāxtan*) is considered the best food. Cold meats included a calf (*gawdar*) whose meat is rubbed with sour vinegar (*sig ī truš*), then cooked as potted meat (*halām*). As for sweet-meats each season a different set of sweet-meats must be served. In summer time almond-pastry (*lōzēnag*) and walnut-pastry (*gōzēnag*) were desired. In the winter juicy (*šiftēnag*), cool (*wafrēnag*) pastry made of crystal-sugar (*tawarzad*) and flavored with coriander (*āčārag*) was desired. But the most desired was *pālūdag* (Persian *pālūde*) which was made from apple juice, sugar and cardamom. As for jam, red and white orange (*wādrang ī wahrman ud spēt*) and above all a jam made from Chinese ginger and myrobalan preserved in sugar (or honey) (*sinjīwēl ī čīnīg ud halīlag ī parwardag*) were desired. Fruits (*šawēnag*), pistachios (*bistag*), and dates (*xormā*) are also mentioned. As for drinks, wine appears to have been the beloved choice. Grape wine (*may ī kanīg*) from different regions was desired, but Assyrian wine (*may ī āsūrīg*) and Basarangian wine (*bādag ī wāzarangīg*) were deemed the best.[53] Both red and white wine (*may ī suxr/may ī spēd*) were consumed, and their clarity and taste judged.[54] Again, variety and access to exotic foods and drinks signaled a prosperous empire which had everything and was to be emulated by its neighbors.

The chase or the hunt was another favorite activity of the nobility in which women participated also.[55] The hunt mirrored warfare in the off season, and symbolically signified the battle readiness of the warriors. Parallel ideas developed in Europe with the coming of the Germanic people, where the hunt became the accepted activity of the warrior aristocracy. These hunting programs could also have been quite extravagant if the Taq-ī Bustan scene is accurate in depicting such scenes. While the king was hunting on the boat, there were rows of harp players, elephants, attendants and others before the king. Silver plates also mostly depict the ancient Near Eastern image of the king as hero who either slays a lion or is on the hunt, killing the game with his arrows or the sword while riding the horse. The image of the king as the ultimate hero is not only depicted, but mentioned in Shabuhr I's inscription at Ka'ba-i Zardosht. In this inscription he mentions several times his heroic deeds and taking the Roman emperor by his own hand, but also in another inscription at Hajjiabad, Shabuhr I again states that in front of the nobility he made a shot with bow and arrow that went quite far and challenges anyone else to be able to make their shot go further.[56]

Wahram II was especially keen on showing himself on plates and inscriptions along with his family. His rock relief at Sar Mashhad are among the most interesting, since not only is he shown killing lions, which reminds us of the Assyrian and more importantly the Achaemenid artistic representation, but there is also the depiction of the royal family and the queen(s). At Barm-i Dilak also Wahram II is shown with his family and the courtiers along with women together.[57] By comparing the inscription of Shabuhr I at Ka'ba-i Zardosht and that of Narseh at Paikuli, we get a sense of the ordering of the courtiers and the nobility. The family of the king, rankings, that is the princes of royal blood (*wispuhrān*), the grandees (*wuzurgān*), and the nobles (*āzādān*) appear to be the most important of them. They are, however, preceded by the local kings and queens, and the family of the King of Kings. The grandees appear to include the viceroy (*bidaxš*); the Chilarch (*hazārbed*); chief of cavalry (*spāhbed*); the noble families of Waraz, Suren, Undigan, and Karen; followed by other title holders which included satraps (*šahrāb*), counselors (*andarzbed*), sword bearers (*šafšēlār*), master of the servants (*fristagbed*), master of ceremonies (*grastbed*), chief scribe (*dibīrbed*), chief of prison (*zēndānīg*), gate keeper (*darbed*), castle lord (*dizbed*), treasurer (*ganjwar*), local rulers (*framādār*), eunuch of the harem (*šabestān*), judge of the empire and other lesser functionaries. These officials were ranked and distinguished by their clothes, bonnet and belts which were given to them by the state. We should mention that we come across later sources which supply other official titles such as the chief usher or master of the ceremonies (*andēmāngārān sālār*), the stablemaster (*āxwarbed*), the Chiliarch (*hazārbed*), the Cupbearer (*taghārbed*) who may have served as a eunuch. The *darīgbed* which according to the Greek sources was equivalent to *kouropalátēs*, a palace superintendent, and the chief physician (*drust-bed*) were also present.[58]

SCRIBES

The scribes' (*dibīrān*) function and importance became increasingly greater as the bureaucratic apparatus of the Sasanian government grew. They performed a variety of functions and needed to have various skills. Some scribes accompanied the Sasanian army[59] and were in their service (**dibīr-spāh* and **gund-dibīr*)[60] while other scribes were in the employment of the local provincial kings. The royal scribes were also responsible for ordering the writing of the imperial inscriptions, and then written drafts were translated into Greek, Arabic, Sanskrit and other languages.[61] Some had to be bilingual for translating and writing in other languages and probably some were drawn from Rome, Arabia and other regions. The scribes have left us seals which demonstrate their rank and the region they covered, from simply *dibir* to the chief scribe (*dibīrbed*). At schools (*dibīrstān*),[62] the *dibīrān* were expected to be able to learn different forms of handwriting, such as calligraphy (*xūb-nibēg*), shorthand (*rag-nibēg*), subtle knowledge (*bārīk-dānišn*), and to have nimble fingers (*kāmgār-angust*).[63] They appear to have had knowledge of different scripts employed for writing which included the religious script (*dēn-dibīrīh*), i.e., the Avestan script which was invented in the Sasanian period; a comprehensive script (**wīš-dibīrīh*) whose nature and function is unclear. The Islamic sources state that it was used for physiognomy, divination and other unorthodox purposes. A third, known as turned or cursive script (**gaštag-dibīrīh*) was used for recording contracts and other legal documents, medicine and philosophy; the secret script (*rāz-dibīrīh*) was for such affairs as secret correspondence among kings. The sixth was script for letters (*nāmag-dibīrīh*), and the seventh was the common script (*hām-dibīrīh*). The *dibiran* were to draft letters (*nāmag*) and correspondence (*frawardag*) and we posses a specimen of such a manual about the manner in which one should write for different purposes and occasions.

Thus there was a formula for each type of correspondence to the grandees or lords (*xwadāyān*), first to inquire about the state of their well-being (*bēš-pursīšnīh*) and happiness (*hunsandīh*) and then how to begin and finish the letters.[64] This formulaic system of letter writing is also clear from the seventh-century papyri which exist from the time of the occupation of Egypt by the Persians. They usually start with reverence (*namāz*) and salutations (*drōd*) to the receiver and/or the date (*rōz*) when the letter was written.[65] Some of these scribes included the accountants (*āmār-dibīr*) who used a specific script known as *šahr-āmār-dibīrīh*/(Arabic *kātib al-xarāj*). The court accountant (*kadag-āmār-dibīr*) used the *kadag-āmār-dibīrīh*, the treasury accountants (**ganj-āmār-dibīr*) used the *ganj-āmār-dibīrīh* (Persian *dabīr-ī xazāna*) script, and the accountant of the royal stables (*āxwar-āmār-dibīr*) used the (*āxwar-āmār-dibīrīh*) script. There were also accountants connected with the fire-temples, the (*ātaxšān-āmār-dibīr*) who used the (*ātaxšān-āmār-dibīrīh*) script. The accountants of the pious foundations (*ruwānagān-āmār-dibīr*) used the (*ruwānagān-dibīrīh*) script. The royal tax collectors sent to the provinces of the empire were known as (*šahr-dibīr* Arabic *kātib al-kūra*).[66] The judicial decisions were written down by the legal scribes (**dād-dibīrān*) who used the *dād-dibīrīh* script.[67] The documents or contracts drawn up by these scribes in relation to legal matters were taken from a known legal phraseology and then signed with wax and seal (*gil ud nāmag*),[68] and copies were kept in the different archives (*nāmag-miyān*).[69] They also had to keep a record of the minutes in tribunals of inquiry. They were probably drawn from the clergy and dealt with the Zoroastrian law. There were several kinds of contracts and documents which included royal decrees (*dib ī pādixšāy-kard*),[70] treaties (*pādixšīr*), the certificates of divorce (*hilišn-nāmag*), manumission certificates (*āzād-nāmag*), and title deeds for the transfer of property for pious purposes (*pādixšīr*),[71] ordeal warrants (*uzdād-nāmag*)[72] as well as an ordeal document (*yazišn-nāmag*) drawn up for the guilty.[73] In relation to the holy-scripture, the copiers of the scripture (**dēn-dibīr*) used the *dēn-dibīrīh* to copy what had been committed to writing in the Sasanian period.[74] The head of the scribes like any other profession held the title with the suffix "master" (*bed*), i.e., *dibīrbed*. The scribes would have a very important presence in the court and with the coming of the Arabs, they were to stay and render their service to the Caliphate.

Many of the local kings who were from the family of Sāsān had their own retinue including a councilor (*andarzbed*); a priest (*mow*); a scribe (*dibīr*); knights/nobles (*āzādān*); messengers (*frēstag*), and chiefs (*sardārān*).[75] This last group had further subdivisions, such as master of the house or clan leaders (*kādag-xwadāyān*); and the landed gentry (*dehgānān*) who rose in prominence by the late fifth or early sixth century as a result of the reforms of Kavad I and Khusro I. We should remember that because of the Mazdakite revolt, Kavad I got the chance to reduce the power of the upper nobility and in return empower the lower class of the nobility, the *dehgānān*. By the sixth century CE the landed aristocracy or gentry became the backbone of the state and the state became dependent on these small landowners. The status of *dehgānān* grew at the expense of the nobility, because they acted as collectors of taxes from the peasants and served in the military. This ultimately must have given rise to localism, where the local landowners saw their interests as more important than that of the Sasanian state and when the Arab Muslims began the conquest of the region, they were willing to pay *jizya* (poll tax) to stay in power and function similarly under the new masters. The *dehgānān* are also known to have been the conduits of Persian ethics, ideals, and social norms which were captured in the epics and romances of Medieval Islamic Persia. The epic texts demonstrate their taste for the heroic and a class consciousness which must have been different from the city dwelling population, where probably the stories of kings and heroes were retold differently emphasizing other functions which was appealing to the population at large.

THE CITIZENS OF THE EMPIRE

The citizens of the empire known as "flocks" or" masses" (*ramān*) constituted the largest group of the society. We should also mention that among them there were non-Zoroastrians, i.e., the Jews and Christians, who probably had their own dwelling quarters. We know for example that the city of *Gay*, which was close to Isfahan, was the city of the Jews. This city which was on the western side of the Zayandeh Rud in the Islamic period and was called al-Yahudiyah "the Jewish town," which was larger than the part on the east side of the river.[76] In Susa as well there appears to have been a large number of Jews living, where the important tomb of the Prophet Daniel was nearby. For the Christians, after the recognition of the Persian Christian church (Nestorian) and its split from the Byzantine church, the situation became much better.[77] The establishment of a diocese and the existence of seals can tell us of their prominence and where the Christians were most numerous. For example in Persis, in six districts Christians administered dioceses.[78] This toleration may have been the reason for which such a proselytizing religion was becoming successful even among the nobility, especially the royal women, such as Shirin, and Gulinduxt, whose martyrologies are numerous for this period.[79]

The Christian subjects of the empire were of two groups: those Christians who were Persian who were probably much more influential in Sasanian affairs and established the Nestorian church, and the second group which consisted of the Roman war prisoners and those captured in Syria and deported to the Sasanian empire. For the second group the architectural remains at the city of Bishabuhr and roads and bridges which demonstrate Western taste and technology suggest that they were used in the building activity, and their engineers were used for building the infrastructure. By the late sixth century the issue of the conversion of Sasanian nobility to Christianity and the amount of hagiographies and martyrologies suggest that the Christians had penetrated the core of Zoroastrian society. More importantly the evidence that Yazdgerd III and his son Piruz commissioned the building of Christian Churches in China suggests the tide of conversion among the royal family.[80] The non-Zoroastrian women, especially the Jews and Christians did marry Zoroastrians, particularly the nobles and the King of Kings as well. For example the mother of Wahram V was Jewish and the favorite wife of Khusro II, the mother of Queen Buran, was Christian. This may have made the situation of their respective communities safe, as such women would represent their concerns.

By the fifth century CE, the state had realized the importance of the religious minorities and attempted to co-opt them into a system of governance where according to legal precepts, all would be considered simply as *mard / zan ī šahr* "man/woman citizen (of the Empire)." Each community was bound by their local religious tradition and under the jurisdiction of their Rabbi and/or Priest. When there were cases which were between people of different religious communities, the state court had precedence. Although Zoroastrian law was the basis of state law, the imperial system had created a system to co-opt all citizens of the empire. This way, one could be considered as *ēr* "Iranian," and the community of the *Iranagan* "Iranians." The Jews and Christians in turn accepted the idea of *Iran/Iranshahr* as they had become part of it, but the Manichaeans who were persecuted never did. In this way the idea of *Iran* left its Zoroastrian roots and thanks to the Sasanians lingered on even after the fall of the Sasanians and Zoroastrianism as a state religion.[81]

THE POOR, THE NEEDY AND THE REBEL ROUSERS

The other largest part of the society was the poor, the downtrodden, and the mob. We should however, according to Shaki make a distinction between those who were seen as the needy poor, which the religion stipulated should be helped and protected (*driyōšān*), and the abject poor who were insolent and unhappy with their state (*škōhān*). The worthy poor whose name renders the medieval and modern *darwīš* are usually praised in the Zoroastrian texts and consisted of women and men, and as the texts tell us were people who were content with what they had and lived with basic subsistence.[82] There were injunctions to aid them, and those who did not would be punished in hell and receive eternal torment.[83] Shaki believed that the *driyōšān* were a class of learned clergy,[84] and this would make it even more possible that they were the precursors to the *darvishes* of the Islamic period. On the other hand the abject poor, the *škōh* must have been as numerous as in any other late antique societies. They were the ones who may have caused most of the tensions within the society and hence were treated badly in the Zoroastrian Middle Persian texts. From the language of the texts which cover the abject poor, it appears that they were discontent not only with their own miserable situation but also with the Sasanian State and held the richer folks in contempt. Mostly they would be the common thieves and criminals who stole and caused disturbance for safety of the urban population and distant trade of the empire. If they were captured, they were branded (*drōš*) and thus identified as deviants from the Ohrmazdian society. Just as the *driyōšān* had become a group, the *škōhān* must have organized in some fashion not only to help themselves but their kind. A person who was dissatisfied with what he had or was contemptuous of his situation[85] would easily be persuaded to steal from the rich. The *škōhān* may have been from the fourth estate, those laborers or simply the unemployed who worked hard and were looked upon with suspicion by the priests and the state. According to Adurbad i Mahrspandan one of the five great calamities which can befall people is the uprising of the *škōhān* against the Lords (*xwadāyān*).[86]

This brings us to another group in the Sasanian society and those are the *mard i juwan*, known in the Islamic period as the *Jawan-mardan* (literally "young men") or the *männerbund*, who represented the discontented youth. The Islamic sources give us more positive information in regard to these discontented youth which the Sasanian state saw as mob. They had their own code of conduct and were not bent on pillaging anyone in sight, but rather had a directed aim of aiding the poor and the downtrodden in society. In the Middle Persian sources they are fleetingly mentioned and from the few passages that these texts provide, one understands their crime as stealing from one group (the rich) and giving it to another (the poor). What is more interesting is that they considered it to be meritorious to rob the rich and give to the worthy poor.[87] They may be compared with the social groups known in the Islamic period as the *'ayyarun* which with some stretch of imagination have some similarities with Blue and Green circus factions in the Eastern Roman empire. The reports about the Mazdakite activity has a similar ring to the activity of this group, since during the early sixth century it was the followers of this sect that worked to divide the property of the rich among the poor. This of course stemmed from their religious belief that Ohrmazd had given the worldly goods to all to be shared equally, but some had done wrong and had taken the wealth and property of the others.[88] Thus it appears that these people acted according to a set theology which was different from that of State Zoroastrianism.

The Zoroastrian religion had an institution which aided the poor and the downtrodden. This institution was implemented by individuals for the sake of the soul of the departed ones (*ruwānagān*). According to Sasanian law, one's wealth could be divided into three categories, and one third could be used for the preservation of the soul. Building infrastructure and money and food for the poor were distributed under the protection of designated persons by the person who had established the charitable foundation for his/herself or his/her family member. This institution certainly appeased some of the misery and tension which were not mentioned in the surviving Middle Persian texts.[89] The creation of the late office of the "Protector of the Poor and Judge" (*driyōšān dādwar ud jāddag-gōw*) was also a reaction to the social and economic problems during the time of Kawād I. The societal tension went against the idyllic representation of the Zoroastrian society, where everyone had their place and order was given prominence. Thus the law and the state dealt with these individuals and others who went against the norms by being punished. For example criminals who were considered to be the citizens, i.e. men and women of the empire *mard/zan ī šahr*, were branded, as the Sasanian legal texts state as well as being subject to flogging (*čūb zandan*), amputation (*borīdan*), and imprisonment (*zēndān*).[90]

SLAVERY

There were a large number of slaves who were classified based on their function, origin, and gender. The typical slave (*bandag*) was the household servant who worked in the domestic domain, but also worked at the fire-temples. The women slaves in the household (*bandag paristār*) were common and the man of the house had complete control over them and could procure children with them as is evident from the many legal cases which involved slave girls and free citizens and the issue of the status of their children. People who were in debt or had a religious decision to give some of their time to a fire-temple can also be placed in this category. Foreign slaves as well as others who were simply used as slave labor on farms and manual labor were known as captive slaves (*wardag*). These were the most common slaves, but there was a more basic class of slaves who were known as body (*tan*) who were delivered as security. Slaves could be freed at the time of the death of the master or simply if the owner decided to release them. The slaves also received wages and were able to have their own families.[91]

GENDER AND SEXUALITY

In relation to gender, women's positions depended on their class. Women of high rank such as the queen and the mother of the king were much freer in the scope of their activity and decision making. Their seals demonstrate their importance as is also evident on the rock-reliefs which demonstrate their presence in the royal *bazms*. As mentioned before, they engaged in hunting, drinking and feasting with men, wore elaborate costumes, and two women were able to rule in the seventh century CE. Although by all accounts Queens Borān and Azarmi(g)dukht were the only legitimate surviving members of the Sasanian family in the seventh century, the acceptance of their rule and the benevolent remembrance of them by the Sasanian sources suggest that they were accepted by the clergy as well. The other queens remembered but who did not rule were Ardashir-Anahid, Wahram II's sister and wife, and later Shabuhrdukhtag, his other wife who is the only queen whose portrait was on the coins beside Wahram II.[92]

The Zoroastrian Middle Persian texts were written for the community to know how to function in the society and since male priests wrote them, it was their opinion that is known.[93] According to de Jong the one word that best describes what priests wanted from women was "obedience."[94] Common women were considered to be the property of men and fetched a certain price (500 *stēr*). Many of the religious injunctions against women firmly applied to women of non-noble category. The priests took much pain in describing in detail every aspect of the life of women and their rites and rights. One can not give a detailed discussion here in regard to the position of women in Sasanian society, but rather a survey of the different issues will be highlighted here. Women were seen as creatures that could bring destruction to society, like their counterpart in the cosmological world of Zoroastrianism in the character of the female demoness, *jēh*.[95] The *Bundahišn* has a fascinating reference to the inability of Ohrmazd to find any other creature to bear children than woman, and that if it were otherwise Ohrmazd states he would have done so. This gives us the sense that women were not all together of "Ohrmazdian" realm in the mind of Priests or men.[96]

Zoroastrian Middle Persian texts tell us that women had to dress and look modest. By this it meant that covering one's head and feet were important.[97] Makeup and wigs were probably forbidden for the common women, since a passage in the *Ardā Wirāz Nāmag* states that certain women were cast into hell who were those "women who painted (their faces) (*rang nihād*) and used the hair of others (*mōy ī kasān*) as ornament and led the eyes of pious people astray."[98] Laws forbidding women from taking part in daily activity, such as cooking, cleaning and coming into contact with the sacred fire during the time of menstruation (*daštān*) are detailed and abundant. Women who engaged in intercourse during the period of menstruation (*daštān-marzān*) were worthy of death (*marg-arzān*). Men were to avoid women during their menstrual period, because this was the time when women were seen as most contagious and dangerous to every living being. According to the *Wīdēwdād* they had to be kept in an enclosure (*daštānestān*) where they would not be seen until their menstruation cycle was over.[99] Detailed discussion exists for what type of utensils and trays should be given to the menstruating woman and how for her to be purified after that period. This menstrual cycle also gave a sense of when the women would and would not be fertile, as the texts tell us, ten days after the end of the menstruation (*daštān*) they were able to become pregnant. These legal and mythological injunctions mainly arose from the dread of pollution of blood which appears to have been the main source. Abortion (*wišūdag*) was also seen as a sin which would make a woman worthy of death.

Legally, women were seen as equal to children and slaves and the dowry of a women was about 2000 *drahm*, equal to the price of a slave. Once a girl reached the age of nine it was believed that she had to be married, and a boy when he was fifteen. This was the ideal age for humans, and at the end of the world they would dwell in heaven at the same age. The women were required to kneel before their husbands three times daily and ask what his wish was and how she could make him happy.[100] There were several forms of marriage according to Zoroastrian law. The principal wife of the man with full rights was called a *pādixšāy* wife, who had many more rights than other wives. If the husband (*šōy*) was not able to procure offspring, he could give his wife as *čagar* in which she entered into a levirate marriage to procure a son. This type of marriage was usually undertaken with a close relative which also made sure that it was a familial affair. If the man died without a male heir, it was up to the daughter to become a *stōr*, meaning it was her obligation to provide a successor by procreating a child with another member of the family, who would inherit the property of the deceased man and hence protect the familial continuum.[101] If she was harmed (*rēš*) when she left her husband to procreate a child for another person, she would be returned to her husband.[102] The term designated for a daughter or sister who is to enter this type of marriage in order to fulfill the "obligation of successorship" is *ayōkēn*.[103] Still, however, the wife could ask for divorce (*hilišn/ abēzārīh*) and receive a certificate of divorce (*hilišn-nāmag*). Both men and women could ask for a divorce.

A man could divorce his wife if she was thought to be barren (*starwan*), if she committed adultery (**gādārīh*), sorcery (*jādūgīh*), failed to fulfill the obligatory duties, refused to submit herself to her husband, and failed to observe the period of confinement during menstruation (*daštān*),[104] and a *čakar* wife could be divorced much more easily. If she had just reached puberty and abandoned her husband, she would be deserving of death (*marg-arzān*).[105] If she wanted to marry someone who was not authorized by the family head, i.e., the father of the woman (*xwarāyēn* lit. "self-guardian")[106] it was considered a misunion (*jud āyōzišn*). The idea of the girl simply leaving the house (*bēastān*) to marry was also unacceptable.[107] There were certain measures to protect the wife. For example if the man unlawfully divorced his wife, the wife would still receive some compensation, even if the man had left his property as alms. The law required that a portion of that wealth be returned to the wife. It appears according to the *Mādayān ī Hazār Dādestān* that if the woman decided to divorce, the property (*wāspuhragān*) or dower (*pēšīgān*) which she brought with her into the marriage could be kept by her, but the earnings from it were to be kept by the husband.[108] Woman, depending on their age and status, could ask and be granted a divorce.[109] But the more privileged men would have two wives (*abōg*, Persian *havū*) and even more by several Sasanian kings. Thus, the *pater-familias* was all-powerful and could even sell his wife and children if he was unable to support his family (*adbadāt*), or because of death or hardship (*margīh ud raxtagīh*).[110] If a married woman was raped, she would receive 300 *stēr*s and 500 *stēr*s for being kidnapped,[111] and if raped before coming of age (*aburnāyag*) she recieved 1,200 *drahms*.[112] Union (*āmēzišn*) out of wedlock was considered a theft (*duz*).[113]

As the Middle Persian texts demonstrate, sexuality was an important issue in the Sasanian period. If we are to believe, according to the *Bundahišn*, that women were the progeny of the evil demoness, their actions would also be dangerous and had to be controlled. Women were seen as potent forces in making man deviate from his religious obligations and duties, primarily through her sexuality. This does not mean that the good religion prohibited the bearing of children. On the contrary, it was a *mitzveh* that men had to engage in the act of procreation. In fact if a man had intercourse with a sterile woman, it was considered a sin, since he had wasted his semen. According to *Zādaspram*, women's wombs were seen as receptacles where man's seed was placed and from which the child was born. Thus the wasting of one's semen was seen as a sin against the religion and caused all sorts of difficulties, including the loss of strength and intelligence. But the injunction to marrying at an early age (men at fifteen and women at nine) was to ensure this process of procreation. We also come across passages where the idea of the ideal woman is presented. This includes the following women: "who in her mind loves her husband" (*pad mēnišn mard-dōst*), "who has good words in bed for her husband, but does not talk shamefully (dirty)," (*pad wastarg ī mard hu-saxwan [ud] nē ašarmīhā gōwēd*). In her looks she must be one whose stature is middle-sized and whose chest is broad and whose head, buttocks, and neck are well-formed and whose legs are short and waist slender and soles of the feet arched and whose fingers are long and whose limbs are soft, smooth, and fleshy and whose breast is quince-like and whose body down to the toes' nails is snowy-white and whose cheeks are pomegranate-red and whose eyes are almond-shaped and lips coralline and (eye)brows vaulted and whose denture is white, fresh, and brilliant and locks black and bright and long (*bālāy mayānčīg u-š war pahn ud sar ud kūn ud gardan hambast uš pāy kōtāh ud mayān bārīg ud azēr ī pāy wišādag ud angustān dērang u-š handām narm ud sād ud āgand ud wehīg-pestān u-š hamvg tan tā nāxūn ī pāy wafrēn u-š gōnag anārgōn u-š čašm wādām-āyēn ud lab wassadēn ud brūg tāg ud gāz spēd ud tarrūg ud xwašāb ud gēsūg siyā ud rōšn ud drāz*).[114]

Those women who did not follow the social norm were punished under a variety of reasons, the most common being sorcery, and blasphemy which all probably meant being disobedient to their husbands, which was punishable as well. A woman or young girl who did not want to marry was also worthy of death. There are a host of negative proclamations against women in Middle Persian texts as well which show the relative uneasiness of the priestly class with the female. Some are quite common and can be found in other societies as well. Only a selection of such sayings will be given here to demonstrate the general view of men in regard to women. In general men were expected to beget such women as ideal for marriage: *šarmgēn zan dōst bāš* "love a woman who has shame,"[115] *zan juwān pad zanīh gīr* "take a young wife for marriage."[116] The negative dictums give us much more evidence of the male view of women in Sasanian society. The most common sayings include *zanān rāy xird nēst* "women have no intelligence,"[117] *rāz ō zanān ma bar* "do not tell secrets to women,"[118] *ud ān zan nē pad zan abāyēd dāštan kē framān burdār ī šōy nē bawēd* " and one should not marry that woman who is not obedient to the husband,"[119] *pad zanān wistāx ma bawēd kū ō šarm ud pašēmānīh nē rasēd* "do not be trusting of the woman so that you do not become shamed and repentant."[120] Other things that should be avoided include *juwān mard kē zan ī pīr pad zanīh gīrēd* "a young man who marries an old woman."[121]

The other important sin which carried the death penalty was sodomy, which was known under several terms such as "sodomy" (*kun-marzih*), "unnatural lust" (*waran ī abārōn*), and "sinful copulation" (*abārōn marzišnīh*). There are a number of laws and cases which refer to this practice which suggest that it occurred. The *Mēnōg ī Xrad* relates that the evil beings were created in this manner: "The evil Ahreman created the demons (*dēwān*) and deceiving ones (*drōjān*) and other evil offsprings through the act of self-sodomy."[122] Then first this act is given as a vehicle in which evil was able to reproduce more evil in universe, and secondly Ahreman is seen as a homosexual/sodomite. In the *Wīdēwdād* (VIII.32) it is stated that if men engaged in passive and aggressive sodomy unwillingly, they are worthy of lashes, but if they are willing, they would be worthy of death. It appears that passive sodomites were seen as more evil than those committing sodomy with women as evidenced by the *Ardā Wirāz Nāmag*.[123] Many texts demonstrate that the reference is about a man and a woman, but there are instances in which we gain insight into the world of homosexuality of the Sasanian era. These laws were spelled out in a portion of the *Avesta* which is now lost. The eighth book of the *Dēnkard*, in which chapter XXXIV is about legal precepts against offenses and other matters as they appeared in the *Hūspram Nask* of the *Avesta*, states there were such laws: "About the immoral desires of the (*wiftag*) "passive sodomite" and (*wiftīnag*) "aggressive sodomite," their tyrannical lust, and corrupt activity, and blighted glory, (and) corrupt and polluted bodies."[124] In the *Ardā Wirāz Nāmag* one of the most imaginative texts of the Middle Persian corpus, we find the punishments which are given against homosexuals and sodomites. Wiraz in his journey to hell sees that a man is being punished by snakes entering into his anus and coming out of his mouth. The Angels tells him the reason for his punishment is that: "this is the soul of that wicked man who committed sodomy in the world and allowed a man over himself."[125] In another chapter a man is punished for the act of sodomy with a woman which was less severely punished.[126] Needless to say the law handed down a swift death sentence for such a practice to those who were worthy of death (*marg-arzān*).[127]

There was only one meritorious act that nullified the "evil effect of sodomy" and that was the practice of "next-of-kin marriages" (*xwēdodāh*). The issue of next-of-kin marriages had been a matter of controversy in the early part of the last century, but anyone who can read Avestan or Middle Persian, along with the attestation of the foreign sources can have no doubt whatsoever that this type of marriage was practiced in Sasanian Persia. *Xwēdodāh* is one of those institutions that has brought about the most fierce debates, on the one side the European scholars and on the other the Zoroastrian.[128] We have evidence from the Achaemenid period which suggests that this was a common practice among the royal family, but there is less evidence for it among the population. According to Frye, its origin, if not Zoroastrian, may be sought among the Elamites, which the Achaemenids may have emulated for keeping the royal blood pure. In time this practice became common among the population, and in the early Sasanian period the Zoroastrian priest Kerdīr tells us that he concluded many *xwēdodāh* marriages as part of his beneficial acts. Not only the third century inscriptions, but also later Middle Persian texts elaborate on the beneficence of such a marriage. These marriages were of three kinds as attested by *Dēnkard* III (Chapter 80), between the father and daughter, son and mother, and brother and sister.[129] Beside its religious significance, one should also realize that *xwēdodāh* was a means of keeping the wealth of the family intact, as opposed to marrying one's daughter to another family, hence giving some of the wealth away. *Xwēdodāh* ensured that not only the family and its wealth were intact, but also the religious affiliation of the family remained Zoroastrian.[130]

PUNISHMENT AND REGULATIONS

Punishment was a device used by the state to control the society. Lashing, cutting of body parts, and branding were practiced in Sasanian Persia. For example for non-appearance in the court at the designated time for theft, or if the husband would not provide food for the wife during her menstruation period and would steal, the punishment was branding (*drōš ī šahr*),[131] and if a person was branded four times for various offenses, the offender would be imprisoned for life.[132] Another type of punishment and humiliation was to have the convicted person placed on an animal, usually a donkey and paraded through the streets. The early reference to this is found in the Parthian epic, the *Ayādgār ī Zarērān*, in which at the end of the battle the Iranians capture the leader of the enemy of the Iranians, Arjasp. One of his hands, legs, and ears are cut off and an eye of his is burnt and he is placed on a maimed donkey and sent back to his city.[133] Based on this passage we may suggest that this was an ancient type of punishment and if one remembers that the Achaemenid King of Kings, Darius I punished Phraortes but cutting off his nose, ears and tongue, and putting out one eye, we see this tradition.[134] Again it is in the fourth century CE during Narseh's attempt at taking power that we hear of such a punishment again. According to the Paikuli inscription, his adversary by the name of Wahnam was captured and brought before him, bound and put on a maimed donkey.[135]

A series of injunctions about purity and pollution also reflect the way in which nature and animals were treated. Cutting down trees, polluting streams and lakes, and the earth was considered a sinful act. These injunctions even with the influx of foreigners who were settled in the empire was a deterrent against ecological distress and made the plagues less current than in the Eastern Roman empire. Of course this obsession of the priests with the issue of purity and pollution caused problems for the population as well. Since water was the manifestation of the deity *Khordad*, its pollution meant a major sin, which the Zoroastrian clergy found ingenious means of getting around, especially for washing or bathing.[136] We are told that in the cities the bathhouse (*garmābag*) was near the fire-temple and the place where the seasonal festivals (*gāhānbār*) were performed.[137]

The dead body also brought about pollution and the deceased body had to be cared for three nights and watched so that the evil spirit would not be able to drag the soul to hell, while the body rotted.[138] The death ceremonies were said not to be solemn occasions, but several sources suggest that mourning rituals were practiced in the eastern part of the empire and that the tearing of one's clothes as an act of passion was looked down upon by the state clergy and the authors of the Middle Persian texts. In fact the *Mēnōg ī Xrad* states that a land is most miserable in which tearing of hair (*mōyag*) in mourning takes place. According to Zoroastrian theology the more the relatives of the deceased cry a larger river will separate the deceased person and the bridge on which he/she can pass to heaven. This religious injunction, however, did not mean that it was applied to every region of the Sasanian empire. While the Middle Persian texts supply the official Sasanian Zoroastrian view of prohibition against mourning, in the eastern territory of the empire we have evidence of mutilating one's self and of mourning ceremonies. According to early Persian texts in Khorasan on a specific day the Zoroastrian priests would mourn the death of the innocent hero, Siyavash, who was killed unjustly. This mourning ceremony is known as the *Sōg ī Siyāwaš* "The Mourning of Siyavash," which resulted in the beautiful work by the Persian literatus, Meskūb,[139] and the ceremonies which are still carried on today in the province of Persis called *suwashun*. The Persian texts tell us that this event was sung with mourning ceremonies known as *Griystan Moghan* "Wailing of the Mowbeds;"[140] and the Persian savant Biruni tells us that the people of Sogdiana on a specific day wail and mourn for their dead and cut their faces,[141] the pictorial representation can be found on a panel in China where a Zoroastrian priest is conducting mourning ceremony.[142]

Burying the dead was also considered a sin, and so the dead body was exposed in open air to vultures and dogs in enclosures called *dakhma*. The reason for this was that it was thought that once the soul left the body, it began to decompose and the corpse was instantly polluting. There are detailed measures which are taken by those who are in charge of carrying the dead and the elaborate cleansing ceremony which they have to go through after their task.[143] In turn the sun was to cleanse the remaining pollution of the bones and then the bones were collected and placed in receptacles, usually found in rock tombs (*astōdān*). By this act the earth was to remain clean and not be defiled. These practices must have seemed strange to say the least for the Romans or those captured during wars when they heard or saw them, and probably could not make sense of them. The question that can be raised is how the Jews and Christians would bury their dead and if they did so, wouldn't they have been considered impure and hence untouchable? In one instance when Yazdgerd I had allowed Christian bodies to be buried they were dug up under Wahram V or Yazdgerd II and the bones strewn about in the sun. We know that in fact that the Christians also made tombs which were over the ground and in rock cut structures which were acceptable to both the Zoroastrians and the Christians. But with the Muslim conquest of the Sasanian empire we hear of the horror of the Zoroastrians in seeing the dead bodies being buried and defiling the sacred earth.

These considerations and others probably caused the segregation of the people based on religious conviction and so each section of a city would have had a quarter which belonged to a religious group, some based on the purity laws of the followers of Zoroastrianism, Judaism and Christianity. It may have been that some of the cities were also dominated by a single religious group such as the town of Gay (Old Town of Isfahan) which was Jewish. We should remember that the Zoroastrians were probably more numerous and so whole cities dominated by other religious groups would have been rare, hence interaction inevitable. For the Zoroastrians, the further one went to the east from Persis, or westward to Mesopotamia, it made their interaction with non-Zoroastrians inevitable. Certainly those who were in Persian colonies in China, in the Far East had to deal with purity and pollution laws in their own way.

Chapter 3

Religions of the Empire: Zoroastrians, Manichaeans, Jews and Christians

EARLY SASANIAN ZOROASTRIANISM

Through Ardashir and the family of Sasan, Zoroastrianism was made the official religion of the empire. This religion certainly had devotees in the province of Persis before the Sasanian period, from where the Achaemenids had ruled and worshipped Ahura Mazda. Coins from Persis, beginning with the second century BCE to the end of the second century CE demonstrate that Ohrmazd (Ahura Mazda) was worshipped and honored. The reverse side of these coins show the king and sometimes two people raising their hands in a gesture of reverence towards a structure which looks very much the Ka'be Zardosht at Naqsh-i Rustam. Above the structure hovers Ohrmazd in his Achaemenid anthropomorphized self. Thus, Ardashir was continuing a religious tradition which had existed from the Achaemenid period in the province of Persis. By all accounts Ardashir's family had a priestly function with the Zoroastrian cult of Anahid and its fire-temple at the city of Istakhr. Their knowledge of the tradition (Zoroastrian religion) made them equipped for attaining political control over the region and eventually the whole of the Iranian plateau. One may make an analogy with the later sufi warriors in North Africa or the Safavīd family in Persia who began as a religious movement and religious leaders who then become leaders of bands of warriors.

We are not sure who the family of Sasan was and what their relation was with the kings of Persis, but there may not have been mutual support or respect, especially since Ardashir's family was an upstart family.[1] Ardashir, in one of his investiture reliefs, erases all doubts as to his religious conviction when he states: "This is the image of the Mazda worshiping Majesty (Middle Persian *bag*; Parthian *xwadāy*), Ardashir, King of Kings of Iran, who is from the lineage of the Gods (*yazdān*), the son of the Majesty, King Pabag."[2] His coins also bear similar titles and suggest that Ardashir minted coins with similar titles before his defeat of Ardawān IV. Then the idea that rulers were from the race of gods had been current in some form ever since the invasion of Alexander the Great. This is manifest from the coins of the kings of Persis who have the Aramaic legend, "from the gods" (Aramaic *zy alahia*). The process of codification of religious knowledge is provided some attention in the Zoroastrian tradition. The Middle Persian text, the *Dēnkard* (Acts of Religion) states that:

> *ōy bay Ardaxšīr šāhān šāh ī Pabagān pad rāst dastwarīh tōsar ān-iz hammōg ī pargandag hamāg ō dar xwāst tōsar abar mad ān ī ēwar frāz padīrift ud abārīg az daswar hišt ud ēn-iz framān dād kū frāz ō amāh har nigēzišn ān-ē bawēd az dēn māzdēsn čē nūn-z āgāhīh ud dānišn aziš frōd nēst*
>
> His Majesty, Ardashir, the King of Kings, son of Pabag, acting on the just judgment of Tosar, demanded that all those scattered teachings to be brought to the court. Tosar assumed command; he selected those which were trustworthy, and left the rest out of the canon. And thus he decreed: From now only those are true expositions which are based on the Mazdean religion, for now there is no lack of information and knowledge concerning them.[3]

The following passage suggests that Ardashir, who was from a priestly family, was not well versed in the religion that was to become the official religion of the empire, so that a priest by the name of Tosar/Tansar was chosen as the religious authority. One may also be able to conclude that Ardashir and his family were knowledgeable about the cult of Anahid but not the Mazdean tradition as a whole. We see the name of Tosar mentioned in the inscription of Shabuhr I although curiously as the father of a member of the court of Ardashir. This part of the *Dēnkard* also gives us another clue which is also corroborated by other sources, which is that Ardashir's religious views were not accepted by all the Zoroastrians in the empire.[4] First the text states that there was scattered information on the Zoroastrian doctrine which may mean that there were different beliefs or understandings of Zoroastrianism. Consequently, Tosar was employed to systematize the doctrine of Zoroastrianism based on the surviving texts, documents and the oral tradition carried by the "reliable" priests. One may make an analogy in bringing together the definitive text of the New Testament and the process in which it was canonized, where some texts and authorities were seen as unreliable and others agreed upon. The canonization of the sacred texts of the Zoroastrians and the Christians was taking place approximately in the same period and would develop in a similar fashion, but the followers of both religions would clash with each other in late antiquity as two different world-views formed, backed by absolutist rulers.

We may even see Ardashir and the religion which he proclaimed to be the official religion of the empire as a deviation from the tradition(s) of Zoroastrianism, hence a heresy. That is, the Zoroastrian religion he proclaimed as "orthodoxy" did not appear to have been accepted by all. This new tradition which the Sasanian invented was adopted by the Sasanian states and priests and the Zoroastrians were made to conform to it. In a sense, with regards to the beginning we should not speak about "orthodoxy," because it probably did not exist. In the *Letter of Tansar*, the king of Gilan and Mazandaran, who was independent of Ardashir, accuses him of being a heretic and bringing innovations into the tradition. Ardashir has to respond that while this is true innovations had to take place in order to bring unity to the "nation" and the "religion."[5] The Zoroastrian clergy supporting Ardashir had to further support Ardashir's claim via supernatural means, such as claiming that his arrival was predicted.[6]

The problem with what was true Zoroastrianism or orthodoxy would not be solved until the fall of the empire, although the Sasanians and the priests attached to the state would have liked to have portrayed a picture of religious solidarity.[7] In terms of the cultic activity Ardaxšir's son, Shabuhr I, left us some detail in terms of such practices. In the early period the Sasanians engaged in establishment of fire temples as a general rule. Shabuhr I states that he founded at least five sacred fires, one in his own name, one in the name of his daughter Shabuhrdukht, and one for each of his three sons who were ruling Armenia, Meshan/Mesene, and Sistan. From the amount of sacrificial material that was dedicated to a temple (20 lambs each day and bread and wine), we may think of a temple economy and the money needed for its upkeep as well as the others that would be established in the future. Each king appears to have established a number of fires and along with them came the care-taking of the fire by priests and people who worked the temple lands in order to keep them functioning and thriving. The idea of temporary servitude to these temples was in existence, and people donated their time working for the temple to cleanse their soul or reach their religious objective. These people were known as "temple-servants," (*ataxš-bandag*) or simply "body," (*tan*) who gave an amount of their time to the service of the fire-temple. A fire foundation had several types of attendants, those of "slaves" (*anšahrīg*); "servants," (*bandag*) and "guardians," (*sālār*) who each had specific functions.[8] These matters should remind us of the ancient Near Eastern tradition of temples and their vast land holdings and power which undoubtedly influenced the Zoroastrian temples as well. This meant the apparatus of the ancient Near Eastern temples would have been a model for the Zoroastrian temple economy and its function.

Thus, in early Sasanian Persia we have a king who is the caretaker of the Anahid fire-temple which was also a warrior of a cultic center. A religious authority by the name of Tosar was brought in to canonize the sacred texts which were said by him to have been kept in the hearts (Persian *dil*) of those who knew about the religion. This suggests the importance of the oral tradition, as is evident from the dialectal differences in the surviving Avestan hymns from Arachosia, Sogdia, and Persis;[9] and finally, the existence of cultic sacrifice and the establishment of fire-temples which took the name of the kings, queens and the nobility. The situation becomes more complicated when we take into account that there were priests or those who honored the cult of Ohrmazd who, like the Sasanians, also dedicated themselves to Lady Anahid. Just like the Sasanians who centered their cult around Anahid, others had centered their activity around other deities such as Mithra, and probably had various ideas as to what "Zoroastrianism" meant and wanted to emphasize the importance of their cultic deity.[10] Thus we may see a religion in which several deities played important roles for people and local cultic activity. Nothing can really be said of the existing non-Iranian deities and temples which were certainly in existence, due to Greek and Mesopotamian influence. These types of worship now either had to be abandoned or incorporated under the religion of Ohrmazd.

MANI: THE PROPHET OF LIGHT

During the rule of Shabuhr I, the prophet Mani appeared on the scene and the king was receptive to his ideas allowing him to move about freely and propagate his religion. Mani had been born in Babylonia and was a physician, as he tells Shabuhr (*bizišk hēm az bābel zamīg*), during the time when the Sasanians were attempting to conquer Persis and challenge the Parthians. His early years appear to have been spent with his parents, religiously focusing on the Baptists in Babylonia who probably came under Christian and Gnostic influence.[11] His religious system was by all accounts dualistic and, as Mani himself explains in the *Šabūhragān*, based on the two principles (*dw bwn*). Thus this system was dualistic and used Zoroastrian terminology to propagate its message to those who were familiar with Zoroastrian deities and doctrine. This should also give us another clue as to the importance and popularity of Zoroastrianism in the third century.

It does not mean, however, that this was the Zoroastrianism of the Sasanians and it appears to be unlikely that in such a short span of time the population of the Iranian plateau was to have become familiar with the Sasanian brand of Zoroastrianism. Consequently we must suspect that Mani propagated his message to the Iranian population who believed in Ohrmazd and other Zoroastrian/Mazdean deities (such as Mihr/Mithra who has an important function in Manichaeism) and who were not altogether accepting of the particular doctrinal nuances espoused by the Sasanians and the religious establishment which now attached itself to the state. The use of *Zurvan* as the great god in the Manichaean texts also indicates the importance of this deity in the early Sasanian period and Mani used this name since he was probably considered the great god, the father of Ohrmazd and Ahreman according to those who followed the ideas of Zurvanism.

This is where the similarity between Manichaeism and Zoroastrianism ends. Mani taught the opposition between spirit and matter. All that was spiritual was good and all that was material, evil. This was contradictory to the Zoroastrian view of the good life, where all that was created in this world which was beautiful to the eye was the work of Ohrmazd and his helpers, the Bounteous Immortals (*Amharspandān*). In Manichaeism, not resisting sexual desires which ultimately led to the entrapment of the particles of light in flesh (one's body), and asceticism for the Elect (Manichaean priests) were central to its doctrine. Pesūs, the evil demoness, created the first couple who entrapped the light particles which represented the spirit, while in Zoroastrianism the act of creation, enjoying the fruits of the world and celebrating the bounty of the earth was celebrated. We may end this religious divide by simply stating that Manichaeism was anti-material and otherworldly, while Zoroastrianism was worldly and let its followers enjoy the creation of Ohrmazd in this world and the next. The Manichaeans had to wait until the time of redemption when Jesus would appear and resurrect the bodies of humans and place the followers of Mani, who had suffered, into heaven.

What made Mani's campaign successful, however, was the fact that he lived in Babylonia, where a large number of different groups and religions existed side by side, each with its own doctrine and god(s). Mani would propagate his religion which may be called anti-material dualism by using the names, terminology and concepts from the native vocabulary of the area to make the population better understand his ideas. Second, he organized scribal teams which undertook not only to translate Mani's ideas into different languages and scripts, but also each book was written in a different language. For Shabuhr I, Mani presented the Manichaean text in Middle Persian, wisely called *Śabūhragān.*[12] Another reason his religion was deemed universal was that he proclaimed himself to be the seal of the prophets/teachers, meaning that he was to complete the teachings of the Zoroastrians, Christians, Buddhists and Mandeans. Mani also incorporated the Gnostic system of Bardesanes of Edessa, Marcion, and others. He had simply come to complete the message of previous wise men and prophets.[13] Mani appears to have been only hostile to Judaism which is interesting because he was from a region where a large number of Jews lived. This may be due to his upbringing where the anti-Judaic views of the Elkaisites made an impact on the young Mani.[14] Another reason may be that the large Jewish community in Mesopotamia were not accepting of his ideas and rejected any of his teachings.

We know that he traveled to India and Central Asia and learned much about non-Abrahamic religions, namely Hinduism and Buddhism. That is why Shabuhr I may have liked Mani's religious syncretism and universalism,[15] and was to live peacefully under the next king as well. By the time of Wahram I, things began to change because of Kerdir's rise to power and his opposition to Mani. It is said that at the time Mani entered the city of Wendoy-Shabuhr (Gundišāpur/Jundīšāpur), which was also to be an important medical centre, his entrance resembled Christ's entrance into Jerusalem and caused much commotion. It was at this time that Kerdir, along with other Zoroastrian priests complained and caused Mani's arrest.[16] We have some detailed information from the Manichaean sources which describe Mani's fateful visit with King Wahram I and Kerdir's plot:

'dy'n qyr(d)[y](r) mgbyd (')[d] 'dy 'wr'n ky
[pr](x)'št prw'n š'h 'nd[yš'd] u rsk [']wd n(b)[yn

Thereupon Kerdir the Magbed (Mowbed) planned with his friends who served before the king, and . . . jealousy and cunning . . .[17]

He was summoned and scorned by the king in the following manner:

> 'wh gwpt kw 'yy pad cy 'b'yšn hyd oo k' ny 'w k'ryc'r
> šwyd 'wd ny nhcyhr kwnyd oo b' 'wẖy 'yn bšyhkyh r'y
> 'wd 'y drm'n bwrdn r'y 'byšn hyd oo 'wd 'ync ny kwnyd oo

> Eh, what are you good for since you go neither fighting
> nor hunting? But perhaps you are needed for this
> doctoring and this physicking? And you don't do even that![18]

He was imprisoned and died there, but this did not finish the Manichaeans' religious activity and now their focus turned to Central Asia where the Turkic tribes and the Chinese found interest in his doctrine. Manichaeism would not have been very successful in the West since Christianity, which was gaining momentum, would have eventually put an end to it, with the exception in Egypt. However, Manichaeans did live in Rome, but they gradually disappear from our sources. From the episode told in a Manichaean text, it appears that Wahram I was angry with Mani, perhaps due to the instigation of Kerdir and others who had precipitated this anger. He may also have been drunk, since the same fragment states that after feasting, he had one hand on the shoulder of the Saka queen and the other over the shoulders of Kerdir, the son of Ardawān, when coming towards the prophet.

KERDIR: THE FORGOTTEN PRIEST

Kerdir rise from the rank of a Zoroastrian teacher-priest (*hērbed*) to an all-powerful chief priest (*mowbed*), and assuming other titles along the way is important for understanding early Sasanian Zoroastrianism. Kerdir has left us his biography in several places in the province of Persis along with the Sasanian royal inscriptions and rock-reliefs. His eventual power and influence in the second half of the third century is apparent in that he is the only non-royal personage in the third century who was given permission to have his own biography written on stone, which was characteristic of Persian royalty.[19] In his biography we may find two different strands of information. One has to do with his political aspiration and the establishment of a unified religious doctrine. Second, we can ascertain what the process of this empowerment was and how Kerdir was able to justify his religious conviction over other subjects of the empire. In his biography, he misleads us into thinking he was active from the time of Ardashir I and that he held much power. Kerdir tells us that under Shabuhr I he surveyed the empire and established fire-temples and that the priests were given monetary and perhaps more power so that they became content and he taught them the correct rites and rituals. He had charters signed for the fire-temples with his insignia, "Kerdir the priest" (*hērbed*) making them more authoritative (perhaps those which accepted Kerdir's conditions and what was to be called Sasanian Zoroastrianism). His title suggests that he was a simple priest at the time or that there was no real religious hierarchy, but this would change. He must have also taken it upon himself to establish religious seminaries (*hērbedestān*) where the priests would be trained adequately in matters of religion. This system would ensure unity in doctrinal matters and the identification of recognized priests, since others now could be labeled as heretics. These seminaries were the religious schools where most of the issues in regard to doctrine and ritual were discussed. It was in the *hērbedestāns* where differences arose and debates took place. By focusing on this imperial religion and its seminaries two problems arise: one being that Kerdir and the Middle Persian texts portray a unified Zoroastrian doctrine which the majority of the Zoroastrians followed at the time. Second, by focusing on these matters, popular religion is neglected and what must have been an eclectic tendency on the part of the populace and the Zoroastrian intellectuals at large is pushed aside.[20]

It is under Hormizd I that Kerdir received new titles and honors. As he states he received the markings of rank for the upper class, i.e., cap and belt (*kulāf ud kamarband*) and he received the title of Chief-Priest (*mowbed*). Kerdir also received a new title which, for a long time was misunderstood, but now thanks to Ph. Huyse we can read the title as "Kerdir, whose soul (the god) Wahram saved, the Mowbed of (king) Hormizd."[21] When we come to the reign of Wahram I we begin to see changes in the status of Kerdir. In describing his feats under the first three kings in his inscriptions, Kerdir describes his work formulaically, where there is little difference with the exception of the new titles which he assumes. When Kerdir describes the time of Wahram I, it is evident that this king bestowed more honor on him. This is clear by what Wahram I allowed Kerdir to receive, first becoming a magnate or assuming their rank, second becoming the Judge (*dādwar*) over the whole empire which suggests that from then on the judges were drawn from the ranks of the priests. Third, Kerdir is given the custodianship of the Anahid fire-temple at Istakhr. One cannot help but feel that something changed in the relation of the Sasanian kings vis-à-vis the fire-temple or their religious functions which were once tied to this important cultic centers. This power base of the rulers was given up altogether to a priest and so a divergence took place in the function of the king and the importance and rise of the professional religious organization and hierarchy in the late third century CE.

There may have been religious doctrinal differences between Zoroastrian schools of thought if such schools existed, since Kerdir states that he put down heresies and tried to put all the different Mazdean thinkers in line with the official state religion: "them (heretics) I punished, and I tormented them until I made them better."[22] Another important but more ambiguous term that Kerdir deals with is *mowestān*, which has been translated differently. I see in this the concept of religious seminaries for the priests (*mowān*) whose chief (*mowbed*) was Kerdir.[23] This confirms the *Dēnkard*'s statement that under Shabuhr I, the *Avesta* was collected and the different schools of thought in relation to religion were brought forth and examined, so there would be no disputation as to the authoritative text, which also suggests unified rites, rituals and doctrine.[24] He also mentions another important term which is *nask* (passage 29 of his inscription) which is of interest. *Nask* refers to each of the sections of the *Avesta* which the Zoroastrian tradition considers to have consisted of 21 *nasks*. *Nasks* were books or collection of texts and so it suggests that the *Avesta* may have been written in one form or another the third century CE.

CHRISTIANITY AND JUDAISM: PERSECUTION, COEXISTENCE AND RECOGNIZED RELIGIONS

The persecution of the other religious groups also becomes evident from the inscription (KKZ 9–10) in which Kerdir states that Jews (*yhwd-y*), Buddhists (*šmn-y*), Hindus (*brmn-y*), Nazarenes (*n'cr'-y*), Christians (*krstyd'n*), Mandaens (*mktk-y*), and Manichaeans (*zndyk-y*) were harmed.[25] The next line indicates that idols existed in the empire or idol worship was in existence which was probably in regard to Christians' and Buddhists' veneration of the image of their respective leaders/teachers. The Persian term of idol, *but* is derived from *Buddha* which gives credence to the fact that Kerdir persecuted the Buddhists. Christians were to be the subject of persecution for several reasons. First, Christianity before the Christianization of the Eastern Roman empire tended to have a universal outlook, much like Manichaeism and always held to universal aspirations. But with Constantine and the adoption of Christianity in the Roman Empire, Persian Christian loyalties were divided between the King of Kings who was not Christian and the emperor Constantine who proclaimed to be the leader of all

Christians in the oikumene.[26] The problem with the issue of Christian loyalty to the King of Kings is also clear in that Shabuhr II in the fourth century had asked a double tax from the Christians for his war campaign. According to the *Acts of Simeon* once the Christian leader had refused to abide by this request, it is said that Shabuhr had said "Simeon wants to make his followers and his people rebel against my kingdom and convert them into servants of Caesar, their coreligionist."[27] Second, Christianity was a proselytizing religion which brought it into conflict with the Zoroastrian hierarchy. After all, who were the Christians in Persia trying to convert? We have many cases in which even people from the noble families converted to Christianity and were martyred for their belief. For the Zoroastrians this would not have gone over well with Kerdir and other priests. The persecution of the Christians from this time took place when the Sasanians fought the Romans, especially in the fourth century CE.[28] This persecution would decrease because the Persian Christian church became officially recognized and its Catholikos was stationed at Ctesiphon from the fifth century CE.

Jews appear to have been treated much better by the Sasanians. When reading through the non-religious Middle Persian texts written during the Sasanian period, one can see the close relations between the Sasanian monarchs and the Jewish population, especially with the leaders of the community. For example in *The Provincial Capitals of Ērān* (*Šhrestānīhānīhā ī Ērānšahr*) a Sasanian king is said to be from the marriage between the Sasanian king and a Jewish woman: "The city of Khwārizm was built by Narseh, the son of the Jewess (10),"[29] or "The city of Šūš (Susa) and Šūštar were built by Shishindokht, the wife of Yazdgerd, the son of Shabuhr, since she was the daughter of Resh Galut, the king of the Jews and also the mother of Wahram Gur (another Sasanian king) (47)." Middle Persian *Reš Galut* is the Aramaic form of *Resh Galutha*, "Leader of the Exile." We know of this close association between the Jews and the Sasanians from non-Sasanian sources as well. These two references are from the time of Yazdgerd I (339–420 CE) who, according to the *Talmud*, was in close contact with the Jewish community. It is even said that Yazdgerd addressed the rabbis with courtesy, cited scriptures to them, and of course married a Jewess, i.e., Shishindokht.[30] This again may be the product of Jewish historiography and propaganda, but one cannot deny the historicity of the contacts between the Sasanians and the Jews. As for Wahram V (Gur), the Zoroastrian Persians could see him as a legitimate ruler and the Jews would see him as a Jewish king. After all, he was Jewish since his mother was a Jewess.

The Jews would have been the most important source of transmission of knowledge about the Achaemenids as well, even if the Sasanians were not informed about the Achaemenids independently. The mention of the Achaemenids in the *Bible* is very important. This would mean that when the Middle Persian versions of the *Bible* were at hand during late antiquity, the Zoroastrian priests would have had access to them. Theodoret in the fifth century CE states that a translation of the Bible was made into Middle Persian.[31] In the *Talmud* as well there is reference to whether the story of Esther could be recited in Persian or not which suggests that orally conveying the stories about the Achaemenids was also possible.[32] The story of Esther was central to this transmission of the memory of the Achaemenids by the Jews to the Sasanians. Not only the *Bible* reflects the Jewish fascination about the Achaemenids but also the paintings at Dura-Europos remember the Biblical story of late antiquity. This brings us to the Dura-Europos synagogue in Syria where another important and vital piece of information is given in regard to Sasanian understanding of the Biblical story of Esther. During the time of Shabuhr I (240–270 CE), Sasanian officials visited the synagogue at Dura-Europos. One of the best preserved and elaborate frescos represents the story of Esther. The scene represents Ahasuerus (Artaxerxes) on a throne who is receiving a message in the presence of the Jews. Mordecai is on a royal horse which is held by Haman. What is important is that several Middle Persian graffiti can be found on the scene which has been attributed to the third century CE. These were inscriptions placed by the Persian emissaries of Shabuhr I who visited the synagogue where the date is also given (255 and 256 CE).[33]

Elisaeus tells us that during the time of Yazdgerd II (438–457 CE), the court and the king were told about the stories of the Bible regarding the Persians and the treatment of the Jews by the Achaemenids.[34] The translation of the *Bible* into other Middle Iranian languages is still in existence and was probably the work of Christian missionaries in the Sasanian empire and in Central Asia.[35] The Judeo-Persian tradition is certainly rich in Achaemenid stories,[36] which demonstrates the continuity of this memory among the Jews of Persia.[37] The Jews must have reminded the Sasanian Persians of this glorious past when they ruled Asia and were tolerant of all people, especially the Jews. This would have made the Jews much more secure than their rival community, the Christians, but in the end it was the Christians and their religion which captured the attention of the Persians.

BEFORE DANTE: TRAVELING TO HEAVEN, HELL AND PURGATORY

We should turn back to Kerdir and discuss the second significance of his inscriptions in the third century. This has to do with his religious mission and his journey to the other world to find out matters about the true religion and the correct way in rites and ritual.[38] In his inscription he has a fascinating account of his vision of heaven, hell and purgatory. F. Grenet has, however, suggested that the idea that Kerdir himself had made the journey is wrong and placed someone else,[39] a young boy (*rahīg*) in a squatting position (*nišast*) to have the vision.[40] M. Schwartz has shown that this vision of the other world was made possible through the reciting of the mantra while the young boy stared into a mirror (*ēwēn mahr*).[41] This method of divination is not Iranian in origin and is found in the Mediterranean world in Late Antiquity, and thus it demonstrates a foreign borrowing by the Zoroastrian priesthood in the early Sasanian period. This fact suggests that Zoroastrian ritual and tradition had not yet been formed and was susceptible to foreign influence. Second, I believe the adoption of such a non-Iranian method of divination caused Kerdir to be wiped from the memory of the Zoroastrian tradition and the Sasanian historical tradition.

Then what is the Iranian manner of divination and journey to the netherworld? In a Middle Persian text which deals with such a journey, the righteous Wiraz takes a drink called *mang ī wištāpān*, which was a hemp or henbane potion in order to travel to heaven and hell to inform the Zoroastrian priests.[42] In a Zoroastrian apocalyptic text, the prophet Zoroaster is also able to see what will happen in the future by drinking water which Ohrmazd had given him in order to achieve "all knowing wisdom" (*xrad ī harwisp āgāhīh*).[43] Long ago H.S. Nyberg had suggested that this Zoroastrian tradition is part of the Central Asian heritage which is still common among the Shamans of Siberia.[44]

Kerdir, however, was able to see the correct conduct of rites and rituals through "incorrect" means, but it made him certain of the existence of heaven and hell. This moral power which Kerdir received from his visionary activity was used as a weapon which he unleashed to combat not only the heretics, but also Mani who had become important in the empire and needed to be dealt with swiftly during Wahram I's rule.[45] Other religions were not immune to this persecution either, as his inscription attests to this fact. With Narseh coming to the throne, the power of Kerdir may have lessened and by this time he must have been very old. We see that Narseh not only mentions Ohrmazd but also Anahid in his inscription at Paikuli which suggests his particular interest in her cult from which his grandfather Ardashir I had gained his power.[46] He makes the point of mentioning Ardashir and Shabuhr as the rightful rulers of the Sasanian Empire, while leaving Hormizd aside and the three Wahrams who interceded between his father and his rule. At Naqsh-i Rustam he had a rock relief carved which shows him receiving the diadem of sovereignty from Lady Anahid, thus making her cult not only important once again but perhaps paying personal attention to the fire-temple at Istakhr which had fallen into the hands of Kerdir and company.

POST-KERDIR ZOROASTRIANISM

We should also say something about the nature of "official" doctrinal Zoroastrianism that was upheld in the Sasanian period. The Middle Persian sources, which are the product of priestly tradition, lead us to believe that the path to the Zoroastrian religion was one (*rāh ī dēn ēk*)[47] and that the priests tied to the state were its representatives. That this religion was connected to the state and that they were deemed inseparable is mentioned in a famous passage in the Dēnkard (*Dēnkard* Madan edition 470.7):

> *hād xwadāyīh dēn ud dēn xwadāyīh . . . pad awēšān xwadāyīh abar dēn ud dēn abar xwadāyvh winnārdagīh*
>
> Know that kingship is religion and religion is kingship . . . for them kingship is arranged based on religion and religion based on kingship.[48]

Even if we do not have much information about the Zoroastrian sects, however, the Zurvanite and monotheistic forms of Zoroastrianism were present. For some time it has been suggested that Zurvanism was the dominant mode of thought among certain Zoroastrian *mowbeds* and kings in the Sasanian period. For the early Sasanian period it is not the Sasanians who tell us about this orientation, but rather it is inferred from the Manichaean sources. Mani, in relating his doctrine in Middle Persian and Parthian (obviously written or aimed at the population of the Iranian plateau), does not use Ohrmazd as the supreme deity but rather Zurvan who in he mentions as the highest god. Based on this evidence it is thought that the early Sasanian kings and even Kerdir may have been followers of Zurvan, although this is speculation based on the Manichaean sources. Kerdir could very well have been anti-Zurvanite and thus saw Mani as further endangering Zoroastrianism. It is again during the middle of Sasanian period, during the rule of Wahram V and Yazdgerd II that we hear through the famous prime minister (*wuzurg-framadār*), that Zurvanism was in vogue (he had named one of his sons Zurvandad "created by Zurvan"). Also such Armenian sources as Ełishe and Eznik of Kolb inform us of Mihr-Narseh and his efforts to force Zoroastrianism upon the Armenians, where the Zurvanite form was being propagated. Certainly traces of Zurvanistic thought are apparent in some of the Pahlavi texts, such as the *Mēnōg ī Xrad*, although there was a campaign to cleanse it by the scribes who wrote down the tradition in the early Islamic period.

Zurvan was the god of eternal time who had existed from time immemorial. The priests who had Zurvanite leanings basically believed that the evil spirit, *Ahreman* came to the world as a result of Zurvan's doubt, followed by Ohrmazd. Thus, in this system Ohrmazd and Ahreman became brothers or twins. This idea may have had its origins in a passage from the Gathas of Zoroaster (Yasna 30.3), where there is a reference to the two spirits being born and being in opposition to one another in thoughts and deeds.[49] Now the interpretation may have been false because in the Gathas the opposition is between *Spenta Mainiuu* (Amharspandān) and *Angra Mainiiu* (Ahreman), and not between Ohrmazd and Ahreman. In the original Zoroastrian doctrine of the Gathas, Ohrmazd in this opposition and dualism is above and beyond the two spirits, but the former is the arm with which Ohrmazd creates and propagates his ideas. The Zoroastrian priests of the Sasanian period, however, had elevated Ahreman to such extent that he was now equated with Ohrmazd. More will be said of the Zoroastrian priests' infatuation with evil, Ahreman, and the campaign to cleanse the world of it with a host of purity laws. These ideas made a deep impression on the people, who also turned to non-Zoroastrian religions for aid. It should, however, be stated that since no reference is made to Zurvan in the Sasanian sources and since Ohrmazd is the deity that is venerated in the inscriptions, we should not give too much weight to the Zurvanite hypothesis as a distinct school of thought. This may be an infatuation of modern scholars with Zurvan rather than a reflection of its importance in the Sasanian period. As Sh. Shaked has mentioned, this creation myth which was projected onto the Sasanian state religion probably never existed as a distinct doctrine of Zoroastrianism in this period.[50]

Armenian and Classical sources inform us that the Persian kings worshipped the sun and the moon, and Roman sources state that Shabuhr II claimed to be "brother of the Sun and the Moon" (Latin) (*frater Solis et Lunae*) but which does not appear in the Sasanian sources themselves.[51] There are two possibilities. One is that this may be a reference to the deity Mithra. A more interesting answer is that it may be an Indo-Iranian trait in which it was believed that their ancestors were descended from Manūčihr (Indic *Manu*) and his father Wiwahvant (Indic *Vivasvant*) who were identified in India with the Moon and the Sun respectively.[52] Otherwise the dualistic form of Zoroastrianism in which Ohrmazd and Ahreman were at battle and where humans must choose between the two was the dominant form of Zoroastrianism. Now in the intellectual circles, there may have been differences and this may have been due to foreign influences, since the *Dēnkard* states that during the time of Shabuhr I non-religious writings were collected and added to the *Avesta*:

> *Šābuhr šāhān šāh ī Ardashirān nibēgīhā-iz az dēn bē abar bizišgīh ud stargōwišnīh (ud) čandišn ud zamān ud gyāg ud gōhr (ud) jahišn ud bawišn ud wināsišn ud jadag-wihērīh ud gōwāgīh ud abārīg kirrōgīh ud abzār andar hindūgān ud hrōm (ud) abārīg-iz zamīhīhā pargandag būd abāz ō ham āwurd ud abāg abistāg abāz handāxt ud har ān ī drust paččēn ō ganj ī šāhīgān dād (ān) framūd ud ēstēnīdan ī hamāg arist (ag)- ān abar dēn māzdēsn ō uskār kard*
>
> Shabuhr, the King of Kings, son of Ardashir, further collected the non-religious writings on medicine, astronomy, movement, time, space, substance, accident, becoming, decay, transformation, logic and other crafts and skills which were dispersed throughout India, Rome and other lands, and collated them with the *Avesta*, and commanded that a copy be made of all those writings which were flawless and be deposited in the Royal Treasury. And he put forward for deliberation the annexation of all those pure teachings to the Mazdean religion.[53]

This passage is important in that it tells us that the king ordered that ideas should be drawn from Greek and Indian sciences and incorporated into the *Avesta*. Thus, the Sasanian *Avesta* was a mélange of ideas and learning from the world which seemed useful or in accordance with the Zoroastrianism in which Shabuhr believed or was creating. What is also apparent is a lively atmosphere of reflection or discussion (*ūskārišn*) at the court of what is reliable and what is not. Finally a copy (*paččēn*) of this written *Avesta* is deposited in the royal treasury. This will not be the last time that the Sasanian *Avesta* would go through redaction. This may also signify Shabuhr I's decision not only to allow Mani, who had eclectic ideas to be active, but also to make the *Avesta* a compendium of foreign and domestic learning in an era of universalism. In fact the *Dēnkard* demonstrates Aristotelian and Neo-Platonic influences and Greek thought in general which must have entered the empire and which some priests had accepted or incorporated into their belief.[54] One can not help but to see the situation as such that while the Zoroastrian priests and the state hammered in the idea of an "Orthodoxy," they were the real innovators and architects of an eclectic tradition in the name of tradition. We should also mention the influence of the Jewish religion on the intellectual life of Zoroastrianism. In some passages of the Middle Persian texts we do have statements which suggest a strong Semitic presence in the Zoroastrianism of the Sasanian and of the early Islamic period. For example in a strange account of the creation it is said that the first man, Gayōmard, was created from clay (Middle Persian *gil*), hence receiving the epitaph "King of clay" (Middle Persian *gilšāh*).[55] The other is in regard to the sin committed by Mashya and Mashyane, the first couple in the Zoroastrian religion, whose lives at times take on Biblical coloring becoming similar to story of Adam and Eve.[56]

ADURBAD I MAHRSPANDAN AND THE SEARCH FOR ORTHODOXY

Of course no foreign influence is needed to cause divergent interpretation among the Zoroastrian priests. Adurbad i Mahrspandan is another important figure in the history of Zoroastrianism who is also credited with the further codification of the *Avesta* and the Zoroastrian law in the fourth century CE. He was the chief priest during the time of Shabuhr II in the fourth century CE.

> *Šābuhr šāhān šāh ī hormizdān hamāg kišwarīgān pad paykārišn yazdān āhang kard ud hamāg gōwišn ō uskār ud wizōyišn āwurd pas az bōxtan ī Adurbād pad gōwišn ī passāxt abāg hamāg ōyšān jud-sardagān ud nask-ōšmurdān-iz ī jud-ristagān ēn-iz guft kū nūn ka-mān dēn pad stī dēn dīd kas-iz ag-dēnīh bē nē hilēm wēš abar tuxšāg tuxšēm ud ham gōnag kard*
>
> Shabuhr, the King of Kings, son of Hormizd, induced all countrymen to orient themselves to god by disputation, and put forth all oral traditions for consideration and examination. After the triumph of Adurbad, through his declaration put to the trial by ordeal (in disputation) with all those sectaries and heretics who recognized (studied) the Nasks, he made the following statement: "Now that we have gained an insight into the Religion in the worldly existence, we shall not tolerate anyone of false religion, and we shall be more zealous." And thus did he do.[57]

In this passage we are told that there was a great synod or council in which all people (*kišwarīgān*), probably meaning Zoroastrian theologians, discussed the material at hand. We also still see the "oral tradition" (*gōwišn*) at work here along with the *Avesta* which was already committed to writing deposited in the royal treasury. The oral tradition may be referring to *zand*, commentary of the *Avesta* which caused so much discussion. This is because we are supplied by a host of terms for "different [Zoroastrian] sects" (*jud-ristagān*), such as those of "different groups" (*jud-sardagān*), and those who "study the Nask" (*nask-ōšmurdān*) of the *Avesta*. From the point in which Adurbad i Mahrspandan is successful, all other sects beside what the State religion is, are called a false religion (*ag-dēnīh*).

The way in which Adurbad i Mahrspandan proves the truthfulness of his ideas over other Zoroastrian sects and theologians is also instructive about the nature of religious life. It is mentioned that Adurbad i Mahrspandan also went through an ordeal the components of which are made clear in another text. In the *Book of Righteous Wiraz* (*Ardā Wiraz Nāmag*), it is said that before Adurbad i Mahrspandan, the people and the priests were in doubt, and as a consequence of Alexander's destruction of the *Avesta* and the killing of the priests there were doctrines (*ēwēnag*), faiths (*kēš*), heresies (*jud-ristagīh*), and doubts (*gumānīh*) and contradictory laws (*jud-dādestānīh*). Then Adurbad i Mahrspandan appeared to set the religion straight by going through the following ceremony:

Adurbād ī mārspandān kē-š padiš passāxt ī pad dēn kard rōy
widāxtag abar war rēxt ud čand dādestān ud dādwarīh abāg
jud-kēšān ud jud-wurrōyīnān be kard

> Adurbad i Mahrspandan about whom the ordeal according to the Religion was performed: melted copper was poured on his breast, and he held several processes and (passed) judgment (on) the unbelievers and heretics.[58]

Thus he was able to prove his point by going through an ordeal which, according to the Zoroastrian tradition, proved one's truthfulness or lying. This reminds us of the ordeals that people of ancient Mesopotamia went through in order to prove their innocence or guilt, by such means as being thrown into the river. Here, however, molten metal was poured on one's chest and survival was proof of truthfulness. The molten metal ordeal certainly invokes Gathic imagery of the end of time when the righteous walk on molten metal as if walking on warm milk, while the sinners burn. This is only of the six ordeals by heat (*6 war ī garm*) which were used in ancient Persia.[59] In another Middle Persian text, (*What is*) *Licit and Illicit* (*Šāyest nē Šāyest*) the story is related that Adurbad i Mahrspandan poured molten metal on his chest (*āhan ī widāxtag*), but since he was sincere it felt as if milk had been poured on his chest. But those who were followers of the Lie would burn and be killed.[60] There was also the placing of hot iron on the tongue and other ordeals which were to prove one's innocence which basically meant a person was guilty until he/she were dead from the ordeal or lived through it. Still another way in which the Persians proved the truthfulness of their statement was by the ritual drinking of sulfur which was thought to be connected with the Persian "to take an oath" (*Sōgand Xwardān*)[61] but this connection has been disproved by M. Schwartz.[62]

MAZDAK Ī AHLOMOGĀN AHLAMOG: THE HERETIC PAR EXCELLENCE

Thus, the problem of "heresy" in the eye of the Sasanian church was serious enough to have had one priest using foreign tradition of vision of heaven and hell, and another pour molten metal on his chest to combat heretics and make others believe in their ways and to codify the Avestan *nasks*. Of course for the Zoroastrian priests tied to the state the arch-heretic was no other person than Mazdak who appeared in the late fifth/early sixth century CE. Regarding Mazdak we must discuss another issue which is the interpretation of the *Avesta*. Even when the *Avesta* was codified and written down, most of it was unintelligible to the priests so commentaries (*zand*) were written in order to make it understandable. There is no reason to doubt that there were various *zand*s or interpretations of the *Avesta*. Consequently those who made unacceptable interpretations of the holy text were labeled "heretic" (*zandīg*) or (*ahlāmoγ*). Some of the commentaries probably had a Gnostic interpretation of the *Avesta* which may have seemed repugnant to the courtly priests, as Mani and his doctrine had been. This foreign influence on certain Avestan interpretations caused the religious body to slander those of "mixed doctrine" (*gumēzag dād*) which was leveled at a certain heretic named Sēn, as well as Mazdak. The doctrine of these heretics was assumed to be in opposition to those who espoused the "good religion" (*weh dēn*). But one has to remember, there was ample opportunity for the Zoroastrian theologians to draw from foreign religions and sources as evidenced by the passages of the *Dēnkard*. Esoteric interpretations of the *Avesta* existed which have left traces in the Middle Persian texts, specifically in relation to such terms as *raz* "secret,"[63] and the Mazdakite belief in the "hidden" (*nihānī*) meaning of the *Avesta*.[64]

By all accounts the social message of Mazdak was the creation of an egalitarian system of the distribution of wealth at a time of famine which must have created further social tensions. Zoroastrian Middle Persian sources of course see Mazdak as the heretic par excellence (*ahlāmoγān ahlāmoγ*) who commanded that women, children, and property be shared among the population, which resulted in social chaos. The Middle Persian sources inform us that sons did not know who their fathers were and so they could not determine their class affiliation. P. Crone has suggested that Mazdak generalized the institution of levirate wife (*stūrīh*), in which a man without male issue can give his wife in levirate marriage to another man.[65] This means that the Mazdakites would have made *stūrīh* possible between classes as well, and maybe forced such an issue with the backing of Kavad. What seems novel here is that Mazdak was probably going against the time-honored dictum "take a wife from your own relatives," (*zan az paywand ī xwēš kunēd*)[66] i.e., the institution of next-of-kin-marriage (*xwēdodah*).[67] The lower classes must have favored this (Mazdak) mowbed's proclamations and ideas which he claimed were based on the *zand* or the interpretation of the *Avesta.* In fact Mazdak's ideas then were not totally foreign, only that his interpretation of the *Avesta* was disliked by the nobility and the priests who were attached to the state.

According to the Middle Persian and other sources, Mazdak's ideas were influenced by a man named Zardosht from the city of Fasā whose followers were called those who follow "the right religion" (*drist-dēn*).[68] He was probably living in the fifth century CE and was a predecessor of Mazdak who now reformulated and furthered his ideas. The Mazdakites who followed the teaching of this Zardosht and then Mazdak and are said to prescribe all the good qualities asked from a Zoroastrian, that is preaching righteous deeds, abstaining from sin and the practice of sacerdotal functions. What they lacked, however, was that they were less bent on following rites and rituals and the most important sentence about them in the *Dēnkard* declares their primal sin:

> *pad dēn ī māzdēsnān ēd ku pad dēn be niger u-šān čārag-xwāh*
>
> Regarding the Mazdean religion they are of the opinion that by interpreting (the Religion) they seek to remedy it.[69]

This means that their *zand* or interpretation was a means of remedying the social and economic hardships of the period after the Hephthalite onslaught, famine, and social tensions. The Mazdakites believed in matrilineal descent, recognizing descent from the mother which was contrary to the Zoroastrianism which the Sasanians had established.[70] He may have been among those heretics who were known as those "who distort a precept as it has been taught by the ancient teachers through interpretation."[71] It is here that Shaked's beliefs in esoteric interpretation of the *Avesta* become all the more valid. Mazdak is said to have distorted the precepts of the religion which seems to mean that he gave an esoteric interpretation to the *Avesta* and favored ascetic practices and maybe even vegetarianism.[72] If the Mazdakites were vegetarians, and believed that through good acts and without proper ritual they would reach salvation, their views was not very different from the common or state-sponsored priestly one. According to tradition it is said that Adurbad i Mahrspandan said "Firmly refrain from eating the flesh of cows and sheep" (*az pid ī gāwān ud gōspandān xwardan pahrēz saxt kunēd*).[73]

There were also differences in many other aspects of the state-sponsored Zoroastrianism, which were similar to Indian and Greek philosophical and cosmological ideas.[74] Here the development in Islamic history may serve as an example: while the Caliphate espoused the rigid doctrine and ritual of Islam, some of the Muslims felt that the state-sponsored religion lacked the humanity and spirituality which was in existence in the beginning. Hence, local anti-establishment Islamic practices were espoused and became popular, especially Sufīsm and Sufī practices which were persecuted by the early Caliphs. This persecution had a point besides its religious implication and it was that by controlling religion, the Caliphs controlled the political allegiance of all people through religion. We may see a similar development with Mazdak and his travails with the Zoroastrian state church and the King of Kings.

Kavad I used Mazdak in subverting the power of the nobility and priests who had weakened the power of the king, which also brought him popular support and made him and Mazdak a populist king and priest. We can tell that Mazdak was populist and that his doctrines were supported by the lower classes when the *Dēnkard* states that Mazdak had styled himself the spiritual leader of the Zoroastrian religion, bringing aid to the hungry and the naked (*gursag ud brahnag*). Other people from the lower classes, according to the text, seem to be the young mob, i.e., the *Jawan-mardan* who plundered the rich in the cities, to feed the poor.[75] Also the king established an office dealing with the downtrodden masses who needed aid, i.e., the office of the "Protector of poor and the judge" (*drīyōšān jādaggōw ud dādwar*).[76]

We also know that during the late Sasanian period charitable foundations were established for the sake of one's soul and the money was used for the poor or public construction projects that benefited the community and were a model for the later Islamic *waqf*.[77] From this time Mazdakite propagandists went as far as the Arabian Peninsula, supported by Kavad I, and where the empire established its base the Mazdakites were able to establish themselves. How much influence these Mazdakites had on Arabia and the Islamic doctrine cannot be known but their presence in Mecca is assured. Even when the anti-Mazdakite Khusro I came to power the Mazdakites were able to survive in the distant places away from Persia, specifically in Arabia.

At the end of Kavad's life there were conflicts in terms of succession and the Mazdakites chose the wrong contender, Kavus. Once Khusro I, aided by the anti-Mazdakite faction, came to power he made good on his promise to his constituents, and Mazdak and many of his followers were killed in a gruesome fashion. As a result the interpretation of the *Avesta*, and the teaching of their *zand* was restricted if we are to believe the Middle Persian texts:

> *pad zand ī wahman yasn ud hordād yasn ud aštād yasn paydāg kū ēw bār gizistag Mazdak ī bāmdādān ī dēn-petyārag ō paydāgīh āmad u-šān petyārag pad dēn ī yazdān kard ud ān anōšag-ruwān husraw ī Kavadān māhdād ud Shabuhr ī dādohrmazd ī ādurbādagān dastwar ud ādur farrbay ī a-dro ud ādurbād ādurmihr ud baxtāfrīd ō pēš xwāst u-š paymān aziš xwāst kū ēn yasnīhā pad nihān ma dārēd be pad pywand ī ašmā zand ma čāšēd awēšān andar husraw paymān kard*
>
> In the zand of the Wahman Yasn and the Hordād Yasn and of the Aštād Yasn it is revealed that once the accursed Mazdak son of Bāmdād, the adversary of the religion appeared. And (his followers) brought detriment to the religion of the yazads. And Xosrō of immortal soul, son of Kavad summoned before him Māhdād Shabuhr of Dādohrmazd, Dastur of Ādurbādagān, Ādur Farrbay the honest, Ādurbād of Ādurmihr, and Baxtāfrīd. And he asked an agreement from them, "Do not keep these Yasnas in concealment, but do not teach and zand outside your offspring." They made the agreement with Khusro.[78]

We realize that Mazdak's religious views based on his zand were so divergent from those of the other Zoroastrian theologians, that once Khusro I had suppressed his activities that he called all the religious authorities and specifically asked them not to teach the zand (*zand ma čāšēd*) to anyone outside of their circles. From this passage it appears that a kind of exclusion appears in terms of the *zand* and the worries of the Sasanians with proliferation of Zoroastrian sectarianism. In the *Dēnkard* we have another testimony about the religious policies of Khusro I which is worth noting:

im bay xusrōy šāhān šāh ī Kavadān čiyōn-iš ahlamōγīh ud sāstārīh spurr-hamēstārīhā wānīd pad paydāgīh az dēn andar har ahlamōγīh ī 4 pēšag āgāhīh ud uskārišn ī gōkānīg wasīhā bē abzūd ud ēn-iz pad gēhān hanjamanīh guft ku rāstīh ī dēn māzdēsn bē dānist ōšyārān pad uskārišn ōstīgīhā tuwān pad gētīg bē ēstēnīd.

His present Majesty, Khusro, the King of Kings, son of Kavad, after he had put down heresy and evil dominion with the fullest antagonism, according to the revelation of the Religion he greatly promoted detailed knowledge and investigation in the matter of all heresy within the four estates. And at an assembly (of the representatives) of the realm he declared: "We have recognized the truth of the Mazdean Religion; and the wise can with confidence establish it in the world by discussion."[79]

Here we are dealing with heresy in the eyes of the established Zoroastrian church tied to the state. For them the heretics (*ahlāmoγān*) were of several kinds; those who were unobservant of ceremonies and rituals; those who had secret doctrines, and those who interpreted the *Avesta* very differently. There were even theological differences among the priests tied to the state and the state nominally supported these priests and allowed them to function. However, others were not so fortunate, probably because their ideas or *zands* were far off the acceptance scale of the established doctrines or interpretations. We know of one other priest whose judgments and beliefs were denounced by the priests. In the *Šāyestnē Šāyest* we read that the Zoroastrian priests were at odds with Sēn, stating:

abēzag dād ud weh-dēn amā hēm ud pōryōtkēš hēm ud gumēzag dād sēnīg *wišgardīh hēnd ud wattar dād zandīg ud tarsāg ud jahūd ud abārīg ī az ēn awēšān hēnd*

We are of pure law and good religion and we are the first teachers of the Mazdean religion, and of mixed law are the followers of Sēn and of the worse law of heresy and Christians and Jews and others of these sorts.[80]

Now there may be several reasons why Sēn was seen as a heretic (*zandīg*). It may be that the priests believed his doctrine was of "mixed law/doctrine," which could mean that he used Gnostic or foreign theological sources, as the Christians and Jews were condemned in the next passage of the same text. It also may be that plainly put his zand was so different from the official theological teachings of Zoroastrianism which are known as the three doctrines (*sē čāštag*),[81] he was seen as a heretic. In the *Dēnkard* he is also mentioned and labeled a heretic because it is said that the followers of Sēn thought they were superior to other priests turned to the teachings of the ancients, meaning they have given it a new interpretation.[82]

There is other evidence to demonstrate that other priests also were not so fond of the courtly priests. If we assume that the courtly priests had their center in Persis we know of a group of priests who lived close to the city of Ray, in Media, whom the Middle Persian text accuses of heresy. In the *Bundahišn* the priests of the region are said to bring doubt upon the deities and since they are themselves of evil thought they convert others through religion to evil thoughts.[83] The Islamic sources state that during the eighth century CE there was a fortification at Ray where priests lived which was also the seat of the great Zoroastrian priest *masmoɣān*.[84] The location of this fort was said to be by the Damāvand Mountain. The Abbasid Caliph al-Mahdi destroyed the fort and had the *masmoɣān* killed.[85] Could this be the source of negative reference to the north in the Middle Persian texts when dealing with heresy and bad religion? Even in the Pahlavi *Anti-Demonic Law* (*Wīdēwdād*), one of the best lands created by Ohrmazd, Rāy, where Zoroaster is also believed to have come from, the evil spirit brought opposition in the form of "extreme unbelief" (*wattar gumānagīh*) by those "who themselves are skeptic and make others also skeptic" (*kū xwad gumānomand ud kasān-iz be kunēnd*).[86]

While the problem of zand was to plague the state church, there is one other group which had a very different view of the problems. These Zoroastrians may be called the "anti-Zand" faction which, of course, the *Dēnkard* takes as heretics. According to them, with the exception of the Gāthās of Zoroaster which was the word of God, other sections of the *Avesta* as well as the commentary were the work of humans and so susceptible to corruption.[87] Thus, on the one hand, the priests tied to the church had to fend for themselves against those Zoroastrians who had allowed foreign ideas enter their religion, or from those whose *zand* was different from theirs. On the other hand they had to defend themselves from a group of Zoroastrian theologians who rejected all interpretations and the *Avesta* which was compiled by Tosar and company and went through changes through the centuries. The problem is that by looking at the translation of the Gāthās we realize that the Zoroastrian priests at the time had a very imperfect knowledge of the Avestan language, hence a poor understanding of the Gāthās as well.

THE SIGNS OF BEING ZOROASTRIAN

What has been discussed so far relates to the intellectual history of Zoroastrianism. We can now turn to the realm of popular religion, which was somewhat different from the intellectual battles of the priests. Sh. Shaked's paradigm is useful here. He states that we can perceive three layers or types of Zoroastrian religion current in the Sasanian period: 1) The official, state sanctioned religion; 2) The popular type which was based on magical practices, and 3) What he calls common religious practices which shared aspects with both of these mentioned above.[88] Mazdak was a populist leader and people probably continued to support his doctrine and even after his death, after the fall of the Sasanian dynasty pro-Mazdakite forces would challenge the Caliphate.[89] In this case then intellectual discourse led to populist movements.

The state sanctioned religion prescribed for the believer a specific set of rituals besides beliefs. In the morning one had "to wash the hands and face with the urine of the sheep and cleanse them with water" (*dast ud rōy pad gōmēz ī gōspandān šāyēd ud pad āb pāk šāyēd*).[90] As for prayer and worship one had to perform often: "three times a day, everyday go to the house of fire and worship the fire" (*har rōz sē bār andar ō mān ī ātaxšān šawēd ātaxš niyāyišn kunēd*).[91] As a Zoroastrian one had "to memorize the Yašts and Hādōxt and Baγān Yasn and Wīdēwdād like the hērbeds, (and) from passage to passage hear the Zand" (*yašt ud hādōxt ud baγān-yasn ud jūd-dēw-dād hērbedīhā warm, gyāg gyāg zand niyōxšīd ēstēd*).[92] As a sign of being Zoroastrian, one had to wear the *kūstīg* "sacred girdle." Before the priest he/she had "to undergo penance, or confession one's sins" (*pad patīt būdan*). He/she had to celebrate the six *gahanbar* "seasonal feasts," and upon death had to be placed in the *dakhmag* which is a building where the corpses were exposed to dogs and vultures.

Popular religion had certain characteristics which the priests probably tried to curtail. For example the issue of magic, which one cannot ignore, especially since recent studies have brought to light magic amulets and bowls of the Sasanian period. In the ancient Near East we can divide the types of magic practiced into white and black magic. Textual sources for the Sasanian period are meager in this regard, while the material culture, especially seals throws light on the subject which has been the subject of study by R. Gyselen.[93] Charms and amulets used in white magic were geared towards averting evil, disease, and death. There are many surviving Pazand texts that give us a flavor of white magic which again have varied aims, such as combating toothache, headache, fever; the stopping of noxious and evil creatures, such as rats, cats, snakes and wolves. The "evil eye" is an important concept which also was a point of concern as is still today in the modern country of Persia. For example such a hero/king as Fredon/Feraidun is invoked by a charm to close the evil eye and to bring prosperity to the person.[94] Of course the reason for which Fredon appears as a healer in this prayer is that in the Iranian tradition, he plays a tri-functional role as a priest, Avestan *paraδāta*, Sanskrit *puróhita* "officiating or head priest;"[95] as a warrior-king who battles against (Middle Persian) Dahag, (Persian) Zohhak and the *Maznian Dews*; and finally as promoter of agriculture, where his epithet *Aptiya* suggests that he is connected with water which associates him with the third class of the society. With this prayer we are safely in the Zoroastrian religious world, where white magic is under the tutelage of the Zoroastrian priest who probably has written the piece. After all for a spell to work, it needed to be written by the hands of a religious authority or someone who had religious powers.

We have less information on black magic and devil worship, although certainly it did exist as one can deduce from the evidence on white magic. One must have been able to put a curse or evil eye on another in revenge as we note in some texts. The Middle Persian term for sorcery or witchcraft (*jādūg*) is often met in various texts, and if Zoroastrian hagiography (*Dēnkard* VII which contains the life of Zoroaster) is a reflection on Sasanian society, one can gain some ideas about the function of sorcerers in Sasanian society.[96] In the *Dēnkard* in the episodes relating to Zoroaster's life there are constant references to the evil Kavis and Karapans, the ancient Indo-Iranian pagan priests who tried to destroy the prophet through magic which was ultimately unsuccessful. These magical practices which can be called black magic include providing chants which hypnotize the hearer. It is in this context as well that we hear in the Middle Persian text of "aiding the demons," (*dēw-ayārīh*) and "devil worshipping" (*dēw-yasnīh*). In offsetting these acts of the demons, the Zoroastrian priests appear to have had an important part as well. They were the religious and moral guardians of their community, especially after the fall of the Sasanian empire in the seventh century, when the Zoroastrian state was not in existence. At this time, devil-worship or demon-worship was equated with the religion of the new invaders. Consequently, the idol-temple (*uzdēszār*) was equated with the mosques which were built over the Zoroastrian fire-temples. It is for this reason that in Zoroastrian apocalyptic poetry there was a longing for a reversal of this process (*Abar madan ī Wahram ī Warzāwand*.22-23):

mazgitīhā frōd hilēm be nišānēm ātaxšān
uzdēsparistīh be kanēm ud pāk kunēm az gēhān

We will bring down mosques, establish the fires,
we will raze idol-worshipping and wipe it from the material world.

At this time when the demons had become physically manifested, and went about not in concealment, and now that the religion was in danger, according to the Middle Persian texts, it was only the Zoroastrian priest who could guard the people with his eloquence, true-speaking and bring health to the people and the land.[97] This is, of course, what the Zoroastrian priests would have liked the people to believe.

We also find some seal-amulets and incantation bowls which are of interest in terms of popular religion and magic. The amulets suggest that a variety of people, belonging to different religious confessions may have used them.[98] We should say that the prominence of these bowls and amulets is in Mesopotamia and the surrounding region where there is evidence of this type of practice from the Neo-Assyrian and Babylonia period, but their prominence in the Sasanian period is from the fifth to the eighth century CE.[99] From reading the inscriptions on the seals or on the bowls it becomes clear that the line of religious affiliation became blurred when it came to magic and popular religion. For example a Zoroastrian might want a priest (maybe a sorcerer!) to prepare for him/her magic formulas to ward off demons and evil spirits. The use of magic then could have come from Mesopotamia, the Mediterranean or the Near Eastern tradition,[100] and the native Persian tradition. Zoroastrianism has no shortage of evil creatures which appear as various manifestations of social and moral taboos in Middle Persian texts.

The twelfth/twenty seventh chapter of the *Bundashišn* is an exposition on the evil creatures which cause various problems for humanity. For example there is a demon which causes evil thoughts (*akoman*); *nanhais* who causes unhappiness; *mihwakht* the demon of lies and bad thoughts, *rashk* who causes animosity and the evil eye; *chashmag* who causes earthquakes and storm; *panī* the demon who causes one to store food and not eat it and not give it to anyone else; *āz* who causes men to become unhappy with their wives and seek other women; *agaš* the demon which strikes people with the evil eye; *astwihad* who is an evil air (*wāy ī wattar*) as opposed to beneficent air (*wāy ī wehttar*), whose shadow causes fever.[101] Some of these demons mentioned in the Sasanian period appear not to have Iranian names and so we may suggest that they are from Mesopotamia or other regions.[102] It can be demonstrated that when it came to magic the lines of religious conviction were blurred. A seal amulet which was recently published has the following formula:

> *Š-RM-OLK MN yy yynw L yyyy W mlgy ŠYDA KON h'ny cygwn ZNE n'mky HZYTN'y ADYNt ZK 'ndlcy 'byd't 'yw [YHW]WNt ZY cygwn-m t [xx] [xxx] m 'lt'dy APš BREryn 'ndlcy krty KON ZNE pylwcdwhty MNW AMY ŠM Apš ABY ŠM W MN MTA mklsy AL YHWWNš Apš AL OHDWN Apt H[t?] OHDWNt HWEt ADYNcš zwty LHLA ŠBW(!)WNn AYKt LA TWB OHDWN Apt PWN LOYŠE pl(?)wt(?) [p't?]pl'sy LHYK xxxx [xxx] Baš KON (kwn?) 'cšc BRA OL cyly AYKš byšzyhy W dlm'n YHWWt PWN yšwdy ŠM*
>
> "Well-being be upon you, from Yahwe Adonai to . . . . . and death to the demon. Now, just as you may see this inscriptions, then for you that . . . . righteous, and he admonished his sons, now this Perozduxt, whose mother's name and her father's name . . . And be not from the village Miklas, and do not seize her/him and if you have seized her/him, then I too shall quickly leave her/him to . . . so that she/he will not take you again, and at your head downward . . . punishment far . . . ., but now from it, too, out to . . . So a healing and a remedy for her there may be in the name of Jesus."[103]

What we have here is a mélange of Irano-Semitic ideas brought together under Sasanian rule. The name of the person mentioned is Perozdukht, a Persian for certain, but the deity who is asked to help her and anyone else and who may carry this amulet is Christian or Manichaean. This, as has been argued, does not necessarily mean that the owner was a Christian or a Manichaean Persian, but it also could be a Zoroastrian, where the name of Jesus was used as a "power name" in this period.[104]

The saying of specific mantras or spells in the Zoroastrian tradition can be classified as white magic. These spells are said to ward off the evil spirits which as mentioned above are in constant action against humans and their environment. The best known of these mantras is the *Yatha Ahu Vairiio* prayer of which is said that reciting it twice it will ward off demons.[105] In a hagiographical text, when the demon *būd* which is characterized as a secret-moving pestilence and deceiver was to attack Zoroaster by his chanting aloud *Yatha Ahu Vairiio*, the demon was confounded and rushed away.[106] Other times the chanting of this prayer causes the demons' bodies to be shattered[107] and more interestingly in one passage it caused all of them to be seized and buried in the earth.[108]

On the eastern frontier religious ideas were also in flux and change. Here Hinduism made an impact as Buddhism certainly did. Popular religions of Central Asia also mingled with Zoroastrianism and this caused the growth of curious and interesting religious practices. For example in the Zoroastrian text we read that mourning for the dead in the form of crying (*grīstān*) and lamentation (*mōyag*) was a sin, in which the deceased was prevented from crossing the river and reaching the *Činwant* bridge because the river had become filled with the tears of those who had lamented. On the other hand, early Islamic sources on eastern Persia and Central Asia tell us that the Zoroastrian priests on a certain day lamented the death of the Persian hero, Siyāwaxš. This event, which has come to be known as *Sog i Siyawash* was popular in Central Asia, where wall paintings at Panjekent show the lamentation scenes. Also songs were sung in Bukhara in memory of the story of Siyawash, by minstrels who were called "the Lamentation of the Mages [Zoroastrian Priests]" (*griyistan ī moγān*)[109] exactly what was forbidden by the Zoroastrian Middle Persian texts. We now have other pictorial evidence of this ceremony or similar one in a panel relief from the Shumei collection. The relief shows a Zoroastrian priest tending the fire at the center of the picture and a group mourners behind him who are cutting or slashing their faces with knives or sharp objects.[110] In this regard the Persian scholar Bērūnī states that in Sogdiana, on the last day of the month of *Khshum* people cried for the deceased people and lamented them and cut their faces, which goes well with this Shumei relief.[111] This example should suffice to demonstrate the diversity of religiosity in the Sasanian empire which held Zoroastrianism as the official religion. Probably there was diversity from province to province and more influence from the neighboring regions in the provinces bordering the Sasanian empire, than the heartland where the Zoroastrian priests must have been able to propagate their religion more forcefully. The Zoroastrian religion, however, was never unified in the Sasanian period and no matter how much the Sasanian state and church and our Middle Persian sources try to portray such unity, the textual evidence as well as the evidence from the early Islamic period suggests the contrary.

In conclusion one must also take into consideration not only the difference and development between early and late Sasanian Zoroastrianism, but also regional variations of the religion. F. Grenet's work on Central Asia which is really the Eastern Iranian world demonstrates Zoroastrianism in its eastern context, different from what was practiced in Fars/Persis and the western Iranian World. Thus, one should take into mind variations for the different parts of the empire, the north which still held to pre-Zoroastrian Iranian ideas mingled with Sasanian Zoroastrianism; the south-east which was probably also influenced by Buddhism and Hinduism; and the West influenced by Hellenism, Semitic religious traditions in Arabia, Syria and Mesopotamia, as well as Judaism and Christianity. In this variation the Sasanian dynasty attempted to choose and pick its version of the "truth," namely the search for an orthodoxy. However, the reality showed a much more diverse view of Zoroastrianism than what the Sasanian wished for, but in this way Zoroastrianism influenced other traditions as it interacted with them on the periphery of the empire.

It is to the credit of the Sasanians that the *Avesta* as a corpus was collected and created in late antiquity. This above all created a structure by which Zoroastrianism would survive till today. Of course the institutionalization of ritual and laws are the other important aspect of any religions. Certainly till today the largest numbers of manuscripts that are found in Iran are the ritual and purity sections of the *Avesta*, i.e., the *Wīdēwdād*. The Sasanian state promoted Zoroastrianism, but by the fifth century it realized that Christianity had become a universal religion and in order not to be the religion identified with the Eastern Roman Empire, a Persian Christian church would be beneficial. Although most people today identify Christianity with the Eastern Roman Empire in late antiquity, there were many Christian groups who were not in or part of that tradition. The Christians along with the Jews created a pluralistic society which was headed by their religious leader, but ultimately answerable to the king and the state. As long as order was kept, all religious communities prospered, but disorder brought persecution. While the Sasanians began as a Zoroastrian dynasty, in time, they became the mediator and arbiter of justice and order among the Jews, Christians, Mandaeans, Buddhists, Hindus, Zoroastrians and other religious communities in the empire. The universality of the Sasanian Empire, unlike the Eastern Roman Empire, was not translated into a Christian order but rather an order with Zoroastrianism at its core, but also with a universal multi-ethnic and multi-religious aspect.

Chapter 4

Languages and Textual Remains of the Citizens

LANGUAGE

Persians were always willing to use the languages of other people in order to further their cause in state building and effective administration. This is clear from the Achaemenid period from the sixth BCE when, while Old Persian was the language of the ruling elite and the king, Elamite was used for economic matters and Aramaic was the imperial language used for communication throughout the empire. Even then, the imperial inscriptions were given in three versions: Old Persian, Elamite and Babylonian, the languages of the inhabitants of the immediate region with whom the Persians had been in contact since their arrival on the plateau. With the conquest of Alexander the Great, Greek replaced Aramaic as the imperial language and it was only in the second half of the Parthian period from the first century CE onwards that Parthian also came to be inscribed on coins and inscriptions along with their Greek version. This multilingual view of the empire was not lost to the Sasanians either and we see that the early Sasanian royal inscriptions provide bilingual or trilingual testimonies, reminding us of the Achaemenid inscriptions. However, now the dominant language along Middle Persian was the language of the preceding dynasty, i.e., Parthian and Greek. Greek had remained the language of science and knowledge from India to the Mediterranean basin for centuries. Ardaxšīr I and his son Šābuhr I both used this trilingual mode of writing, as the Achaemenids had done with other languages. Middle Persian was becoming the dominant language at the heart of the empire which gives us certain insights into the linguistic and cultural preoccupation of the Sasanians.

One can also see that the religious apparatus (Zoroastrian church and priests) from its first literary evidence was anti-Hellenic and had nativist tendencies. Kerdīr only had his inscription carved in Middle Persian in the third century CE which may be an indication of the change in not only linguistic taste, but a purposeful reaction to foreign languages and ideas. If we discard the notion that because of the economy of space Kerdīr did not choose to have his inscription in other languages, then we can gain some ideas about the religious and imperial policies in relation to language and culture. Middle Persian was perhaps the language used by the Persian Zoroastrians, and Kerdīr did not need to communicate in any other language. The King of Kings, however, had to convey his message to all of his people, whether Persian Zoroastrians, Parthian soldiers and the nobility in the court, or the Greek prisoners and colonists of old who were *phihellen*. At the time of Narseh in the beginning of the fourth century, Greek was no longer utilized for imperial inscriptions which indicates a waning of Greek culture and/or a successful anti-Hellenic campaign by the Zoroastrian priests and the state. We should remind ourselves that Greek was also the common language of the Persian nemesis to the West, namely the Eastern Roman empire. With this scheme in mind we can create a chart in terms of the languages used by the priesthood and the imperial court in the third and early fourth centuries (see Table 4.1)

Table 4.1 Language used in Sasanian Inscriptions

Ardashir I	*Shabuhr I*	*Narseh*	*Shabuhr II and III*	*Kerdīr (Priest)*
M. Persian	M. Persian	M. Persian	M. Persian	M. Persian
	Parthian	Parthian		
Greek	Greek			

Our discussion, however, has focused on the imperial languages and the center of Persian civilization which gives us a false picture of the linguistic diversity in the Sasanian Empire. While those who were familiar with Greek or were Greek themselves were present in the empire during the Parthian period, Mesopotamia was dominated by Semitic speaking people, and the Persians were only a minority. These Semitic speakers included the Jews who wrote the *Babylonian Talmud*, and the Syriac speaking population and people who spoke various Aramaic dialects. Arabs resided in southern Mesopotamia, and Arabic was then known in the empire from the third century, when Ardashir I had conquered northern Arabia. In the northwest, Armenian and Georgian were dominant, but since the Parthian nobility had taken refuge in Armenia, the Parthian language became even more influential and the basic vocabulary for institutions, such as religious and administrative terms entered the Caucuses.

In Persis, Persian had been dominant since the Achaemenid period and was probably prevalent in Media and the adjoining regions. There were, however, dialectal differences of which, unfortunately, we have very little evidence, and what evidence there is, is from the early Islamic period. Still, one may hazard a hypothetical picture by drawing on the situation in the early Islamic period. One is reminded of the language known as *fahlaviyāt* and the language of Baba Taher in his poetic masterpiece to understand the complexity of linguistic diversity on the Iranian plateau.[1] In Adurbadagan/Azerbijan, Azari was spoken and one of its dialects, Tati, is well attested and again in the Islamic period there are specimens of Azari in existence.[2] Even today in the Republic of Azerbijan where Turkic is the language of the state and most people, there are villages and towns such as Siyahzan, north of Baku which has a sizable Tati speaking population. In the Caspian region of Gēlān and Māzandarān, again there were distinct language and dialects which is evidenced by the early Islamic attestation and was much more isolated because the mountainous region separated it from the rest of the Iranian plateau. In Xūzestān, Neo-Elamite (not to be confused with the period) or the language of the Elamiyas was in existence in the Sasanian period. Even in Shiraz, the heartland of the Sasanians and Persians, we find variant dialects which, although essentially Persian, still present problems.[3]

In the east we are better informed where Parthian, Sogdian, Bactrian and Xwārazmian were in use by these Iranian speaking people. In the southeast, the Sīstānī language was known to have been dominant, and a recent find of the translation of the Qur'an into the Sīstānī dialect (known as *Qur'an-e Quds*) gives us a clue to the language of southeast Persia.[4] But these are the only languages of which we have some information and there were many more dialects and languages which have been lost to us. The nomadic people and their languages are more difficult to gauge, but certainly the Kurds had been present on the plateau, and Kurdish, with its various dialectal variances, existed, perhaps along with Luri and few others which have been lost.

To make matters more complicated, we should remember that with the capture of Roman soldiers and their relocation along with the Syriac-speaking population of Syria into the Iranian plateau, some Latin, Greek and Syriac was used, especially in the royal cities where masses of Roman soldiers were employed to work as engineers, builders, craftsmen, and on imperial farms as laborers. We should not lose sight of the fact that the Goths and other Germans, along with some Slavic-speaking people who had enlisted in the Roman army and were captured, were also placed in Sasanian Persia. So in a sense, one can state that since there were Germans, Germanic languages were being spoken in Persia by the third century CE. By the fifth century CE, when the Turkic tribes began entering the empire, be it through raiding or by being used as a military force by the state, Turkic languages also must have been known, especially in the northeastern region.

The Sasanians had to establish a certain structure to connect the various provinces linguistically, so there would be a common mode of communication. This must have been done through the establishment of Persian and non-Persian speaking administrators and natives who were bilingual in order to be able to deal with imperial orders and the local administration. While the princes of the blood, the *Wisphuragān* ruled the different regions, a local administration of scribes, priests, and others were in existence as evidenced by the fourth century inscription of Shabuhr Sakan-Shah, the King of Sistan. Otherwise, in such lands as Armenia, Zoroastrian priests and tax-collectors were sent to administer the province. A system of standardization of weights and measures was created and the silver *drahm*s indicated Middle Persian as the dominant language of the empire. This relative standardization and the beginning of a process of homogeneity by the Sasanians also was the beginning of the influence of Persian language in the whole empire. Now we will turn to the Middle Persian language which was to become the dominant mode of imperial communication and much of the religious corpus of Manichaeans, Christians, Jews, and, of course, the Zoroastrians.

Middle Persian or Pahlavi refers to the stage of Persian language which was in existence between the Old Persian (550–330 BCE) and Classical Persian (1000 CE) periods. This division, though, is to a large extent arbitrary and used by scholars as a nice way of demarcating the different stages of the Persian language. This language was probably current from the first century to the tenth centuries CE, although by the late Achaemenid period one can already see that the Old Persian inscriptions were hinting at the transition to Middle Persian. In the eleventh century CE, priests wrote in Middle Persian while Persian and Arabic had become current. Hence, the language of texts that were written in this language is known as Middle Persian. This historical division of Persian is similar to the tripartite division of the English language into Old, Middle and Modern English. In comparison with English, however, Persian demonstrates that it is very conservative in nature and in its development. Persian, which is an Indo-European language, is part of the Iranian languages whose closest kin are the Indic languages. In fact there are only minor differences in phonology and grammatical endings between Old Persian, which was used for Achaemenid Royal inscriptions (550–330 BC), and Classical Sanskrit. Any student of first year Sanskrit or Old Persian realizes this fact. For example the Old Persian verb "to seize," *grab-* is equivalent to Sanskrit *grabh-* and English "grab." Another example would be the word for "door," *duvara-* which corresponds to Sanskrit *dvár-*, English "door;" Old Persian word for "name" is *nāman-*, Sanskrit *nāman-*, English "name;" Old Persian word for "father" *pitar-*, Sanskrit *pitár-*, Latin *pater*, Gothic *fadar*, English "father." These examples demonstrate the connections between Persian and other Indo-European languages. In terms of the development of the Persian language, we can again use some of the same words in their development during the three stages. "Door," Old Persian *duvara-* > Middle Persian *dar* > Persian *dar*; "name," *nāman-* > Middle Persian *nām* > Persian *nām*; "father," Old Persian *pitar-* > Middle Persian *pidar* > Persian *pidar*.

MIDDLE PERSIAN INSCRIPTIONS

Middle Persian literature includes inscriptions and texts which survive from the third to the tenth century CE. Pazand texts which are written with the Avestan script, *Zabūr* texts which are the Psalms (Hebrew *mīzmōr)* written by the Christians, and the Manichaean texts from the late antiquity are also among them. The Middle Persian inscriptions are mainly from the third and the fourth century CE which were commissioned by the kings and by Kerdīr. They are formulaic in structure and their compositions resemble Achaemnid inscriptions. Some have suggested that this was part of the oral literary tradition which was prevalent in ancient Persia and used by the writers of the inscriptions and texts.[5] Others have even gone further to state that these inscriptions are replete in historical data and rather are stories which were inscribed to legitimize the kings through the use of the traditional epic framework of the ancient Near East.[6] The later Sasanian inscriptions (post fourth century) are rarely royal, are shorter, and are commissioned by individuals or local lords for remembrance, building campaigns, and funerary dedications which are much shorter. The script used for the inscription represents the archaic version of the Aramaic script which may be a continuation of tradition which was first developed by the Achaemenids for their royal chancery. The characters are written separately from right to left, while the later inscriptions are almost "Arabisque-like" and the letters are joined, and much more cursive which is similar to the Book Pahlavi or Middle Persian texts which were written in the late Sasanian and post-Sasanian period.

The content of the early inscriptions are boastful and the structure is such that first the king makes sure that it is known that he is a Zoroastrian (*Māzdēsn* = worshipper of Mazda), then his genealogy is given; and next are the territories under his rule. Then a narrative story appears as in the case of Shabuhr's Naqsh-i Rustam inscription, in which there is a story of the defeat of the Romans and what became of them which is told as a result of Roman aggression. By the middle of the inscription, we find the boastful nature of the king and his epic actions: "We searched out for conquest many other lands, and we acquired fame for heroism, which we have not engraved here, except for the preceding. We ordered it written so that whoever comes after us may know this fame, heroism and power of us."[7] This seeking of heroism is also apparent from a short inscription of Shabuhr at Hajjiabad as well, where he tells us that he has shot an arrow which has gone very far: "[Now] whoever may be strong of arm, let them put (their) foot in this cleft [on this rock] and let them shoot an arrow to(wards) that cairn. Then whoever cast [send] an arrow (as far as) to that cairn, they are [indeed] strong of arm."[8]

Then Shabuhr turns his attention to religion and the establishment of fire-temples for the souls of the members of his family, sacrifices are made, and the priests were made content. The rest of Shabuhr's inscription is an exposition of the offices that were in existence during the rule of his grandfather and father. This is followed by an end formula which recounts his zeal towards the gods, and again mentioning his bravery and wishing those who come after him to know about him and follow in his footsteps. He also has several shorter inscriptions at Naqsh-i Rajab (ŠNRb), at Hajjiabad, and at Beshabuhr which really is the most productive period of inscriptions.

The other long inscription is that of Narseh from the fourth century CE which begins the inscription in the same way, but his concern here is to justify his taking of the throne from Wahram, king of the Sakas. Narseh plays the dualism of Zoroastrianism very well in this period, portraying himself as just and the forces of Wahram and his accomplice Wahnam, son of Tatrus with falsehood. He tells us his election was the result of the grandees' election of him over his opponent, where they met him and asked him to become the King of Kings. Finally we are told that Wahram was humiliated by such a measure:

"Take and bind Wahram and [put] him on a maimed donkey [and] bring him bound to Our Court."[9]

Narseh does not portray himself as the hero type, rather making himself the one that has been wronged in the succession and that he was instigated to take the throne by the nobility and the grandees which reappears in Iranian history again and again (one can point to the election of Nadir Shah and the institution of the Afsharids). Even at the end of the inscription after he has punished and killed the supporters of the king of the Sakas, he portrays his family as the most righteous and hence fit to rule. He gives a long rendition of the goodness of his family, certainly playing on his connection with Shabuhr I and the he has to finally come to power because he is told by the nobility: "nobody else has been similar to You [whom . . .] the gods have favoured (?) [and (who) by Your ?] fortune (?) and wisdom and Own [courage (?) have kept ?] oppression [away from Ērān?]šahr."[10]

After Narseh in the fourth century CE, the economy of the inscriptions give us very little historical information with the exception of the time of Shabuhr II, and while the royal inscriptions such as those of Shabuhr II and Shabuhr III at Taq-ī Bustan are formulaic, because of the economy of the non-royal inscriptions such as that of the grand Wazir, Mihr-Narseh and the *astōdān* (ossuary) inscriptions, they provide very little historical information. The subject of the two inscriptions at the time of Shabuhr II is quite valuable and interesting for several reasons. Both of these inscriptions were commissioned by local kings at Persepolis, one by the king of the Sakas, Shabuhr Sagan-Shah and the other by a Seleukos the scribe. These inscriptions reveal the territorial extent of the Sasanian empire in the fourth century CE, the local administrative and military apparatus of the Sasanian kings, and finally the importance of Persepolis for the Sasanians. In the Sagan-Shah inscription, he and his retinue have lunch at the palace and perform a ritual of *yazdān kardagān* "ritual for the Gods," but also blessing his father and forefathers at this place which makes one suspect that the Sasanians knew the builders of this structure as their ancestors.[11] This of course does not mean that we can tell that the Sasanians at this time knew that the Achaemenids were the builders of this structure, but since the *Kārnāmag ī Ardaxšīr ī Pābagān* (The Book of the Deeds of Ardashir, the son of Pabag) mentions that Ardashir I was from the *nāf* "lineage" of Darius III, it can mean that they knew something about the Achaemenids. The other possibility is that they had already begun to identify this structure with the Kayanids and see them as their forefathers. This certainly is clear from the later Sasanian period when the palace at Persepolis came to be known as *Taxt-ī Jamšīd* "Yima's

Throne," and the memory of the Achaemenids was given to oblivion under state propaganda.

The interesting point of Shabuhr II and Shabuhr III's short inscriptions is not their content, rather their location which is away from the traditional place where we find the early royal inscriptions. These Two Kings of Kings chose to have their short inscriptions telling about their fathers and ancestors in Taq-ī Bustan located near Kermanshah. The two fourth century Kings are set side by side, suggesting their closeness. This is because after Shabuhr II, Ardashir II came to power and placed himself at Taq-ī Bustan in a relief beside his brother. This location is also interesting because Narseh has a rock carving and later Xusro II as well, and what can be said is that it may have been a sanctuary dedicated to the deity Anahita. Here we have a relief of Narseh and Mihr or Mithra being given the diadem of sovereignty. The largest relief belongs to Khusro II from the late sixth/seventh century and his grotto which represents the armored custom of the Sasanian cavalry from this period, where his horse (Shabdiz) is also covered with armor, reminding us of Medieval European knights and jousting scenes. Above Khusro II's grotto, there is also a scene of Khusro II's investiture not only Ohrmazd, but by Anahid who is pouring libations. Other pillar fragments from Taq-ī Bustan also contain pictures of Lady Anahid which attests to the importance of this deity. This is interesting, since the triad deity of the Achaemenid period, such as Ohrmazd, Anahid, and Mithra are here represented at Taq-ī Bustan and demonstrates the continuity of Persian belief system.

Mihr-Narseh, who was the grand Wazir or minister *Wuzurg-framādār* in the fifth century has left a short inscription by a bridge which he commissioned for the sake of his and his son's souls which attest to the Zoroastrian conception of building for salvation in this period, be it a common person or a grand Wazir.[12] By the end of the Sasanian and the beginning of the early Islamic period several small private inscriptions exist of which the most prominent include the two inscriptions at Maqsud Abad which relate the issue of ownership of land and a well. These inscriptions deal with the owner of a piece of land, it's well, and reconstruction of castles. Other inscriptions have been found in Byzantium,[13] and east in India[14] and as far as China[15] which are from the late Sasanian period when there was intense contact with those regions or a later migration as a result of the Arab Muslim conquest of Persia. Another group of inscriptions belong to the graves of individuals (*astōdān*).[16] These inscriptions relate the name and information on the family of the individual whose bones lay there and the date of their

Plate 1 Ardashir's victory scene at Firuzabad

Plate 2 Bust of Khusro II at Taq-ī Bustan

Plate 3 Bust of Shabuhr II from Hajjiabad

(a) (b)

Plate 4 Sasanian coin a) Obverse b) Reverse

Plate 5 Fire-temple of Tape Mill at Ray

Plate 6 Hormizd II jousting at Naqsh-i Rustam

Plate 7 Ka'be-ye Zardosht at Naqsh-i Rustam

Plate 8 Zoroastrian priest Kerdir at Naqsh-i Rajab

Plate 9 Gilded dish portraying Khusro I at National Museum of Iran

Plate 10 Khusro II flanked by the deities Anahid (Anahita) and Ohrmazd at Taq-ī Bustan

Plate 11 Khusro II at the hunt at Taq-ī Bustan

Plate 12 Khusro II with full armor at Taq-ī Bustan

Plate 13 Manichaean manuscript showing a feast

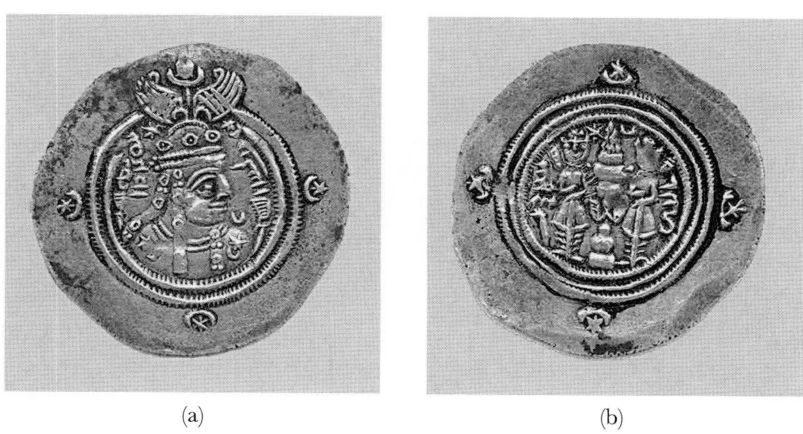
(a) (b)

Plate 14 Silver coin of Queen Buran a) Obverse b) Reverse

Plate 15 The arch of the palace of Sarvestan in the province of Fars

Plate 16 The palace of Sarvestan in the province of Fars

Plate 17 Remains of a Sasanian bridge in Fars

Plate 18 Bust of an armored king at Taq-ī Bustan

Plate 19 Sasanian stucco at the National Museum of Iran

Plate 20 Sasanian figurine at the National Museum of Iran

Plate 21 Sasanian fresco from Hajjiabad (after Azarnoush)

Plate 22 Sasanian silver dish: the king at the hunt. National Museum of Iran

Plate 23 Sasanian stucco underneath of the Masjid Jame in Isfahan

Plate 24 Bullae with the impression of the priest (magi) of the city of Shiraz

Plate 25 Part of Shabuhr I's Middle Persian inscription at the Ka'be-ye Zardosht

Plate 26 Victory scene of Shaubhr I with Valerian and Philip the Arab at Naqsh-i Rustam

Plate 27 Silver vase at the National Museum of Iran

Plate 28 Sasanian stucco at Tape Mill at Ray

Plate 29 General view of the Sasanian complex of Takht-e Suleyman

Plate 30 Wahram II and his court at Naqsh-i Rustam

Plate 31 A woman at the city of Bishabuhr

Plate 32 Harp players during the hunt of Khusro II at Taq-ī Bustan

passing away to the spiritual world. The general impression that we can get from the picture of the Middle Persian inscriptions is that while early on only the king and the high priests were able to leave a record, by the fifth century the *wuzurg-framadār* and the sixth and the seventh centuries we have the mushrooming of smaller private inscriptions. The question is why is it that the populace did not leave such inscriptions only in the sixth and seventh centuries and not earlier? Could this phenomenon be connected to the issue of literacy and the passing away of a society from orality to a literary tradition? These are difficult questions to answer but it does tell us that the populace besides the court and the Zoroastrian church were using inscriptions and writing for memorial inscriptions by the late Sasanian period.

Seals are also important because while they usually contain a slogan or the name of the owner, they can give us an idea of the relevant number of women to men who were involved in business transactions (since these seals were used as signature), the religion of the owner of the seal and the headdress and fashion of the time. The seals with longer inscriptions also give us much more information on the religious preoccupation of the owner of the seal or his/her office and rank. The coinage on the other hand represents the image which the imperial government wanted to portray to the populace and the legend on them is usually the name and a formulaic slogan inscribed, either "King of Kings of Iranians (and non-Iran), from the race of the deities," or the title of "Kay" and a few others. These two types of material culture which contain Middle Persian writing give us information on the public and governmental domain and as to how writing was utilized in those places. While we see diversity among the slogans and names on the seals, the coinage give us the formulaic and somewhat static legends, where they change slowly and represent the changing character of the imperial image.

MIDDLE PERSIAN TEXTS

In relation to non-monumental and non-religious Middle Persian literature we also should mention papyrus, and ostraca, as well as writing on silver vessels. The papyri are important because they give us information on the Sasanian military and in the way in which letters were composed. The papyri were mainly the product of late Sasanian period, specifically the product of the period in which King Khusro II had conquered Egypt and the military apparatus were in charge of that region. The papyri include the list of foodstuffs to be transported, which give us some insights into the diet of the Persian soldiers abroad. This consisted of bread (*nān*), meat (*gušt*), and wine (*may*), and sometimes fowl. Also the title of several officers and typical salutary formula are found with the word of praise (*namāz*).[17] These documents also tell us something about the nature of writing and literacy in the Sasanian world, where at least those serving as officers knew how to read and write. The formulaic manner in which the letters are composed also tell us that they were probably schooled in the art of writing. The letters also use the Zoroastrian calendar system and most names are Zoroastrian. However, we should remember that by the late Sasanian period, Christians and others could also have had Iranian names. We also find non-Iranian names such as Samuel (Shamuel) as merchants who appear to have cooperated with the Sasanian forces in Egypt. The recent Middle Persian documents found and housed at Berkeley informs us that within the Iranian Plateau parchments and leather were used for writing. These documents are also economic in nature and appear to be mainly related to central Iran.

The Middle Persian texts are the main corpus of our study.[18] They are mainly the product of Zoroastrian priestly writing and so they are colored by a religious outlook, where the idea of "profane" does not, if rarely, exist, although some have been seen as less theological than others.[19] We can firmly believe that there was a larger amount of Middle Persian literature in various genres, but because of the hardship on the Zoroastrian community throughout the ages, only those books that were of utmost importance for the religion and communal solidarity were copied by the priests and the rest were lost. Personal choice and taste were also to preserve some of the more rare texts that do survive. Even within the surviving texts, there are different genres which are dealt with separately in their appropriate headings below. They are, however, diverse enough to give us an understanding of Persian mentalities, views of the Persian view of life, religion, and the cosmos according to men. We will divide this large corpus into the following categories:

- Commentaries on the *Avesta* (*zand*).
- Philosophical and debate texts.
- Apocalyptic texts.
- Didactic texts (*andarz*).
- Geographical and epic texts.
- Legal texts (*dādīg*).
- Cultural texts.
- Dictionaries (*frahang*).

Commentary on the *Avesta*

By far the largest group of corpus are commentaries and elaborations on the Zoroastrian holy text which was put to final writing in the sixth century CE, probably during the reign of Khusro I and his high priest Weh-shabuhr. The *Avesta* is said to have had 21 chapters (*nask*) of which most are now lost, but it is the *Zand* or Middle Persian commentaries which gives us information on the lost portion of the *Avesta*. The major text which is important for the understanding of Zoroastrian world-view is the *Bundahišn* (The Book of Primal Creation). In the preface of the text the scribe mentions that he is redacting this Zoroastrian learning in a time of hardship, when the number of adherents are dwindling in the face of conversion to Islam. Hence what we can gain from this text is the sense of urgency by the priest to hand down what he thought was most important for the preservation of the good religion. The text indeed supplies a medley of topics, from cosmology and cosmogony, a good deal of information on deities and demons; an encyclopedia of botany, zoology, ethnography, geography, and history.[20] The other copious work is the *Dēnkard* (Acts of Religion) which is another encyclopedic work, at times written in a difficult and cryptic language and hence consequently the understanding of the text has remained less than satisfactory.[21] The *Dēnkard*[22] originally was composed in nine books, where books one and two have been lost. Book three[23] concerns itself with a host of issues, from the composition of human body to opinions in regard to church and state in the Sasanian period, where one finds the famous Persian dictum of the inseparability of church and state which still rings true in the religious circles: *hād xwadāyīh dēn ud dēn xwadāyīh . . . pad awēšān xwadāyīh abar dēn ud dēn abar xwadāyīh winnārdagīh* "Know that kingship is religion and religion is kingship . . . for them kingship is arranged based on religion and religion based on kingship."[24] Book four has been called the Book of Manners or Customs *ēwēn-nāmag* and is perhaps the most difficult book, since it deals with not only the history of the sacred texts, but also Greek and Indic science which will be dealt with below. Book five[25] begins with a series of questions put forth by a non-believer to a Zoroastrian sage, and it deals with different issues, especially the idea of *xwēdodāh* or consangnious marriages. Book six may be called a Book of Counsel *Andarz-nāmag*,[26] while Book seven particularly deals with the story of Zoroaster, from his birth to his death.[27] Book eight is important because it is a description of the contents of the 21 sections (*nasks*) of the *Avesta*. Each section (*nask*) is named and its content briefly mentioned, while Book nine concentrates on three sections or *nasks*.[28] There are other encyclopedic works such as the *Wīzīdagīhā ī Zādsparam* (The Selections of Zādsparam),[29] and *Mēnōg ī Xrad*,[30] however, they need not be repeated here. The other important genera is known as the *Pahlavī Rivāyats* which concern themselves with legal precepts but also with history, mythical creatures, and customs.[31] These legal texts give us some understanding of the Zoroastrian life in late antiquity, drawn from the *Avesta*, which can in turn be compared with Christian and Jewish legal texts such as that of the Syriac *Law Book of Yišoboxt* and the *Babylonian Talmud*.

Philosophical and Debate texts

Several texts in Middle Persian which mainly are the product of the eighth to ninth centuries CE and represent the end stage of the era of Middle Persian literature. The *Draxt ī Āsūrīg* (The Assyrian Tree) is, however, outstanding in its content and antiquity.[32] The vocabulary of the text suggests its Parthian antecedents and its content its Mesopotamian influence. This text presents a debate between a date tree and a goat, typical of the ancient Mesopotamian debate poetry used during banquets. The debate is about which of these two (the date or the goat) are more useful and their products are enumerated. Other texts are from the early Islamic period, such as the important *Škand ī Gūmānīg Wīzār* (Doubt Dispelling Explanation), recount the supremacy of Zoroastrian theology and the deficiency of such religions as those of the Fatalists (*Dahris*), Manichaeans, Christians, Jews, and Muslims.[33] The author systematically tackles the tenants of these religions and sometimes quotes verbatim from the holy texts of these religious traditions. The method of argumentation is also noteworthy which resembles the analytical method of debate known in Islamic Theology (*'Ilm al-Kalam*) and may have been influenced by that tradition of Islamic thought and literature, most probably as a result of contact with the Mu'tazila. *Gizistag Abāliš* (The Accursed Abāliš)[34] is a short text about the debate between Abāliš who appears to be a heretic or atheist (according to Shaki) and the Zoroastrian high priest and the leader of the Jewish, Christian and Muslim theologians at the court of the Caliph Ma'mun in the ninth century CE. The last text has survived in its Pazand form (Middle Persian written in the Avestan script). The text known as *Pus ī Dāneš Kāmag* (The Youth in Desire of Knowledge) is written in the same vain as the *Škand ī Gumānīg Wīzār* but there is little reference to the Islamic period and is concerned with

Zoroastrian matters such as the reason for the wearing of the sacred belt, the *kustīg*.

Apocalyptic and Visionary texts

This genre of Middle Persian literature is the most imaginative and interesting of the Middle Persian corpus. These texts predict the way in which the world will come to an end and the fate of the people and that of *Iranshahr*, the empire of the Sasanians. *Ardā Wirāz Nāmag* (The Book of Righteous Wirāz) is about the journey of a righteous man, Wirāz, to heaven and hell which may be compared with Dante's famous work, the *Divina Commedia*. Not only the journey itself is interesting but also the preparation for the journey into paradise and hell by Wirāz. He is properly cleansed and laid on a bed when he is given a concoction of hemp called *mang ī wištāsp* "hemp of Wištāsp" which enables him to make the journey.[35] This practice of taking hallucinogens to travel to the netherworld betrays the ancient Shamanistic tradition in the Iranian world which goes back to the Indo-Iranian period. By taking on these hallucinogenic drinks, be it the sacred Haoma/Soma, *mang* or *bang*, the Indo-Iranian priests were able to have visions and compose hymns to various deities. We see that this tradition was alive and well in the Sasanian period and in several apocalyptic texts the various means of achieving this travel is mentioned. In the apocalyptic text of *Zand ī Wahman Yasn* (The Commentary of the Wahman Yasn) Zoroaster is given the *xrad ī harwisp āgāhīh* (Wisdom of complete knowledge) by the means of Ohrmazd pouring it in the form of water onto his hand to drink which induces seven days and nights of dreaming, as in the cases of Wirāz. Then Zoroaster is able to see the future in a mysterious form (a tree with seven trunks) which is explained to him to be seven eras (in another part there are four eras which sound very much like Hesiod's division in his *Theogony*). These eras begin from the beginning of Zoroastrianism to the time of Turkic conquest of Persia.

These texts predict the fate of the Zoroastrians which will eventually face hardships and will only achieve supremacy at the end of the world when the sinners will be punished and those Zoroastrians who have endured hardship will go to heaven, the heaven about which Wiraz had seen and told the believers. There are few people who are given the power to look into the future through the means of hallucinogens, such as Zoroaster, King Wištāsp, his minister Jamasp, and Wiraz. Also one must mention Kerdir whose inscription suggests his campaign be included in the host of righteous personages who were able to make the journey.[36]

The *Jāmāsp Nāmag* is another one of these texts which was especially popular among the Pārsīs in the past century.[37] Again, Jamasp is endowed with a vision of what is to come along with all of its calamities. This text along with that of the *Zand ī Wahman Yasn* portrays a great deal of natural and political disasters until the saviors appear, and men and women arise from the dead and are judged. Finally, evil is destroyed and molten metal will extrapiate all that is evil and send it into the womb of the earth. Those who have been good walk in this molten metal as if walking through warm milk. Then the earth becomes flat, and all returns to how it was in the beginning.

Didactic Texts

Andarz texts or wisdom literature are abundant and are usually attributed to wise sages or people of authority according to the Zoroastrian religion. There are, however, also anonymous *andarz* texts which are found in the sixth book of the *Dēnkard*.[38] These texts give didactic ordinances about religion, social order, good and bad conduct, and proper rules. Priests, kings, important people and wise men all are given credit for these *andarz* (wise sayings). The importance of this genre of Middle Persian literature is that it was liberally used and translated into mainly Arabic and Persian. Thus a major corpus of Arabic *andarz* texts are translations of these works from the Sasanian period. Ibn Miskawayh in his work, which from its title suggest its Middle Persian origin, the *Jāwīdān xrad* (the Eternity of Wisdom), is the best example.[39] The author mentions the genealogy of the text and its translation to another famous Muslim author Jahiz who had found the original text in Middle Persian in the province of Persis/Fars with the Zoroastrian priests. Other Arabic texts also relate the *andarz* of Sasanian kings such as those of Ardashir I, Kawad, Khusro I, and Khusro II. These texts discuss the effective means of ruling over the subjects and how to keep the empire in order. It is for this very reason that this genre found favor with the Caliphs at Baghdad in the Islamic period, who drew from the example of the ancients to keep their Caliphate in order and prosperous. In this manner the *andarz* genre are important and have lasted in the Persian and Arab and Turkish world as a major body of literature of the Medieval Islamic world.

Geographical and Epic texts

There is little material for this genre in terms of complete texts describing the geography of a region. Still, chapters in the *Bundahišn* provide a detailed description of the Persian universe. These include climes of earth, the people, lands, mountains, rivers of Asia and eastern Mediterranean. This would partly be in the tradition of the *Avesta* where a chapter in the *Wīdēwdād* gives us information on the different regions and people who inhabited them. After all we must remember these Middle Persian texts were aimed as commentaries on the *Avesta*, but they took into account the realities of the late antiquity. Still the *Bundahišn* takes notice of the geo-political realities of the Sasanian period and for this reason it is worthy of study.

A short text known as *Abādīh ud Sāhagīhā ī Sīstān* is concerned with the Province of Sistan which had special importance for Zoroastrianism in the Sasanian period and at this time it was thought to be the backdrop of Zoroaster activity and the homeland of the Kayanid king, Wishtasp.[40] The text may be seen as a progenitor of the later Islamic geographical texts and local histories such as *Tārīx-e Sīstān* (History of Sīstān) which is related to this text, and other local histories and geographical texts. There is one text known as the *Šahrestānīhā ī Ērānšahr* (The Provincial Capitals of Iranshahr) which discusses the different capital cities in the different regions. All the cities are mentioned as part of the Sasanian empire which include Mecca, Medina, and parts of Africa. The author mentions the builder and rebuilder of a specific city and the important events which took place there. The text is not an exact geographical-administrative history but contains an imperial outlook which is enforced by Zoroastrian dogma.[41]

There are specifically two texts which may be considered as epic texts. The older one is a Parthian epic entitled the *Ayādgār ī Zarērān* (Memoir of Zarēr)[42] which focuses on the court of King Wištāsp, the patron of Zoroaster and the bloody war with their enemies, the Turanians. The epic is certainly tragic and victory will come to the Zoroastrians only after many heroes and princes have fallen. The epic is more tragic because the minister of Wištāsp, Jāmāsp who is endowed with the knowledge of the future, again in the Indo-Iranian Shamanistic style, tells the king what will happen. The text is set in a poetic style, indicating that it would have been performed and, in a similar way that *Bacche* was performed at the Parthian court, this epic was made into a play. The story survived the Sasanian victory and was written in Middle Persian and then translated into Persian which was incorporated into the Persian epic, the *Šāhānme-ye Ferdowsī*.

The other text which is pseudo-historical is about the career of the founder of the Sasanian dynasty, Ardashir I Pabagan. The *Kārnāmag ī Ardaxšīr ī Pābagān* (The Book of the Deeds of Ardaxšīr, the Son of Pābag) is a sixth century epic which describes Ardaxšīr's origins, as a descendant of King Dara, i.e., Achaemenid Darius. His father's noble origin is found out by Pabag and so Ardaxšīr's turbulent adventures as a man who is good at all that he does, from polo to board games to the challenging of the last Parthian king, Ardawan (Artabanus) is chronicled.[43] This story has also found its way into the Persian epic and so we may assume most of what survives about the ancients in Persian epical form were translations of the Middle Persian version.

Legal texts

The *Wīdēwdād* part of the *Avesta* is mainly concerned with the laws of purity and pollution, and the Middle Persian translation of this text also adds commentaries as glosses in the text. There is an even more copious *Zand* of the *Wīdēwdād* which has not been translated. If we are to accept the contents of *Dēnkard* (Book eight) as having been the topics of the lost portions of the *Avesta*, we realize that much of this text was concerned legal matters as well. The Middle Persian texts also have a prodigious output of legal commentaries. The most important legal text of the Sasanian period is the *Madīyān ī Hazār Dādestān* (The Exposition of One Thousand Judgments)[44] written during the late Sasanian period which deals with legal cases brought to the court. The *Šāyest nē Šāyest* (*Licit and Illicit*)[45] is another important text dealing with judgments of the Zoroastrian judges and theologians who sometimes disagree with one another over legal injunction. Other legal texts are mainly the product of the early Islamic period where the community was shrinking in numbers and there were especial needs to inform and protect the now subaltern community. They still give us insights to the legal mentality of the Zoroastrian priests and the concern with purity and pollution, the rights of men, women and children.

Cultural texts

The texts which tell us much about the cultural life and social norms of the Sasanian period are mainly short works. They include a variety of subjects such as the different types of food, games, ideas of beauty, giving speeches, table manners, and how to write properly. The most interesting is the text of *Xusrō ud Rēdag* (King Khusro and the Page), in which the many courtly ideals of the "good living" such as best meats, fowl, deserts, wines are mentioned. The page recounts his training not only as a chef, but also as a calligrapher, his athletic prowess, as a master polo player and horseman, his religious upbringing, and his morality, which suggests an ideal Zoroastrian man in late antiquity.

The text also mentions Indian and other board games such as chess which is the subject of another small work in Middle Persian known as *Wizārišn Čatrang ud Nēw-ardaxšīr* (Explanation of the Game of Chess and Backgammon). Here the reason for the invention of these games and rules are given which are put in a Zoroastrian perspective and cosmological setting.[46] *Sūr ī Suxwan* (Banquet Speech) is another text which sets out to describe the old Near Eastern banquet etiquette and the list of people who sit before the royal table, from the King of Kings (*šāhān šāh*), to the Grand Wazīr (*wuzurg-framadār*), and lower ranks.[47] There is also a text on how to write properly *Abar Ēwēnag ī Nāmag Nibēsišnīh* (On the Manner of Book/Letter Writing). These remains suggest the sophistication of the Persian culture and society, where every aspect of life was discussed and standards were established.

Farhang or Dictionaries

There are two dictionaries that have survived which have different functions. The *Farhang ī Pahlawīg* is mainly concerned with the understanding of the difficult words which were written with the Aramaic ideogram. The authors took pains to show the Middle Persian word in question in its usual ideographic and its simple representation. For example the word for "night" was written with the Aramaic ideogram *LYLYA* which was read as Middle Persian *šab*. Now to demonstrate that this word stood for night, the author wrote the word without the ideogram as *šb* next to the ideogram. The glossary also demonstrates the Ancient Near Eastern tradition in the way the subject headings are discussed, based on cosmology, waters, fruits, metals, etc. A more recent recession of this glossary exists which approaches the words alphabetically.[48] The other major dictionary or glossary is the *Farhang ī Ōīm-ēwag* which is a dictionary of Avestan words. In the preface the author states that the work is intended to understand the *Zand* (Middle Persian translation of the *Avesta*).[49]

CHRISTIAN AND MANICHAEAN LITERATURE IN MIDDLE PERSIAN

A relatively large number of Christians appear to have lived in Persia by the late Sasanian period which was the result of first the influx of Christian captives and their settlement into the empire, along with later conversions. Second, Mesopotamia had a large number of Christians, and also then the Persian (Syriac Persian) Christian community who were able to attract converts from the royal family, became subjects of martyrologies and hagiographies of late antiquity.[50] The Christians were also active in translating the Christian texts, especially the *New Testement*, into Middle Persian where such specimens exist. The *Zabūr* or Psalms are translations of these Biblical texts into Middle Persian.[51] These texts are the non-Zoroastrian Middle Persian texts that survive, with the exception of a few Christian funerary monuments. They were probably done for and by the Nestorian community, using the Syraic translations of the Bible. There is also evidence of translation of the *Book of Enoch* and other Christian apocryphal works, as well as other hymns which suggest the importance and number of the Christian community in Persia.

The last group of texts in the Middle Persian language are the product of the Manichaean religious life who were an important community in the Near East and the eastern Mediterranean region in the late antiquity. A large corpus survives, but most of the texts are fragmentary in nature and few are complete. These texts are usually called Manichaean Middle Persian texts as much for their language. They are quite varied in topic and parallel the Zoroastrian texts in content matter. The most important Manichaean Middle Persian text is the *Šābuhragān* which was written by Mani for his patron Shabuhr I. This text summarizes the teachings of Mani in the language that was the court language of the Sasanian empire, although the text is difficult, esoteric and apocalyptic.[52] There are other fragments and texts in Middle Persian which may be called Manichaean hagiography and martyrology. There are also sermons and addresses by Manichaean leaders (the Elect) after Mani's death to the adherents.

PARTHIAN, SOGDIAN, KHOTANESE, AND BACTRIAN LANGUAGE AND LITERATURE

From the beginning of the Sasanian period, Parthian was one of the major languages that was used for imperial inscriptions, in addition to that of Middle Persian and Greek. We could guess that indeed Parthian remained spoken and written in the east, the homeland of the Parthains. This is evident by the new discoveries of a number of graffiti found at Lāx-Mazār close to the City of Birjand which have remained unpublished in a Western language.[53] Parthian literature, be it oral or written, made an impact on the Middle Persian literature in the form of two important texts mentioned, the *Ayādgār ī Zarērān* and *Draxt ī Āsūrīg*, where their vocabulary betray their Parthian origin. Still other Persian poetic texts such as the famous, *Vīs u Rāmīn*, also demonstrate its Parthian origin, which also survives in the Georgian version as well.[54] But the most prodigious type of Parthian literature during the Sasanian period was written by the Manicheaens from the third century onwards. Most of these texts are fragmentary and were found in this century which took the attention of the great Iranist W.B. Henning,[55] along with his outstanding pupil, Mary Boyce.[56] W. Sundermann has been the leader in the past decades in dealing with Manichaean material.[57]

As for Sogdian, whose homeland is further east of Parthain, again the Manichaean material gives us the greater amount of evidence, but Buddhist and Christian material also exists. These texts were written in three different scripts which consisted of the "Samarqand type" and was in use in the Sasanian period. The second script which Sogdian was written with was the Palmyrene script which the Manichaeans adopted, and we find stories such of as the "Pearlborer," and "The Three Fishes," having had their origins in India, from Sanskrit literature.[58] The third is the Estrangelo script used for the Christian texts. The majority of the Sogdian Christian texts are translations from Syriac originals and are parts of the new Testament (Matthew, Luke, John, I. Corinthians and Galatians), as well as later Sogdian material which was written from the second to the fifth centuries CE.[59] The Buddhist texts are numerous, of which the most famous is the *Sūtra of the Cause and Effects of Action* (*'krtyh 'n 'nt ptwry pwstk*).[60] What is most interesting in Sogdian is a fragment of the Rustam epic which differs from what has remained in the Middle Persian and Persian tales of this hero in the *Šāhnāme*.[61]

Khotanese which was the language of the Saka, the homeland of Rustam, unfortunately gives little information on the Sasanian empire. The script is a daunting script to learn and is akin to *devānagrī*. The longest work is the *Book of Zambasta*[62] and this work along with most others are Buddhist, some being translations of Buddhist Sanskrit texts.[63] There is also a medical text and other translation of Sanskrit texts which are really concerned with the Indic world. While less was known about Bactrian, mainly on legends on coins, and some inscriptions,[64] we are fortunate that recently Nicholas Sims-Williams has published a series on leather documents written in Bactrian, mainly dating from the Sasanian and the early Islamic period.[65] The script used for Bactrian is the Greek alphabet, probably due to the fact that this was the location where Greeks came and settled after Alexander the Great's conquest. There were other languages of which we have still less information, such as Kharazmian whose language is mainly ascertained from Arabic and some Persian texts written in the Islamic period in that region.[66]

FOREIGN INFLUENCES

The Middle Persian texts, however religious in nature, were not immune to outside influence. In the fourth book of the *Dēnkard* (Acts of Religion), we find the influence of Greek, specifically Aristotelian ideas,[67] where the author(s) tell us that they studied Greek and Indic texts on medicine, geography and other sciences. The narrative of the texts are diverse and demonstrate this foreign influence. In the *Gizistag Abālīš* (The Accursed Abālīš) we find a kind of analogical argumentation which does not appear to be Zoroastrian in origin. Even more obvious is the *Škand ī Gūmānīg Wīzār* (Doubt Dispelling Explanation), where the mode of argumentation is analytical, resembling those who used the method of *'Ilm al-kalam* in the early Islamic period.[68] Thus not only the content, but also the style of these texts were subject to foreign influence. Still, overwhelmingly, the subject matter is religious and the texts provide commentaries and explanation of the Zoroastrian sacred text, the *Avesta*. The *Pazand* texts, are Middle Persian texts written in the Avestan script which made it much easier to read. Some of the *Pazand* texts are simply the rendering of the Middle Persian texts in the Avestan script, but there are many more that are original and provide important information on the folk belief/popular religion of the Zoroastrians and popular belief in the Middle Ages. Unfortunately, they have been neglected by the philologists and have been seen as of little use. Since most are composed after the Arab Muslim conquest, they are not directly related to our topic.

The intellectual life in the Sasanian period has received much less attention than other fields and this is because what has remained of the Middle Persian texts are religious texts and difficult to understand. Still, from the surviving material we know that the Sasanian empire was a meeting ground of Hellenic, Mesopotamian, and Indian scientific and philosophical ideas. While on the surface it appears that the Zoroastrian priests were anti-Hellenic, this anti-Hellenism was not the dictum in regard to learning. The *Dēnkard* is an important text which supports this evidence. In the fourth book of *Dēnkard* in regard to the *Avesta*, we read that during the reign of Shabuhr I texts on medicine, astronomy, movement, logic and other crafts and skills which existed in India and Rome and other lands were gathered and a copy of them were made.[69] As to the nature of these texts, we do have some ideas. For example in another part of Book four of *Dēnkard* the name of the texts are given, these being the Indian *Kāla Kośa* (Treasury of Astronomy), and (Middle Persian) *Magistīg* of Ptolemy.[70] This suggests that the *Avesta* incorporated foreign learning and was not only a religious text. Second, the Persians were familiar with Indian and Greek writings from the third century CE onwards. This is important because while this period has been seen as a time of anti-Hellenism and phobia against foreign influences, we can see that learning and science was not subject to this antagonism.

There is other evidence for the dissemination of Greek knowledge in the Sasanian empire, specifically through Greek and the Syrian Christians whose presence in the city of *Weh-andīōg-šābuhr* (Gundēšābuhr) is well known. This city, which was built during the reign of Šābuhr I, was composed of the Syriac speaking Christians of the city of Antioch who established the famous medical center there. It was in this place that Greek medical books were translated into Syriac in the sixth century CE by Sargis, while Indian medical treatise also reached this location.[71] Thus, the Sasanians made possible the meeting of Greek and Indian sciences and their absorbtion in Persia. Also Aristotelian texts and other Greek texts dealing with (Middle Persian) *bawišn ud vināhišn* "on coming to be and passing away," (Middle Persian) *Jatag-wihīrīh* "change of form," (Middle Persian) *nibēg ī zamīg paymānīh* "measurement of the earth," i.e., geometry were written.[72] Books on logic were written by Paul the Persian, and Priscianus Lydus, who wrote a book on Aristotelian physics, theory of the soul, meteorology, and biology when they were expelled by Justinian in the sixth century CE and found their way to the Persian court.[73] After Šābuhr I's redaction of the *Avesta* and the entering of foreign teachings, the time of Xusrō I may be seen as the second major period of influence. Perhaps this second period of intense contact was felt more and had a stronger impact on Mazdean learning, since it coincided with the writing of the Middle Persian text of which we have access to the surviving portions.

Persian knowledge of Indian learning is known, mainly in the field of philosophy, and astronomy. Books on logic called (Middle Persian) *tark* (Sanskrit) *tarka* were translated from Sanskrit into Middle Persian.[74] Indian influence on astronomy (Middle Persian) *āwyākrn* (Sanskrit) *vyākarana* is well known. One can state that Persia was a conduit for the transmission of knowledge between the Hellenic and Indic world in late antiquity and consequently it became a meeting ground of old and new ideas. All of this would be inherited by the Muslim civilization which transmitted these ideas to the West when it had forgotten its own philosophical and scientific tradition.

The elements which made the deepest influence from India on Persia were, however literature and the arts. As part of education (Middle Persia) *frahang* we know that certain games such as chess (Middle Persian) *Čatrang* (Sanskrit) *caturanga*, which was based on the composition of the Indian army consisting of four divisions, were played in the Sasanian period and came to Persia.[75] Other Indian board games such as (Middle Persian) *haštpāy* (Sanskrit) *aṣṭāpada*, as well as backgammon which was Persianized (Middle Persian) *nēw-ardaxšīr* were known to have come to Persia during the reign of Khusro I as part of the great number of works which were transmitted in the sixth century.[76] These included such texts as the *pañcatantra* which according to tradition was translated into Middle Persian by the famous physician named Borzoye.[77] While the Middle Persian version is now lost, the Syriac translation made from the Middle Persian in 570 CE exists under the name *Kalilag ud Damnag*, this being the name of the two main player "jackals," in the Sanskrit text, *Karataka u Damanaka.* This text was also translated from Middle Persian into Arabic by Abdullah ibn al-Muqaffa in the eighth century CE, also known in Persian as the *Dāstānhā-ye Bīdpāy* (The Fables of Pilpay). This is the version which was first translated from Sanskrit into Middle Persian and then to Arabic and then into Persian.[78] These stories were taken from another Indian text called the *Hitopadesa* "Book of Good Counsel." This book was part of the Indian genre known as *nīti-śāstra* "mirror for Princes," which also existed in Persia, and in Middle Persian was known as *ēwēn-nāmag* "book of manners."

As mentioned earlier, astrology[79] played a prominent part in the society where its importance can be seen from the number of terms used for those professions such as *star-gōwišnīh* "star-telling," *axtar-āmar* "zodiac-teller," *stār-hangār* "star-reckoner," and *hangām-šnāsag* "time-knower." The Sasanian king we are told consulted fortune tellers or astrologers as to find out about the future and the courses of action which should be taken. The best example is found in the Ardashir

Romance, *Kārnāmag ī Ardaxšīr ī Pābagān*, where Pābag has a series of dreams about the progenitor of the house, i.e., Sāsān. One night Pabag had a dream that the sun shone from the head of Sāsān, the second night he saw Sāsān sitting on a white elephant and everyone in the empire was paying homage to him, and a third night he dreamt that the three sacred Zoroastrian fires were shining on Sāsān's house. Pabag had to ask the "dream interpreters" *xwamn-wizārān* to tell him the meaning of his dreams.[80]

As for the nobility we know that some of the basic learnings were acquired in *frahangestān* "House of Culture" which included memorizing the sacred utterances, scribship and calligraphy, horsemanship, jousting, polo, playing musical instruments, singing, poetry, dancing, astrology and being master of playing board games.[81] Naturally the warriors were trained in the art of combat as well as other sports, which not only including shooting, but also horse racing and jousting. In fact it is in Persia that we find some of the earliest reliefs of jousting scenes and the art of one-to-one combat. These are all familiar to the Medieval European world, where their Persian equivalent, i.e., the knights (Middle Persian) *āzādān* did the same, except much earlier.

TRANSLATION TECHNIQUES

In the Middle Persian texts we come across word compounds which appear to define technical religious and scientific terminology and which were foreign to Persian. These terms are also another evidence for the translation of foreign works in Middle Persian. Some Syriac and Greek words which were translated in Middle Persian are as follows: *dašnēzādagān* for Syriac *banyā yāminā* "righteous ones," *gēhān ī kōdak* for Greek *mikros kosmos* "microcosom;" *xrad-dōšagīh* for Greek *philosophia* "Philosophy," and *zamīg-paymānīh* for *geōmetria* "geometry."[82] This among other evidence suggests a vibrant translation campaign by the Sasanian scholars to understand the world and their neighbors which is contrary to the common view of the Sasanian world which is that it was static and reactionary to non-Zoroastrian ideas.

In conclusion one can observe that what remains of Middle Persian texts and Sasanian literature is only a fraction of what existed. The reason for this loss is mainly due to the fact that it was translated into Arabic, especially the wisdom literature, above all to instruct the Caliph on how to rule and how to deal with his subjects. What remained of Middle Persian texts was because of the diligence of a number of priests who wanted to keep the tradition alive and give answers to their dwindling community in the face of conversion and loss of status and wealth in the new Islamic empire which stretched from China to Spain. Thus, what was important for religion was copied by the priests from generation to generation, and the burden of time destroyed other parts of it, along with fires and bigoted amirs who had forgotten that the Zoroastrians were also people of the book.

Chapter 5

The Economy and Administration of *Iranshahr*

THE ADMINISTRATION AND ADMINISTRATORS OF THE EMPIRE

The organization of the provinces of the Sasanian Empire is not completely clear, since many of the sources contradict each other. This is the product of two phenomena. The first has to do with the layers of reforms, meaning that the early Sasanian system was complemented by the reforms of Kavad, and then of Khusro I in the sixth century CE. The second problem has to do with the very nature of the sources which give ample description of the Sasanian administration. Since most of the information comes from the Islamic period, one should be hesitant and cautious in using this information, because the description seems to be closer to the Abbasid administrative division of the eastern caliphate than to the late Sasanian period.[1]

For the Middle Persian sources, the most important text is *The provincial capitals of Iran* (*Shahrestānīhā ī Ērānshahr*) redacted at the time of the caliphate of al-Manṣur (754–775 CE.), but may be based on an authentic Sasanian source.[2] Many of the administrative offices and officers are also mentioned in the *The Book of a Thousand Judgments* (*Madīyān ī Hazār Dādestān*) which was redacted in the reign of Khusro II (590–628 CE.). More importantly, there are administrative seals and coins which represent primary sources. They are invaluable in providing the basis for the reconstruction of the administrative system and thanks to the important works of R. Gyselen, they have cleared up much of the situation in late Sasanian period.[3] The literary sources should be used whenever possible to corroborate or question the epigraphic evidence. However, the seal corpus is incomplete, and only with the future discovery of more seals will we have a better grasp of the situation in the sixth and seventh centuries CE.

The administrative and military division of the empire has steadily become understandable. The quadripartition of the late Sasanian empire, that is, its division into four regions, is accepted by all. The textual sources give ample evidence in regard to the quadripartition. This is not only stated in the Middle Persian sources, but also in Armenian sources, such as Moses Xorenats'i.[4] Within this scheme of quadripartition, there are still contradictions. For example, Xorenats'i places Fars and Sistan in the *k'usti nemrog*, while Tha'alibī places Sistan in the quarter of the East (*kust ī Xorāsān)*, and Fars in the (*kust ī nēmrōz*).[5] The reason for the differences may lie in the nature and times of the various reforms and divisions. There seems to be no hint of a quadripartition with regard to the secular administration since there are no administrative seals to support this notion. Militarily and religiously, there was a quadripartition, where a General (*spāhbed)* was in charge of each *kust* "quarter."[6] Religiously, the *kust* was under the control of a *rad* "spiritual master."[7] Before the reforms of Kavad and Khusro I in the late fifth and sixth centuries CE, the General of the Iranians (*Ērān-spāhbed)* controlled the military of the whole empire, but later his power was to be broken up among four *spāhbeds*.

Some numismatic evidence also points to the quadripartition of the empire under Kavad I. The reverse side of Sasanian coins usually notes the date when the coin was struck and the place or mint signature. There are many Sasanian and Arab-Sasanian mint signatures which have not been attributed for certain. Recently, Gurnet[8] has proposed to read the Sasanian mint signature DYNAW which had been attributed to the city of Denavar, as DYW-AO, along with three other signatures that have been found, DYW-AT, DYW-AS, and DWY-KR. In regard to DYW-AO, due to the confusing nature of the Middle Persian alphabet, a letter at times could be read several ways. The first three letters, DYW have been suggested to be the abbreviation for *divan* (*dēwān)*, thus Perso-Arabic *divan*, meaning "government office," and the next two letters acting as suffixes for the region. Gurnet suggests AO for the south west, AT standing for the quarter of north west, perhaps standing for Adurbadagan; AS for the Capital, perhaps for Asurestan; and KR for the south east, standing for Kerman.[9] By identifying AO with the south west the scheme of the quadripartition becomes questionable, but the real question is what does AO stand for. Gurnet does not give a definitive answer to this anomaly, and indeed one can read the suffix as AN, thus DYWAN, but another suggestion may be more suitable. In Middle Persian, initial *aleph* can also be read as *ḥet* and O is written with *waw*, thus it can also be read as *w*. Here one can suggest the reading XW for Khurasan, thus DYWXW "Divan of Khurasan," the north east.

These coins were minted during the reign of Kavad I, which exactly corresponds with the beginning of the administrative reforms.[10] Thus the literary sources can be complemented by the coins, both pointing to the fact that there was indeed a civilian and military quadripartition. The quadripartition was perhaps a reaction to the military setbacks experienced by Kavad I. The incursions from the east by the Hephthalites, as well as the Byzantine frontier wars in the west, and the Arab raids into the empire from the south made it crucial that the empire be able to deal with problems on several fronts. This may have been the cause behind the division of the military power into the hands of four generals, who would thus be able to deal with the invasions and wars. Here we have a division of four quarters, much like the divisions in late Eastern Roman empire, where there was a *Praefectura praetorio per Orientem* "prefecture of the East," *Praefectura praetorio per Illyricum* "prefecture of Greece and the Balkans," *Praefectura praetorio Illyrici, Italiae et Africae* "prefecture of Italy and Latin Africa," and *Praefectura praetorio Galliarum* "prefecture of Roman Britain and the Iberian Peninsula,"[11] which is interesting. Thus we have the old Sasanian divisions of the third and fourth centuries, followed by the quadripartition and later divisions by Khusro I and Khusro II in the sixth and seventh centuries.

Provinces in the third century inscriptions appear as *Shahr* (Middle Persian *štry*), while the districts were also known as *shahr* and a capital city was known as *shahrestan*. The *shahr* was administered by the *shahrdar*, who was probably a local king in the third century. They were rulers of these provinces who were appointed by the King of Kings.[12] The districts or *shahrs* were under the command of a *shahrab* and a *mowbed*. The *mowbed* dealt with property rights and other legal affairs which is attested by the function of the *mowbed* of Ardashir-xwarrah, one of the districts of Fars.[13] There was also an "accountant" (*āmārgar*) who dealt with the financial aspects of one or several districts.

Now we will turn to the administrative division of the districts. The *shahr* or district was further divided into *rustag*s, which perhaps consisted of several villages, and the smallest unit was the *deh* or village, which was headed by a *dehgan*.[14] This division is apparent from a late Middle Persian inscription, where a certain Khordad, son of Hormuzd-Afarid who was a Christian, recalls his home in this order: 1) *mān ī* Ērān-shahr, 2) *rusta* čālakān, 3) *deh* Khisht: "from the dwelling of *Iranshahr*, from the *rusta* of Chalagan, from the *deh* of Khisht.[15] In *Sirat Anushirvan* preserved in Ibn Miskawayh's *Tajarib al-Umam*, the same order is preserved, where Khusro I enumerates the administrative units in the following order: 1) *bilad* "region/country," 2) *kura*, 3) *rustaq*, and 4) *qarya* which is equivalent to *deh*.[16]

In the early Islamic period some of these terms seem to have been confused and used interchangeably. For example the *rusta*, Arabic *rustaq*, was at times thought to be equivalent to a *tasug*, Arabic *Ṭassuj* or a *naḥiya*.[17] There are, however, several accounts that corroborate the survival of the same terms in the above manner in the Sasanian period as well as the early Islamic period. Bal'ami, retrojecting to the beginning of the Sasanian dynasty, states that Ardaxšīr came from the *shahr* of Istakhr, from the land (*bilad*) of Fars. He mentions that Istakhr had a *rusta*, and there was a *deh*. Thus we have the exact division of the Sasanian epigraphic information, 1) *shahr*, 2) *rusta*, 3) *deh*.[18] This may represent the correct division which stayed on in the early Islamic period as well.[19] This is corroborated by other sources, such as *Tarikh Qom* which records that the city of Qom was made of seven *deh*s which were joined together.[20]

Other divisions included the royal lands, the *ostan* which was headed by the *ostandar*. This is in correspondence with Armenia, where the *ostan* was the royal land and in the Marzpanate period (428–652 CE.); some territories were divided into *ostan*, and the *ostan* into *gawars*.[21] The *shahr* and *deh* contained temples which were under the control of the *Mogwed*.[22] Another division was the *tasug* over which we know that a "judge" (*dādwar*) had authority by the seventh century,[23] and that the *mowbed* of the district (*shahr*) had power over the *dādwar* who had power over the *tasug*.[24] *Tasug*, a loan word into Arabic, *tassoj*, has been suggested to be a fourth of a *rustag*. Its meaning is relatively clear, from Middle Persian *tasum* "fourth." The question is that this *tasug* was the fourth of what part of a territory/unit of division? Morony has suggested that the *shahr* or districts were divided into sub-districts around small towns or villages, and that this was called a *tasug*, Arabic *ṭassoj*.[25] One has to ask if there was a difference between these toponyms or not. According to the *Madīyān ī Hazār Dādestān* (MHD100, 5–7), while the *shahr* was under the jurisdiction of a *mowbed*, the *tasug* was under the jurisdiction of a *dādwar*.

IMPORTANT OFFICIALS/ADMINISTRATORS AND THEIR FUNCTIONS

There are several seals which relate several offices/officials for the empire. They are as follows:

- *shahrāb*
- *mow*
- *mowbed*
- *driyōšān jādaggōw ud dādwar*
- *handarzbed*
- *dādwar*
- *āmārgar*
- *dibīr* and *kārframān.*

Shahrab: "provincial governor"

The provincial governors were the ones who administered the great provinces of the kingdom. In the early Persian history (Achaemenid period), the *shahrab* was the head of the domain or guardian of the kingdom. In the Parthian period, the office is also attested in an inscription found at Susa and it seems that the title had already declined since the Acheamenid period. Henning is correct in stating that "the area he (the satrap) now governed was small, scarcely more than a town with its surroundings."[26] In the third century inscriptions, the decline of this office from the Achaemenid period is evident, where in the inscription of Shabuhr I at Ka'ba-i Zardosht a list of *shahrabs* is given, for example that of Hamadan, Niriz, and Weh-Andew-Shabuhr. The *shahrab* is listed in the seventh position, after the "commander" (*framādār*) and before the *dizbed* "garrison commander."[27] In the Paikuli inscriptions, the *shahrab* is mentioned in the eleventh rank after the "lord of the house" (*kadag-xwadāy*)[28] and before (*āmārgar*) "accountant."[29] In the fourth century inscription of Shabuhr II (311 CE) in the list of the retinue of the king of Sistan, the *shahrab* is placed after the *mow* "priest," and before the (*dibīr*) "scribe."[30] This inscription shows the important position of the office within the province, where it is only subordinate to the MLK' "king," *handarzbed* "councilor," and *mow*, and above the (*dibīr*) "scribe," (*āzādān*) "free men," (*frēstag*) "messenger," and (*sardār*) "chief."[31] This may show the resurgence of the office and its importance in the later Sasanian period. The seal of the *shahrab* portrays the person in jeweled cap with pearls, which shows the importance of the office.[32]

Mow: "priest"

The *mow* functioned within the religious and state apparatus. The sheer number of seals with this title attests to the importance of this office for the bureaucracy of the state as well as the temple economy and the size of the religious body in Sasanian Persia. We do have evidence of a *mow* serving a province as early as the fourth century, where one accompanied the king of Sistan.[33] The *mow* was the lowest rank of "priesthood," who functioned in various capacities in the districts, cities, villages, and temples. He seems to have been in charge of controlling economic transactions. On a large jar with a cursive inscription (late Sasanian) a *mow* is said to have been imprisoned because of lying,[34] and committing (*wināh*) "sin," which was a legal term adopted from religious terminology,[35] perhaps lying in regards to the amount or worth of the commodity stored in the jar.

Mowbed: "chief priest"

The title is apparent in the third century, where Kerdir is called an *Ohrmazd mowbed* "the mowbed of Ohrmazd," under Hormizd I. He later achieved the added title of (*Kerdir ī boxt-ruwān-wahrām ī ohrmazd mowbed*) "Kerdir, mowbed of the blessed Wahram and Ohrmazd."[36] The assumption of many of the titles which appear later for Kerdir at one time, show the beginning of these titles under his control. They include (*hamshahr mowbed ud dādwar*), "the Chief priest and Judge of all the empire," and (*ēwēnbed*) "master of ceremony."[37] By the fourth century, the office of *mowbed* had become important and was placed in the list of offices below (*hazārbed*) "chilarch," and above (*shahr-āmār-dibīr*) "secretary of Finances." This growth in power perhaps had to do with the growing strength of the Mazdean priestly organization and its hierarchy. It seems that the *mow* and *mowbed* were the ones who were involved in the administrative aspects of the empire and the province in large numbers. There are seals of the *mowbed* for subdistricts, fire temples, and cities, which show the degree of their involvement and status.

It appears that by the late Sasanian period the *mowbed* dealt with documents and they were signed by him, which was only part of his duty. There was "The Book Regarding the Duties of the Mowbeds" (*xwēš-nāmag ī mawbedān nibišt*) which spelled out their duties and function.[38] The *mowbeds* functioned in several main capacities. The *mowbed* along with the *shahrab* administered a *shahr* or district. Since we do possess a seals for the *mowbed* of cities,[39] we can assume that all districts had a *mowbed* in charge. While the seal for the *mowbedan mowbed* is absent, from the mention of this title in many textual sources we may assume that ultimately such a person also had authority over the *mowbeds.*

This title seems to have been attested as early as the fourth century in the Syriac sources, where there was a *rēšā de maupatē* "head of the mowbeds."[40]

Their growing authority and status is also attested by late Roman sources. For example in the sixth century, Agathias states that "nowadays, however, the Magi are the object of extreme awe and veneration, all public business being conducted at their discretion and in accordance with their prognostications, and no litigant or party to a private dispute fails to come under their jurisdiction. Indeed nothing receives the stamp of legality in the eyes of the Persians unless it is ratified by one of the Magi."[41] They were not only active in administration, but seem to have gained even more power. The Syriac sources even report that *mowbeds* at some time were able to rule over a province, such as that of Adiabene, and others were in charge of the court. This idea is also supported by Syriac reports that in the early Sasanian period, the *mowbeds* and *marzbans* were put in charge of provinces.[42] This may be a retrojection to the past, but it also may reflect the way the *an-Iran* "non-Iranian" provinces were controlled, since we hear from the Armenian sources that the Sasanians put in charge of Armenia along with the *hazarapet*, a chief *mow*, i.e., *mowbed*, who functioned as the judge of the land.[43] Ełishe also reports that the Sasanians governed their empire by the religion of *mow*.[44] In the Middle Persian writings, an interesting passage states that the *mowbed* was in charge of an *awestam* which can be translated as "province," which was larger than a *rustag* and smaller than a *kust*.[45]

Driyōšān jādaggōw ud dādwar: "advocate and judge of the poor."

One comes across this title mainly by viewing the seal corpus, the *Madīyān ī Hazār Dādestān*, and the Armenian sources. According to the *Madīyān ī Hazār Dādestān* (93.7) at the time of Kavad, official seals were introduced for the *mowbed* and the *āmārgar*, and the seal of the *dādwar* was made by the order of Khusro I. There was a *mowbed* for the entire province of Fars, and the title of the *mowbed* was changed to *driyōšān jādaggōw ud dādwar* "Advocate of Poor and Judge." This office seems to be concerned with social, legal, and religious spheres. From seals we know that there were *dādwar*s "judges" functioning in the province, but for the *jādaggōw*, there is no evidence that it was a separate office. It was during the time of Khusro I that the *dādwar* was given a seal, and functioned in districts and cities.[46] The textual evidence may shed some light on the problem, because we do come across the title *jādag-gōwān* "advocates," which is explained as (*ayār*) "helper," and (*panāhīh*) giving "protection."[47] Its sense is not clear, and it may have had the function of intercessor on behalf of people or a cause.[48] In the Zoroastrian world, the *jādag-gōwān* are thought to be placed with the peace-seekers in heaven.[49] De Menasce was one of the first to comment on the function of the office and to show that this office belonged to the *mowbed* of Fars.[50] Now we have as many as sixteen seals with this title. The sheer number of the seals with this title makes Shaked's assumption implausible that this office belonged only to the *mowbeds* of Fars.[51] For Fars, there is a seal for the *driyōšān jādaggōw ud dādwar* who administered the various subdistricts, such as Bishabuhr, Istakhr, and Ardashir-xwarrah.[52] Also a *driyōšān jādaggōw ud dādwar* was in charge of three districts at the same time, those of Darabgerd, Bishabuhr, and Weh-az-Amid-Kavad.[53]

Shaked has shown the moral authority of this *mowbed*, which seems to be concerned with the welfare of the poor as attested in the Middle Persian texts: "The seventh is (*jādag-gōwīh*) advocacy. It is this: One who speaks a word on behalf of a widowed woman, a hungry child, fires, cattle, sheep and other helpless creatures, specifically for the sake of his own soul."[54] Clearly, this official must have had some functions relevant to the title as opposed to other *mowbed*s, such as administration of money received in charity for the poor and the needy.[55] From the title it is clear that the religious authority (*mowbed*) had gained legal authority as well, which is paralleled with the title of St. Nerses in Armenia: *jatagov amenayn zrkeloc* "intercessor for all the deprived."[56]

The *driyōšān jādaggōw ud dādwar* was perhaps the overseer of charitable foundations to help the poor and the needy.[57] This was a religious duty which the powerful should keep as their duty (*Dēnkard* VI.142):

> The powerful means are not harmful to that man or to (other) people. In whatever comes about he is *driyōšān jādag-gōw* advocate for the poor and does good to them. He praises the poor and acts in such a manner that (his) wealth and riches are open to all men, and that they hold them as their own and are confident.[58]

On the local level the *mow* may have been in charge of the religious endowments, which were set up by people *pad ruwan* for the sake of the soul. This is similar with the Catholic foundations and of course ties in with the Islamic institution of *waqf* or religious endowments which had the same function in the early Islamic era.[59]

Handarzbed: "councillor"

The *handarzbed* served in various capacities or as an advisor to persons of rank. In the Persepolis Middle Persian inscription, in the early fourth century we encounter the title *Sistan handarzbed* "chief councillor of Sistan," second only to the king of Sistan, and above the *mow* and the *Shahrab* of Zarang.[60] Thus from early on, he seems to have had an important function within the court apparatus, whose function may have been more concerned with advice, acting as an advisor and dealing with moral causes. We possess a seal of the *handarzbed* of Ardashir-xwarrah,[61] which makes it probable that there were other *handarzbedān* functioning for other districts. Alternatively, there could have been one *handarzbed* administrating several districts at the same time.

The *dar handarzbed* "court councilor," was an advisor to the king and was part of the court retinue, who according to the *Kārnāmag ī Ardaxšīr ī Pāpagān* (X.7) accompanied the *mowbadan mowbed* "chief mowbed," *ērān spāhbed* "chief of the army," *puštaspān sardār* "chief of cavalry," *dibīrān mahist* "chief scribe," and was placed before the *wāspuhragān* "grandees/specials." The *mowān handarzbed* gave advice in legal matters pertaining to marital questions *Madīyān ī Hazār Dādestān* (57.12; 59.10; 98.3). The *mowān handarzbed* had reached an important position by the end of the Sasanian period, perhaps because of the growing power of the religious hierarchy. In one Middle Persian text *Abar Stāyēnīdārīh ī Sūr Āfrīn* (157.9–14), he is listed after the following offices: *šāhān šāh* "King of Kings," *pus ī wāspuhr ī šāhān* "principal son among the princes," *wuzurg framādār* "grand minister," the *spāhbeds* "military commanders" of *Khurasan* "northeast," *xwarwarān* "northwest," and *nēmrōz* "southeast," followed by the *dādwarān ī dādwar* "chief judge." Below him are the *mowān handarzbed*, and the *hazārbed* "chilarch."[62] The *mowān handarzbed* was the councilor to the *mowbedān* and as an explanation or Pahlavi version of the *Yasna*, *mowān handarzbed* is glossed as the teacher of the *mowān.* In the Perso-Islamic literature, the men of religion are placed in the first rank and divided into four divisions, the last being the *mo'alimān*, i.e, the *hērbedān* "teacher-priests."[63] We also have a seal for this office, as well as the *mowān handarzbed* of Sistan. The *handarzbed ī wāspuhragān* "councillor to the grandees/specials" had authority within the king's demesne.[64] There was also a *handarzbed* for the queen at the time of Shabuhr I, *bānūgān handarzbed*, and a *handarzbed ī aswāragān*, "the councillor for the cavalry."[65]

In the Armenian *History of Lazar P'arpec'i*, it is reported that the *movan anderjapet* was sent to a fortress in Nēw-Shabuhr where Armenian priests were held captive. He was to take them to a deserted spot to torture them, but more probably to try to change their mind in religious matters. More importantly, the text states that the *movan anderjapet* was under the authority of the *movpetan-movpet*, i.e., *mowbedān mowbed.*[66] A Middle Persian text states that the *mowan handarzbed* and the *mowbedān mowbed* were set over the *dādwarān* who held sway over the *rustag*, the *mowbedān* who held sway over an *awestām* "district," and *radān* "spiritual masters," over a *kust* "quarter."[67] The *mowān handarzbed* according to the *Madīyān ī Hazār Dādestān* was in charge of establishing guardianship, and administrating foundations for the soul (*pad ruwān*).[68]

Dādwar: "judge"

The judge had to have legal schooling, and they were drawn from the *mowbedān*. The *dādwar* also had a superior, who had the title of *shahr dādwarān dādwar* "Supreme judge of the province."[69] This is also evident from the Syriac text *The Life of the Patriarch Mār Abā* (540–552 CE) where a certain Mār Qardag held two titles, that of *ēwēnbed/āyēnbed* "master of ceremonies," and *shahr dādwar* "judge of the empire." This has been suggested to be the combination or conflation of two titles, the *shahr dādwar* and *dādwarān dādwar* "chief judge." The fact that a chief judge existed is attested by al-Mas'ūdī, who stated that the chief judge, *Qadī al-Qodat*, probably a claque on (*dādwrān dādwar*) was the head of all *mowbeds.*[70] Thus the legal apparatus seems to have been under the control of the religious hierarchy. As stated earlier, the *Madīyān ī Hazār Dādestān* (100,11–15) states that the *dādwar* was under the authority of the *mowbed.* There are only a few seals found with this title, thus we do not know how prevalent the office was from the sigillographic evidence. This perhaps means that by the sixth century CE, the *mowbed* had taken over the function of judges. According to the Middle Persian texts, the *dādwar* dealt with a variety of cases, such as property rights, records and confessions, attended to complaints, broke seals and retained unclaimed property.[71] They had to be well versed in the Zoroastrian law and there were a series of texts which gave them recourse to past legal precepts. For example in case of appeals, he would have had "The Book of Appeals" (*Mustawar-nāmag nibišt*) in order to refer back to past cases.[72]

Āmārgar: "accountant"

From the sigillographic evidence it appears that the *āmārgar* "accountant," and the *dādwar* "judge" controlled economic, administrative, and legal processes. Whole provinces had an accountant, which is manifest from a seal found at Qasr ī Abū Nasr (D209) which supplies the "Accountant of Fars," (*pārs āmārgar*).[73] In addition, there were accountants who held power over one or more *shahrs* within a province. One example is the *āmārgār* of Istakhr and Darabgerd,[74] and the other the *āmārgar* of (B164) "Ardashir-xwarrah, Bishabuhr, and Nēw-Darāb." An āmārgar's jurisdiction could be changed, as is evident from other seals such as (Z3 Gyselen) "Istakhr and Bishabuhr and Weh-az-Amid-Kavad." Beside the accountant for the provinces and the districts there were also a "court accountant" *dar-āmārgar* and an accountant in charge of the finances of the empire, *Ērān-āmārgar*.[75]

Dibīr: "scribe" and *Kārframān/Kārdārn* (MHD A38.16–18)

The *dibīrān* scribes were the ones who had the knowledge of reading and writing for different occasions and matters. A short Middle Persian text title "On the Manner of Writing Letter/Book" (*abar ēwēnag ī nāmag nibēsišnīh*) spells out how letters should be written to people of different ranks such as the lords (*xwadāyān*), and rulers (*pādixšāyān*); for inquring about someone's torment (*bēš-pursišnīh*) and providing happiness (*hunsandīh*) to people who have lost loved ones; and what forms of salutations should be used, and how to end the letters.[76] To learn these matters they attended the *dibīristān*, where from them they were employed in the court and the provincial administration. According to the Islamic sources, those scribes who were selected to serve at the court were required not to associate with many people outside. This may be why we hear of several strange scripts which according to Ibn Nadim were used for writing secretive matters, i.e., the secret script (*rāz-dibīrīh*). Those of lesser knowledge were considered as *kārframānān* or *kārdārān* to enhance their skills.[77]

SASANIAN ECONOMY AND AGRICULTURE

The main mode of production and source of income and livelihood was farming and agriculture. Crops included cereals such as barley, rye, millet, legumes, forage, fibers for spinning, fruits such as grapes, figs, dates, and nuts, and vegetables,[78] as well a rice cultivation, apricot and olive trees. The Sasanians were very much interested in the development of agriculture and we know that there was an expansion of agriculture and cultivable lands in Xuzestān and Iraq. Frye is correct to note that the characteristics of land tenure or "feudal" make up in the Near East is somewhat different from that of the European Feudalism. This is confirmed by the archaeological evidence from southwestern Ērānshahr where there are no villages along castles or fortifications.[79] This is because there were several different types of land-tenure such as "state lands," "endowment land," "land with collective ownership," and one should also mention "land as charitable endowment." But what was more important than land ownership was the issue of water control, making the development and ownership of *qanāt*s much more important.[80] The care and building of *qanāts* tell us the importance in which the Sasanians gave to agricultural development,[81] especially for the arid and hilly regions. Some *qanāts* were several kilometers long and designed to bring water to large settlements.[82] Unlike the feudal society of Medieval Europe, water was a much more important commodity in Sasanian Persia and its source and control are discussed in legal texts. Chapter 22 of the *Mādayān ī Hazār Dādestān* is an exposition on the use of *qanāts/katas* which describes the sharing of and laws cases in regards to disputes among individuals and those who share a *qanāt*.[83]

Xūzestān and Iraq were the two important provinces where the agricultural land was in use. Xūzestān was the richest in terms of fertility of the soil and abundance of water, and it had constructed irrigation systems to assured its utmost use. Here rice, sugarcane, orchard and other crops were grown and exported. This in turn ensured its highest taxability by the government, generating money for the royal coffers.[84] Thus the development of irrigation in Ērānshahr can tell us much about state reaction to agricultural development and its control. Evidence from the Susania plain suggests that smaller irrigation canals gave way to larger ones which cost more money and were more labor intensive.[85]

The highlands were affected by lumbering activity by the pastoral nomads in this region and government schemes for intense irrigation and damn building were to have major effects on the ecology of the region.[86] Because of this level of centralization, the Sasanians were able to tax the nomads and hillside residents of the empire,[87] a sector of the society that has been a constant obstacle to governments in Iran since time immemorial which was only to be controlled during the Pahlavi era.

CITIES

The urbanization project by the Parthians and then the Sasanians brought about an influx of population from other parts of the Iranian Plateau as well as through forced migration from the Near East.[88] Not only later Islamic sources, but also Middle Persian sources attest to the intense interest in the city-building projects of the Persian kings. The *Shahrestānīhā ī Ērānshahr* (*The Provincial Capitals of Ērānshahr*)[89] which is a Middle Persian text naming cities throughout Central Asia, the Iranian Plateau, Mesopotamia, and the Near East, gives us a good view of this Persian campaign. Many of the *shahrestāns* which may be translated as "provincial capitals" or major cities are said to have been built by the Sasanian kings, or rebuilt by them, thus receiving the king's names.[90] Persian Muslim historians, such as Hamza al-Isfahānī also supply a long list of cities built by the various Sasanian kings of kings which corroborates the *Shahrestānīhā ī Ērānshahr*.[91]

The archaeological evidence from southwestern Ērān provides evidence of decline in rural settlement and of migration to the cities in such places as Iraq,[92] Xūzestān,[93] and the Deh Lurān plain further north.[94] Neely's statement that the population increase and urbanization was a direct result of planned expansion and growth promoted by the Sasanian government[95] seems to be accurate for most of the provinces which were developed. The prerogative for such a move was also probably based on the commercial viability of the new sites and their location close to the roads where economic activity was rampant.[96]

This urbanization was done for several important reasons which for one meant that in order for the Sasanians to benefit from taxes, they needed to develop textile, glass, metalwork and other crafts and industries which needed a large workforce which were stationed by them in the cities. The capture of the Roman engineers and skilled workers and craftsmen and their deportation into newly built or older cities brought in new workforces which could augment the shortage of population and train the Persian population. This massive movement into the cities is not only demonstrated by the textual sources, but also the archaeological work done so far.[97] The naming of many cities with the suffix of Ērān or with *xwarrah* suggested the ideological tendencies of the Sasanians as well, where they were used in naming or renaming cities. This harkened back to the Avestan *airyanəm xvarənō* "the glory of the Aryans" connected with the concept of kingship,[98] and the direct control of the cities by the King of Kings.[99] Then the process of urbanization had economical as well as political significance for the Sasanian period.

In order to build new cities and populate the regions, the Sasanians needed to invest in the economy, specifically agriculture in order to feed its burgeoning population. Since agriculture was a main mode of production one needs to view landholding patterns in the Sasanian Empire. From the various sources we can state that there were several types of landholding. Private ownership of a small farm is one type of landholding which became increasingly difficult to maintain, especially with the development of the second type of landholding, i.e., communal ownership. Those involved in communal ownership were of the same religious attitude. For example Jews owned villages in Iraq which employed slave labor to yield its produce. They as well as others had the right to own slaves and sell the town and its surrounding plot of land which they owned. This communal religious ownership of land applies to the Christians when monasteries and churches in Mesopotamia had the same arrangement and used slave labor.[100]

LOCAL AND INTERNATIONAL TRADE

Early Sasanian economic interest is manifested through several major activities. The first factor in the development of Sasanian economy is the control of the Persian Gulf. This we know was done from the time of Ardaxšīr I onwards where ports were established on the Persian and Arab side of the Persian Gulf.[101] We are told that once Ardaxšīr had defeated Ardawān and controlled the plateau, he made incursions into Oman, Bahrain, and Yamamma, defeating Sanatruq, the king of Bahrain.[102] The reason for the establishment of forts along the coast, however, is not clear, since it is implausible that a Sasanian navy would have been present at these forts. Still, they could have acted as hospices or storage. Arabic sources state that during the Sasanian period the Persians controlled the shores and strands of the sea, while the Arabs lived in the mountains and deserts.[103] We have very little information on the Sasanian navy and it does not appear to have been a major force. The sources, however, mention the Sasanian navy several times, once during the time of Ardaxšīr, and again during the time of Khusro I.

In the *Kārnāmag ī Ardaxšīr ī Pābagān* we are faced with one of these ports which is called *Boxt-Ardaxšīr* (modern Būšīhr) which among other evidence demonstrates the importance of the Persian Gulf for the early Sasanians.[104] The importance of this port is that *Boxt-Ardaxšīr* was linked to Kāzerūn and Šērāz inland by road where commodities were sent for export to other regions. Also its closeness to the center of Persis, i.e, Šērāz must have made it an important port.[105] Another important port was Sīrāf which was connected by road to Fērūz-Abād and also to Šērāz, where pottery sherds and coins are among other finds suggesting a Sasanian port.[106] Other ports included the site of Hormuz at the straight of Hormuz, which was connected to the northeast, via Lulfar to Sirjan.[107] Also the port of Guzeran or Kujaran-Ardešīr was located near Bandar ī Lengeh which again had a role in trade and met the needs of the city of Dārāb in Persis.[108] Also one can mention the island of Khārg which appears to have been a late Sasanian settlement in the fourth century CE, 37 miles northwest of Būšīhr.[109]

These ports were probably an important center for trade, where not only commodities were brought to its ports and taken to the inland cities, but also as a stopping place for the cargo going from Mesopotamia to Asia, East Africa and back.[110] We know that in the early Islamic period the houses that were built at the port of Sīrāf were made from a wood called Sāj which was brought from India and Zanzibār which points to the import and export of commodities from Asia and East Africa.[111] Sasanian coin finds at Sīrāf demonstrate the occupation of the site from the Sasanian period as well.[112] It should be mentioned, however, that it appears that this control of the seas was not actively pursued by the Sasanian navy or the state, but rather the Persian merchants dominated the trade without state heavy state intervention.

The Sasanians were competing with the Byzantines and disputing trade as far as Sri Lanka, where it appears there was a Sasanian colony in Malaysia which was composed of merchants.[113] Persian horses were shipped to Ceylon,[114] and a Persian colony was established at that island, where ships came from Persia to its port.[115] Sasanian control of the Sind region is also apparent from the recent coin finds which are copies of the Pērōz type, and suggests fifth century presence and/or influence.[116] The Persians built other ports to expand their trade, in such places as Muscat in Oman during the sixth century,[117] where the importance of this port for Persian traders continued into the Islamic period, as the ships sailing from India to Aden stopped at this port.[118]

At Sūhār, at the mouth of the Persian Gulf in the Sea of Oman, there appears to have been a Sasanian fort which may have participated in trade, as well as at Dama and Jurrafār.[119] There was a Persian outpost at Ghanam in the Strait of Hormuz which may have overseen shipping and those who wanted to enter the Persian Gulf.[120] The same can be said for Banbhore in Sind, at Kilwa on the east coast of Africa, where few Sasanian-Islamic wares were found.[121] In the Umm al-Ma region there is also evidence of Sasanian presence, where green-glazed pots from Iraq were found.[122] There is also evidence of Sasanian material at Salihiyah near Khawran in Ras al-Khaimah.[123] The presence of the Persians at these ports suggests that there was a campaign in controlling the shipping close to these outposts.

By the sixth century it appears that the Persians were not only bent on controlling the Persian Gulf, and the Arabian Sea, but also looked further east which brought them into conflict with Rome. Silk appears to have been an important commodity which the Romans wanted. It seems they were bent on circumventing the Persian traders to get a cheaper price for both silk and other commodities. Consequently, the Byzantines had to seek the aid of the Christian Ethiopians, who were expelled by the Yemenis with the backing of the Sasanians from the region.[124]

We also have information about Sasanian trade with China[125], where imported objects, such as T'ang dynasty export wares, and other items from Rome, were found at the port of Sīrāf.[126] This trade with China was conducted through two avenues, one through the famous Silk Road about which we have much information and the other, the sea route. It should be mentioned that the rate of trade from these two trading avenues were at a different rate and intensity depending on the time period. That is the rate of trade was not constant on either route and it tended to fluctuate. Ammianus Marcellinus tells us that in the fourth century "all along the coast [of the Persian Gulf] is a throng of cities and villages, and many ships sail to and fro."[127] This maritime trade became more important because of the political situation, and hence Persis ports became increasingly central to this trade. From these ports, Persian traders went to China for silk, since the Romans also decided to do the same. The Persian merchants, we are told, did not sit idly by but established their centers in China as well. With the establishment of ports and Persian colonies in east Asia, the Romans were not able to do much, even if Justinian in the sixth century had made the Ethiopians, who engaged in trade, help him. But we are told that it was "impossible for the Ethiopians to buy silk from the Indians, for the Persian merchants always locate themselves at the very harbors where the Indian ships first put in (since they inhabit the adjoining country), and are accustomed to buy the whole cargoes."[128]

Off the coast of China there are finds of Sasanian coins which again suggest the maritime trade between this region and Persia. At least three sites where Sasanian coins were found in southeast China by the sea make it probable that ships from the Persian Gulf came there. These are the sites of Kukogng, Yngdak, and Suikai which had connections with trade in the Persian Gulf.[129] Many of the coins belong to the late fifth through seventh centuries,[130] which again attest to the importance of the Persian Gulf in the Late Sasanian period. The date of the coins demonstrate that they were deposited in the Ch'i period (497–501) at Kukgong and Yngdak which is a coastal province.[131] In return we also have finds of Sasanian coins in the southeast coastal region of China which also attest to this exchange.[132] Although their number is small we may suggest that these coins came through the sea trade. Kavad I's coins were found in the maritime province of Guangdong, where their mint signatures are from Persis and adjoining regions which appear to have come via the sea route.[133] The Presence of Persian colonies in China has also been confirmed by the existence of fire-temples belonging to Zoroastrians found in the Chang'an region in southern China.[134]

Land trade is much better documented and the Silk Road should be mentioned, because it connected the east to the west where Persia became the nexus or middle region of this international road. The various taxes and tolls placed on commodities going from east to west would certainly have benefited the royal treasury which would keep up good roads along with lucrative tolls. Morony has mentioned that we may see the creation of new settlements not only in the campaign of the Sasanians to create new cities and to populate the region but also a shift from remote, less well accessed locations, to locations which lay on the trade routes concentrating on the commercial economy.[135] The one product that was in demand in the Roman Empire and the trade of which the Sasanian tried to control, was silk. The Sasanians created workshops at Susa, Gundē Shabuhr, and Šuštar to rival the Chinese and the Syro-Phoenician workshops, by importing raw silk yarn[136] and creating designs which were to be imitated in Egypt and into the Islamic period.[137]

The large finds of Sasanian silver coins from the end of the fifth and sixth centuries in China suggests intense trade by the Sasanians with the east and was part of what has been called "diplomatic commerce."[138] The important merchants on the Silk Road were the Sogdians who are known as silk merchants and controlled the trade in Central Asia. Although they were active in trading, the change in the monetary policies coincides with Sasanians' economic involvement with the Chinese. Its precise beginning was in the sixth century, and based on the coinage, we can see a new stage in the economic development and trade in Central Asia, specifically in Sogdiana.[139]

The other important point is that rather than engaging in commerce and the purchase of goods from Syria where some of its products such as glass was in demand, the Sasanians had decided that by deporting the skilled workers of the region and their settlement into the newly developed imperial cities they would be able to compete against the Romans.[140] There seems to have been a steady exchange and commerce in late antiquity between the Sasanians and the Romans, but the Perso-Roman rivalry must have brought pressures on various trade routes. For example, Armenia was a scene of rivalry between the two sides which was also a market where trade and exchange took place. Procopious states that Persarmenia (Eastern Armenian under Sasanian control after the middle of the fifth century CE) was an important trading center for the Sasanians and the Romans to trade in Indian and Iberian products.[141]

Now, depending on the political problems in Armenia, Mesopotamia became an important route and increased the volume of trade. Of course during the heated wars in the late sixth and early seventh centuries these routes must have been reduced significantly which in turn would have made Arabia a very important route, which probably had far reaching consequences for the development of the Arabian economy and Islam as well. The two empires had made various treaties and their economic interests became more important and the rivalry more intense as time went by. By the sixth century the *Codex Justinianus* (IV 63/4) mentions that both Roman and Persian merchants must trade in pre-designated areas by the two empires and that each side may not travel into the other empire or go very far.[142] This scheme was devised in order to keep the secrets (economic) of the state and consequently made the Persian merchants stay in Persia and travel east as far as China and for the Roman merchants to stay in the Roman empire and use other subjects such as the Ethiopians to make way to the east via the waterways. The heavy tariffs and tolls placed by both sides, sometimes as high as ten percent at certain regions, where the meeting of merchants were agreed upon,[143] made regions, that were not under Roman and Persian control, such as the market place at ash-Shihr on the southern Arabian coast, much more popular.[144]

THE DOMESTIC ECONOMY

As for the domestic economy, we can rely on the seals and bullae which give some insight into the Sasanian administrative institutions.[145] These sources can tell us about the Sasanian bureaucracy, administrative organization and divisions and, for example, the level of involvement by the priests,[146] the scope and degree of economic activity, who was in charge of these activities, and where they took place.[147] In terms of economic activity we can tell that there was a vibrant domestic exchange based on the placement of bullae and seal finds in the empire with the name of one of the cities or districts of the province of Persis. Four major storehouses of bullae have been found, namely those at Taxt ī Suleymān, Qasr ī Abū Nasr, Āq Tepe, and Dvin, from which we can draw certain assumptions. In Āq Tepe, sealing with the name of Kermān and Ardashir-xwarrah from Persis have been found which should persuade us that Persis had economic relations with the far reaches of the empire, and only Persis can claim this position, because of the numerous seals and bullae found with names belonging to its cities. At Dvin, again sealings from Ardashir-xwarrah have been found. This fact tells us that commodities were brought from Persis, with either Persis acting as a port or from where the merchandise began its route.[148] The bullae were used to seal packages destined for caravan or maritime trade which is supported by later historical evidence.[149] It is also important to note that bullae finds in East Asia, especially in Mantai in Sri Lanka, attest to Persian economic activity as well.[150]

The nature of trade but also who engaged in it is important as well. Trade was conducted by companies and religious communities who combined their resources and formed partnerships. The term used for joint-partnership in the Middle Persian legal texts is *hambāyīh* which really meant holder of a common share whose joint investment would have brought a better return and a larger purchasing power. These joint-partnerships were probably based on religious association as well, where Zoroastrians created their own *hambāyīh*, but may have dealt with other religious groups outside of their regional reach. In regards to this form of ownership which was common in the late Sasanian period, not only the *Madiyān ī Hazār Dādestān*, but also the fifth book of Ishoboxt which was composed in Syriac, is devoted to the principal of company or joint-partnership.[151] We are well informed in regard to the legal aspects of trade and business agreements. Drafts of agreements were drafted, signed and sealed and a copy was kept at the local office of registry *dēwān*. These agreements were legally binding and depending on the violation cases of transgression were taken before a lesser magistrate, *dādwar ī keh*, or a higher magistrate, *dādwar ī meh*, who were certainly high ranking priests.[152]

THE PERSIAN WĀZĀR/BAZAAR: THE MARKET PLACE

The principal economic activity in the cities was performed by the merchants (*wāzārgānān*) who were from the *hutuxšān* estate. Commerce (*wāzārgānīh*) was conducted in the bazaar (*wāzār*) which today is still the economic center of both small and large cities in Persia. Like today, it appears that each group of artisans occupied a specific section (Persian *rāste*) of the bazaar. This information is gained from the *Dēnkard* (VIII Chapter 38), where a specific rule existed "about the series of shops in the bazaar belonging to various artisans" (*abar ān ī kirrōkkārān ēk ēk rastag ī wāzār*).[153] A list of various professions who occupied a section of the bazaar included the blacksmith (*āhengar*), iron molder (*āhen-paykar*), silver-smith (*asēmgar*), silver-molder (*asēm-paykar*), roof-maker (*āškōb-kardār*), string-maker (*bandkār*), those who worked with mortar (spice maker?) (*čārūgar*), iron-smith (*čēlāngar*), tailor (*darzīg*), and dress-maker (wastarg-kardār), porcelin pot-maker (*dōsēngar* or *jāmīg-paz*), carpenter (*durgar*), washerman (*gāzar*), shoekmaker (*kafšgar*), shoemaker of a kind of shoe made of strings (*surgar*), potter (*kulwārgar*), baker (*nānbāg*), book-painter (*nibēgān-nigār*), painter in general (*nigārgar*), cup-maker (*payālgar*), tanner (*pōstgar*), ironsmith (*pōlāwad-paykar*), dyer (*rangraz*), various builders (*rāzān*), barber (*wars-wirāy*), tent-maker (*wiyāngar*), cooks in the sense of making sweets and other finger foods in the bazzar (*xwāhlīgar*), tablecloth maker(?) (*xwāngar*), goldsmith (*zarīgar*), and saddler (*zēngar*).[154]

There were various other professions, but we are not sure if they were in the bazaar or not. Each artisan (*kirrōg*) guild was lead by a head of the guild (*kirrōgbed*/Syriac *qārūbed*). As some of the skilled workers were either settled people from Syria or Roman prisoners, we find that some of the guild masters were Christian. These included Posi and Barāz who served in this function.[155] Of course many of the better craftsmen were settled in the royal workshops who produced commodities for the King of Kings and his family. The activity and the prices of the bazaar were overlooked by a head of the bazaar (*wāzārbed*) who probably represented the artisan class. The office was already in existence in the third century CE, since he is mentioned in the court of Shabuhr I.[156] It was in these centers where local products were produced and commodities from other provinces as well as some of the foreign products entered the cities via the caravans (*kārwān*). These caravans which went into other cities of the empire or farther were lead by a caravan leader (*sārtwā*) who was either hired by the merchant or in joint business with him.[157]

THE MERCHANTS

While there were Zoroastrian merchants as far as China trading in the markets, the merchants were looked down upon, below the three traditional classes of priests, warriors and farmers. This is apparent by looking at the structure of the section in relation to the various duties of men in the Middle Persian text, *Mēnōg ī Xrad* (Chapters. 30–31). In question 30 it is asked what are the responsibilities of the priests, the warriors and the farmers: one to hold the religion, the other to strike the enemy and keep the empire safe and the last class to cultivate the land. The merchants curiously are treated separately in the next question (32) and are spoken of negatively: "The function of the workers is this: that they would not engage in a work with which they are not familiar and do well and with precision what they know, and receive a fair wage."[158] This maybe one reason why the Sogdians and Christians, be they Persians or Roman and Germanic war prisoners who were settled in the empire, engaged in trade in Persia more than the Zoroastrians.

The third important activity has to do with the predatory activities of the Sasanians. From the time of Ardaxšīr I, the Sasanians attempted to exert their influence in Syria and the neighboring region which were not under their permanent control. This was done to plunder the cities, which included not only their monetary wealth, but also their intellectual and scientific expertise and bring it back to their empire. This will be a constant feature of Sasanian activity throughout its lifetime, where cities west of the Euphrates were attacked, their wealth taken and in many instances, their population were deported. These predatory tactics also were used to receive money from the Romans. This of course was done if a Sasanian army was victorious against the Romans, where they had to pay a ransom to escape. During the rule of Shabuhr I in the third century, after the death of Emperor Gordian and the defeat of the Roman forces, Philiph who had been chosen as the new Emperor agreed to pay some 500,000 *denārs*.[159] In the fourth century, the defense of the Caspian Gates became an issue for both the Romans and the Persians. When Jovian ceded territory to the Sasanian in 363 CE which was again renewed in the fifth century by Theodosius II, the Romans also agreed to pay an annual sum to keep up the fortresses to the Persians.[160] While the Sasanians were strong, their appeal to the Romans for monetary aid to guard the Caspian Gates was acknowledged. For example during the reign of the Roman emperor Zeno in the late fifth century, Pērōz was able to convince him to support his activity against the Hephthalites, which was continued during the reign of Kawad I in the sixth century. This aid was, however, dependent upon the strength of the Sasanians and Roman problems with other neighbors in the north, because during the reign of Walāxš (484–488) the Romans stopped paying.[161] Once this aid, which was based on an earlier treaty, was suspended, it gave the Persians the pretext to attack and plunder Syria as Kawad I did in 502 CE, receiving 1,000 lbs. of gold and, for the next seven years, an annual payment of 500 lbs. of gold.[162] When Khusro I came to the throne, in his second year of rule, he made a peace treaty with the Romans in 532 CE which is known as the "Endless Peace" which according to Procopius (*Bell. 1.22.3–5 and 16–18) in return the Romans had to pay 11,000 lbs. of gold. This peace lasted for only eight years and as a result the Persians were able to exhort another 2,000 lbs. for the truce of 545 CE and another 2,600 lbs. in 557 CE.[163] This scenario continued into the seventh century and more gold was taken from the Romans, although never with any regularity.

The question that arises is what the Sasanians did with the gold, since *drahms*, which are silver coins were the dominant coinage in circulation and they struck very little gold coinage which was mainly for ceremonial or commemorational purposes. One can guess that the treasury of the King of Kings was filled with gold, of which the empire saw very little, if any. So we can conclude that there was a steady influx of gold into the empire beginning from the third to the seventh century. Further, the Romans only were willing to pay to an adversary when they felt that they were not able to defeat them or were preoccupied with another enemy. This scheme suggests the strength of the Sasanian military throughout its existence.

MONETARY PRODUCTION

While the barter system was in use at the local levels in villages and the like, the Sasanians brought about a standardization of weights and the minting of coinage which was directed from above and under the control of the imperial administration. The units and types of coins struck by the Sasanian government were the gold *dēnār*, silver *drahm*, one-sixth silver *dang* and copper coins *pašīz* made of copper and used for local daily transaction. While the increase in the usage of copper and bronze coinage in certain parts of the empire attest to the increase in trade and governmental control,[164] the silver coinage was much more prevalent. The use of copper coinage certainly should tell us that during the Sasanian period, especially in the latter Sasanian period there was a move towards a monetary economy. Among these coins the most widely minted and attested in documents is the silver *drahm* which in weight was about 4.25 grams. From the time of Ardaxšīr I we find coins with this uniform weight which typologically vary. On the obverse we find the portrait of the King of Kings along with a name and title, such as "Ardaxšīr King of Kings of Ērān whose race (is) from the Gods." On the reverse of the coinage is a fire-alter sometimes alone and sometimes with two attendants flanking the fire. Until the late fifth century CE the coins did not indicate their place where the coins were minted which makes it difficult to gauge the number of mints and amount of minting at each location. While there are more than 100 mint-marks known, no more than 20 mints were producing the majority of them in the Sasanian empire.[165] This of course can not be said for the early Sasanian period, and, for example, there may have been three different mints in operation, mainly in Fars and the capital.[166]

With the striking of the mint-marks on the reverse and the date in which they were struck (the date indicates during the rule of which monarch the coin was struck), we begin to have an idea of the regularity of the mints and which were most productive and stable. Certainly those which were close to economic centers such as the province of Persis had a huge output which supported the Persian Gulf trade,[167] while the mints of Media had far less output. The other time when mints went into over production was during wars. For example during the reign of Khusro II (590–628 CE) there was a huge amount of coinage production which was used to finance the long war with Rome. Even though the weight of the coinage fell towards the end of Khusro's reign, he kept minting coins to finance his activity.

The silver *drahms* were so well known that places as far as India imitated Sasanian coinage which attests to the economic power and/or prestige of the Sasanian empire in the eyes of their neighbors. It is important that although we do not have an agreement between the Romans and Sasanians in terms of what types of coins should be struck, the Romans used gold as the metal of choice for minting, while the Sasanians used silver. This may have been a tacit agreement between the two empires, where Sasanian silver would be acknowledged as the silver coin of choice as is apparent from its use as far as western China. The purity of the coins also give us some ideas about the mines and where the coins were minted. For example, we know the coins that were produced in the northeast had a higher purity level than the other regions and so their silver must have come from the mines of this region. In fact it is this region that Islamic sources attest to having the largest silver mines extracted by the dynasties which came after the Sasanians. For example among the names which are connected with silver mines, none one can match Panjshīr located in Khurasan which is a located in modern day northeastern Afghanistan. The analysis of the silver there has demonstrated that the silver had exceptionally low gold content, exceptionally low copper content, and abnormally high bismuth content.[168] Presumably much wood was needed to smelt the ore and could have been a reason for the widespread deforestation in eastern Persia and Central Asia.[169] Agapius states that the Zoroastrians *mājūs* were active in the silver mines in Khurasan as well attesting to the importance of this region for silver ore to mint coins.[170] This is especially significant in the face of medieval textual reports which attest to the lack of silver mines throughout the Sasanian empire. How else would the mints of Fars have been able to generate a steady output of *drahms*?

According to the Chinese chronicle *Ko-Ku-Yao*, steel was also produced in Sasanian Persia which was then exported to China.[171] The Romans considered "Persian Steel" to be secondary in quality only to "Indian Steel."[172] This is also confirmed by the Sasanians themselves in the Middle Persian texts where a good Indian sword made of steel is mentioned. In the *Kārnāmag ī Ardaxšīr ī Pābagān*, Ardaxšīr fights with *šamšēr ī hindīg* "Indian sword" which was taken from the Parthian royal treasury.[173] While the tree supply may have been exhausted in Khurasan for smelting silver, in Adūrbādagān we find iron smelting sites in the Qarādāg ranges close to modern day Tabrīz, but also near Rašt and Massula, in Qazvīn. The abundant availability of iron which is suggested by scholars,[174] can be found in many regions of Persia.[175] Textile industry, specifically carpet making was also known in Persia.[176] From the Achaemenid period we are told that the Persians had carpets (Greek, *psilotapis*) which were used by the king, and in the seventh century when Heraclius sacked Khusro II's royal treasury in 628 CE, carpets (*tapis*) are mentioned, which may have given rise to the Byzantine Greek word for carpet weaver (*tapi-dyphos*) from the Persian.[177]

RELIGIOUS ENDOWMENTS

The Zoroastrian institution of charitable foundations functioned in the same way, where the temple owned cultivable lands and slaves and others worked on it. Based on the Sasanian legal texts we know that a host of people from different classes and prerogatives worked on the massive Zoroastrian temples, which were owned by the clerical class or established by individuals as charitable foundations for the sake of one's soul (*pad ruwān*). We know that foreign slaves (*anshahrīg*) caught in wars were used for menial labor and to work on the fields. The term used for slaves or servants in these temples is *ātaxš-bandag* "temple-servant" who did not necessarily need to be a slave and could have been an individual who dedicated part of his or her time as a pious act to cleanse his or her soul or to render service as part of a debt. This and other financial aid kept the priests and the retinue needed to run the temple employed and afloat which although Zoroastrian in character was deeply influenced by the Mesopotamian temple economies of the Near East before it. There was a spiritual side to this communal land-holding and temple economy, as well, which becomes more apparent during the late Sasanian period.

In the Middle Persian encyclopedic work, *Dēnkart* VI, we have evidence of monastic life, if we can use a Christian term here, for two priests (*hērbed*) which is applauded by our author who also gives us some of the flavor of communal monastic life for Zoroastrian Persia.[178] We should remember that the cultivation of the land is very important religiously as well, where according to the fourth chapter of the Middle Persian text, *Dādestān ī Mēnōg ī Xrad*, a list of the times when the earth is most happy or content and the answers given very much reflects the mentality of the Zoroastrian community in Sasanian Persia. The earth would be happy if livestock is on it, the land which has not been cultivated to become cultivated, when a barren land becomes thriving or cultivated. But in relation of temple estates there is also mention that the earth would be content if a fire-temple is built on it.[179]

This form of communal ownership of land also made sure that the progeny of the one who had set up such a foundation would continue to benefit from the inheritance spiritually and financially as well. Also, communal ownership appeased the problems associated with inheritance and the problems with taxation and landholding patterns.[180] The lands that were not owned by a religious community were mainly owned by aristocracy who acted as absentee landowners living in the cities and employed the *dehgāns* "landed gentry," to manage their estate.[181] People worked as share-cropers who turned over a portion of their yield as tax to the provincial or governmental authority, another portion to the landowner and kept the rest. Before the reforms of the sixth century CE, those who leased land did so in return for a fixed annual sum of their produce, but after the reforms, a fixed land tax was applied per unit area.[182] After the reforms of the sixth century, the state was able to have a more reliable and systematic income. Land was distributed and the power of the large landed aristocracy was checked by the empowerment of the small landowners who sometimes had functioned as absentee land owners, i.e., the *dehqān*s. This was achieved since the taxes were levied based on the amount of land and the kind of produce that was grown on it, where in times of drought and disaster the state was willing to remit taxes.[183] This system brought financial stability to the empire for a while, but there were basic problems which would create a "feudal" society in late Sasanian Persia. This was because while the aristocracy was bent on controlling their land and exacting as much income from the peasants who worked on it, if the local officials could be bribed, the laws set by the king and court would have been symbolic at best. Further, the *dehqān*s were the new land owning elite who were emerging which was more loyal to the government as far as it gave them wealth and power against the communal and large land owning aristocracy. The margraves (*marzbān*s) held power over their own domain and when the government was weak were able to become semi-independent and, by using the nomads as a local military force, create another "feudal state" within a larger state. As has been suggested it is quite possible that the chiefs of the nomadic tribes were given land by the *marzbān*s as fiefs, while the cavalry soldiers were given land in return for service,[184] making them attached to a region and locality. Only those who held a communal ownership of land tended to remain unaffected, even into the early Islamic period.

CONCLUSION

While we are dependent on the few Sasanian imperial inscriptions and coins in the first centuries, by the end of fifth century CE we also find bullae and seals as well as texts which help us understand late Sasanian administration. One can conclude that as the empire became established a larger chancery and administration developed. The Zoroastrian priests became of the administration throughout the empire. The system seems to have responded well to the challenges which arose for the administrative system. With the reforms of Kavad I and Khusro I, a major reform took place which is much known, not only through the Sasanian sources and material culture, but also through Islamic sources. This system was adopted and adapted in the Islamic period, where many functions and offices continued into Medieval Iran.

On the other hand Sasanians were able to create a new economic network in the Near East which supplanted the Arsacid economic activity. The Sasanians, however, took an aggressive approach in controlling the waterways and land routes to ensure safety for the traders and in return were able to excise taxes from them. Investment in dams and water projects also demonstrates the state's concern with the well-being of its population. The influx of foreign skilled workers at the royal workshops also brought new ways of production from that of the existing bazaars in the cities where local trade took place. We are ill informed about the local economic activity of the Sasanians, but the use of copper coinage in large numbers suggests a move towards a monetary economy within the empire which was not the case in the Arsacid period. Trade wars with the Romans were kept up in order to keep the Persian traders in healthy competition with the foreign traders. The Sasanian Empire was blessed in that it was the middle kingdom between China and Rome, and so it held the key to trade. With the intensification of the wars with the Eastern Roman Empire, there seems to have been a decline in trade, as well as less investment in water projects, hence a decline in the economic output and naturally, lower state income. What we can see is that at the end of the Sasanian period there is a general economic decline, but what the Muslims inherited from the Sasanian Persians was an already existing economic system that was revived by the Muslims and continued under the Caliphate.

Notes

1

CHAPTER 1: THE POLITICAL HISTORY OF *IRAN* AND *AN-IRAN*

1 The basic outline of Sasanian history is based on Al-Tabarī, *Ta'rīkh al-rusul wa-al-mulūk*, ed. M.J. de Goeje, Leiden, 1879–1901. The English translation with copious notation is by C.E. Bosworth, *The History of Al-Tabarī, vol. V, The Sasanids, the Byzantines, the Lakmids, and Yemen*, State University of New York Press, 1999. Secondary sources, M. Morony, "Sasanids," *The Encycleopaedia of Islam*, 1998; A. Christensen, *L'Iran sous les Sassanides*, Copenhagen, 1944; R.N. Frye, *The History of Ancient Iran*, C.H. Beck'sche Verlagsbuchhandlung, München, 1983, pp. 281–340; ibid., "The Political History of Iran Under the Sasanians," *The Cambridge History of Iran*, ed. E. Yarshater, vol. 3(1), 1983, pp. 116–180; K. Schippmann, *Grundzüge der Geschichte des sasanidischen Reiches*, Darmstadt, 1990; J. Wiesehöfer, *Ancient Persia from 550 BC to 650 AD*, I.B.Tauris Publishers, London and New York, 1996, pp. 151–222; Z. Rubin, "The Sasanid Monarchy," *The Cambridge Ancient History*, vol. 14, 2000, pp. 638–661. For a comprehensive overview and important notices on Sasanian and Roman empire in a comparative perspective see J. Howard-Johnston, "The Two Great Powers in Late Antiquity: a Comparison," *The Byzantine and Early Islamic Near East*, vol. III, ed. A. Cameron, The Darwin Press, Inc., New Jersey, pp. 157–226. For the map of the Sasnian Empire, see E. Kettenhofen, *Das Sasanidenreich*, TAVO, Dr. Ludwig Reichert Verlag, Wiesbaden, 1993.

2 For the latest treatment of the Fratarakas see A. Panaino, "The bagān of the Fratarakas: Gods or 'divine' Kings?," *Religious Themes and Texts of pre-Islamic Iran and Central Asia: Studies in Honour of Professor Gherardo Gnoli on the Occasion of his 65th birthday on 6 December 2002*, eds. C. Cereti, M. Maggi, E. Provasi, Wiesbaden, 2002, pp. 283–306.

3 *Dio's Roman History*, Book LXXX.3, 1–2 mentions that Ardashir was victorious in three battles against the Arsacids; *Herodian*, Book VI.2, 6–7.

4 K. Schippmann, *Grunzüge der Sasanidische Reich*, 1986, p. 70.

5 Agathias, *The Histories*, Book 2.27, p. 61. For Pabag and his relationship to Ardashir see R.N. Frye, "Zoroastrian Incest," *Orientalia Iosephi Tucci Memoriae Dicata*, eds. G. Gnoli and L. Lanciotti, Istituto Italiano per il Medio ed Estremo Oriente, Roma, 1985, pp. 445–455; also M. Shaki, "Sasan ke bud?," *Iranshenasi*, vol. 2, no. 1, Spring 1990, pp. 78–80.

6 For a study on the cult of Anahid see M.L. Chaumont, "Le culte de la déesse Anāhitā (Anahit) dans la religion des monarques d'Iran et d'Arménie au Ier siècle de notre ère," *Journal Asiatique*, Vol. 253, 1965, pp. 168–171; and her "Le culte de Anāhitā à Stakhr et les premiers Sassanides," *Revue de l'Histoire des Religions*, Vol. 153, 1958, pp. 154–175. Tabarī also gives further information, *The History of Al-Tabarī,* translated by C.E. Bosworth, 1999, p. 4.

7 A. Piras, "Mesopotamian Sacred Marriage and Pre-Islamic Iran," *Melammu Symposia IV*, eds. A. Panaino and A. Piras, Milano, 2004, p. 251.

8 V.G. Lukonin, *Tamddun-e Irān-e Sasanī*, translated from Russian into Persian by I. Ridā, Scientific and Cultural Publication Company, Tehran, 1987, pp. 268–269

9 E. Herzfeld, *Iran in the Ancient East*, Hacker Art Books, New York, reprint 1988, p. 309.

10 *Herodian*, Book VI. 2, 2.

11 R.G. Hoyland, *Arabia and the Arabs, From the Bronze Age to the Coming of Islam*, Routledge, London and New York, 2001, pp. 27–28.

12 G. Widengren, "The Establishment of the Sasanian dynasty in the light of new evidence," *La Persia nel Medioevo*, Academia Nazionale dei Lincei, Roma, 1971, pp. 711–782; J. Wiesehöfer, "Ardašīr I," Encyclopaedia Iranica, ed. E. Yarshater, vol. II, 1987, pp. 371–376.

13 Armenia was of course independent of Rome and was able to defeat Ardashir, Dio Cassius, *Dio's Roman History*, Book LXXX, 3, 3.

14 Dio Cassius, *Dio's Roman History*, Book LXXX, 3, p. 483.

15 *Herodian*, Book VI. 2, 4. Roman sources of course make Alexander Severus the victor over Ardashir, Eutropius, *Breviarium*, Book VIII.23, translated with an introduction and commentary by H.W. Bird, Liverpool University Press, 1993.

16 The wars between Ardashir and Alexander are described in *Herodian*, Book VI. and VI.5. For the Persian and Roman wars in this period see E. Winter and B. Dignas, *Rom und das Perserreich, Zwei Weltmächte zwischen Konfrontation und Koexistenz*, Berlin, 2001, pp. 39–40.

17 For a detailed study of the Perso-Roman wars of the third century see, E. Kettenhofen, *Die römisch-persischen Kriege des 3. Jahrhunderts n. Chr. Nach der Inscrift Šāpuhrs I. An der Ka'be-ye Zartošt (ŠKZ)*, Beihefte zum TAVO, Reihe B., Geisteswissenschaften, Nr. 55, Wiesbaden, 1982. In this campaign Shabuhr I, the son of Ardashir was a main actor, p. 19, Winter and Dignas, *ibid.*, p. 40.

18 D.S. Potter, *The Roman Empire at Bay (AD 180–395)*, Routledge, London and New York, 2004, p. 217.

19 For Ardashir's reliefs showing him at the battle of Hormozgan and other reliefs see W. Hinz, *Altiranische Funde und Forschungen*, Walter de Gruyter and Co., Berlin, 1969, pp. 127–134; G. Herrmann, *The Iranian Revival*, Elsevier, Phaidon, 1977, pp. 87–90.

20 G. Gnoli, *The Idea of Iran, an Essay on Its Origin*, Serie Orientale Roma LXII, Rome, 1989.

21 See the "Symposium: Iranian Cultural Identity," published in *Iranian Studies*, vol. 26, nos. 1–2, 1993, pp. 139–168.

22 *Herodian*, Book VI. 2, 2–3; Dio Cassius LXXX 4, 1–2; Zonaras XII, 15.

23 Ph. Gignoux, *Les Quatre inscriptions du mage Kirdīr*, textes et concordances, Association pour l'avancement des études iraniennes, Leuven, 1991, p. 71.

24 M. Alram, "The Beginning of Sasanian Coinage," *Bulletin of the Asia Institute*, vol. 13, 1999, pp. 67–76.

25 For Sasanian coins see R. Göbl, *Sasanidische Numismatik*, Klinkhardt and Biermann, Braunschweig, 1968; M. Alram, *Iranische Personennamenbuch, Nomia Propria Iranica in Nummis*, vol. 4, ed. M. Mayrhofer and R. Schmitt, Vienna, 1986.

26 A. Panaino has emphasized the human character of the Sasanian king and his lack of divine attributes, see "Astral Characters of Kingship in the Sasanian and Byzantine World," *La Persia e Bisanzio*, Accademia Nazionale dei Lincei, Roma, 2004, p. 558.

27 V.A. Livshits, "New Parthian Documents from South Turkemenistan," *Acta Antiqua Academiae Scientiarum Hungaricae*, vol. 25, 1977, p. 176.

28 M. Schwartz, "*Sasm, Sesen, St. Sisinnios, Sesengen Barpharangès, and ... 'Semanglof,'" *Bulletin of the Asia Institute*, vol. 10, 1996, pp. 253–257; *ibid.*, "Sesen: a Durable East Mediterranean God in Iran," *Proceedings of the Third European Conference of Iranian Studies held in Cambridge, 11th to 15th September 1995*, Part 1, Old and Middle Iranian Studies, ed. N. Sims-Williams, Wiesbaden, 1998, Dr. Ludwig Reichert Verlag, pp. 9–13.

29 R.N. Frye, *The History of Ancient Iran*, München, 1983, p. 200.

30 In Shabuhr's inscription at Ka'be-ye Zardosht (ŠKZ 25/20/46), Sasan is called: s's'n ZY MR'HY; *Sāsān ī xwadāy* "Sasan the Lord." While the Middle Persian text *xwadāy* stands for Lord in the political sense, there are instances where it also accompanies Ohrmazd, thus giving the word a spiritual sense. For *xwadāy* see R. Shayegan, "The Evolution of the Concept of Xwadāy 'God'," *Acta Orientalia Academiae Scientiarum Hungaricae*, Vol. 51, Nos. 1–2, 1998, pp. 31–54. The tradition of deification of the ruler/king which became important with Alexander under Egyptian influence may have influenced the Persians as well. See T. Daryaee, "Laghab-e Pahlavī-ye 'čihr az yazdān' va Šāhanšāhī-ye Sasanī," *Nāme-ye Farhangestān*, Vol. 4, No. 4, 2000, pp. 28–32; *ibid.*, "Notes on

Early Sasanian Titulature," *Journal of the Society for Ancient Numismatics*, vol. 21, 2002, pp. 41–44. There is much similarity between the Sasanians and the Seleucids since the latter dynasts represented themselves to their subjects as descended from a god (*theos*) and more importantly god-made-manifest (*epiphanes*), F.E. Peters, *The Harvest of Hellenism, A History of the Near East from Alexander the Great to the Triumph of Christianity*, Barnes and Noble, New York, 1970 (reprint 1996), p. 232; P.O. Skjærvø has made the observation earlier that these ideas were already current during the time of the kings of Persis, "The Joy of the Cup: A Pre-Sasanian Middle Persian Inscription on a Silver Bowl," *Bulletin of the Asia Institute*, vol. 11, 1997, pp.93–104. Also it must be noted that while Ardashir and other early Sasanians called themselves *bay* "god" or "lord," written in the ideographic form *əlh*, in such Middle Persian texts as the *Ayādgār ī Zarērān*, Ohrmazd also bares this title as *ohrmazd bay*. This also suggests the Sasanian belief in their own divinity.

31 T. Daryaee, "Notes on Early Sasanian Titulature," *Journal of the Society for Ancient Numismatics*, vol. 21, 2002, p. 42.

32 A. Gariboldi, "Astral Symbology on Iranian Coinage," *East and West*, vol. 54, 2004, p. 32.

33 According to a later source, when the king died a council would choose the next king and the Chief Priest (Persian *mowbed ī mowbedan*) had to agree with the decision, M. Minovi, *Nāma-ye Tansar*, Tehran, 1352, p. 88; and for the English translation see M. Boyce, *The Letter of Tansar*, Rome, 1968, p. 62.

34 Roman sources are divided as to the cause of death of Gordian. *Oracaula Sibyllina* XIII, 13–20 predicts Gordian's downfall as a betrayal; Aurelius Victor, *liber de Caesaribus* 27, 7–8: 7 states that he was a victim of intrigues of his Praetorian Perfect, Marcus Philippus; Festus, *Breviarium* 22 mentions that Gordian was returning, victorious from his war against the Persians when he was murdered by Philip. For all these sources see M.H. Dodgeon and S.N.C. Lieu, *The Roman Eastern Frontier and the Persian Wars, A Documentary History*, Routledge, London and New York, 1991, pp. 36–45. For details see Kettenhofen, *op. cit.*, p. 31–37.

35 Potter, *op. cit.*, p. 236.

36 Potter, *op. cit.*, p. 236.

37 ŠKZ 5/4/9.

38 Zonaras XII, 19; Evagrius, *Historia Ecclesiastica* V, 7 which talks only about Armenia, see Dodgeon and Lieu, *op. cit.*, pp. 45–46.

39 The concept of lie (*druγ*) is antithetical to the ancient Persian ethics and the idea of order and righteousness (*aša*), see M. Boyce, *Zoroastrianism, Its Antiquity and Constant Vigour*, Columbia Lectures on Iranian Studies, Mazda Publishers, Costa Mesa, California, 1992, pp. 56–57.

40 ŠKZ 12/9/11.

41 ŠKZ 6/4/10. For the campaign see Kettenhofen, *op. cit.*, pp. 38–46.

42 Potter, *op. cit.*, p. 237.

43 In regard to the idea that the Sasanians may have claimed Syria, that is the cities of Carrhae, Edessa and Nisibis by ancestral (Arsacid) rights see Z. Rubin, "The Roman Empire in the Res Gestae Divi Saporis," *Ancient Iran and the Mediterranean World*, ed. E. Dąbrowa, *Electrum* 2, Jagiellonian University Press, Kraków, 1998, pp. 183–185.

44 For the details (including maps) of the campaign and the cities taken by Shabuhr I see Kettenhofen, *op. cit.*, pp. 97–126; ŠKZ 15/11/24–25.

45 For the Perso-Roman wars of the third century see, E. Kettenhofen, *Die römisch-persischen Kriege des 3. Jahrhunderts n. Chr. Nach der Inscrift Šāpuhrs I. An der Ka'be-ye Zartošt (ŠKZ)*, Beihefte zum TAVO, Reihe B., Geisteswissenschaften, Nr. 55, Wiesbaden, 1982.

46 For example Lactantius, *de mortibus persecutorum* 5; Eusebius, *Historia ecclesiastics*, VII, 13, and especially Orosius, *adversus paganos*, see Dodgeon and Lieu, *op. cit.*, pp. 58–65.

47 For the issue of borders and frontiers between Rome and Persia see H. Elton, *Frontiers of the Roman Empire*, Indiana University Press, Bloomington and Indianapolis, 1996, pp. 97–99.

48 Agathangelos, *History of the Armenians*, Translation and Commentary by R.W. Thomson, State University of New York Press, Albany, 1976, p. 35.

49 *The Kephalaia of the Teacher*, ed. I. Gardner, E.J. Brill, Leiden, 1995, 15.28, p. 21.

50 For a list of the functionaries at the Sasanian court in the third century see R.N. Frye, "Notes on the early Sassanian State and Church," *Studi Orientalistici in onore di Giorgio Levi Della Vida*, Rome, 1956, pp. 314–335.

51 Agathias IV, 24, 5.

52 For the role of the priests in the Sasanian period see Sh. Shaked, "Administrative Functions of Priests in the Sasanian Period," *Proceedings of the First European Conference of Iranian Studies*, 1990, pp. 261–273.

53 J.K. Choksy, "A Sasanian Monarch, His Queen, Crown Prince and Deities: The Coinage of Wahram II," *American Journal of Numismatics*, vol. I, 1989, pp. 117–137.

54 A.Sh. Shahbazi, "Studies in Sasanian Prosopography: III Barm-i Dilak: Symbolism of Offering Flowers," *The Art and Archaeology of Ancient Persia*, ed. V. Sarkhosh, *et al.*, I.B.Tauris, London, 1998, pp. 58–66.

55 The only detailed study of the concept of *bazm* and the idea of its significance is that by A.S. Melikian-Chirvani, "The Iranian bazm in Early Persian Sources," *Banquets d'Orient*, ed. R. Gyselen, Res Orientales IV, Bures-sur-Yvette, 1992, pp. 95–120.

56 N. Garsoïan, *The Epic Histories: Buzandaran Patmut'iwnk'*, p. 515; for feasting under Šāpuhr II see Chapter IV.XVI, p. 146.

57 Either a mistake for Cusii, the Kushans, see Dodgeon and Lieu, *op. cit.*, p. 373.

58 *Panegyrici Latini*, III/11, 17, 2, Dodgeon and Lieu, *op. cit.*, p. 112.

59 *Die Chronik von Arbela*, 8,66, ed. P. Kawerau, Peeters, Louvan, 1985.

60 Most sources claim that while Carus was successful, he was struck by lightning. For example see Eutropis, *Breviarium*, IX, 18, 1.
61 Agathias also provides the same title for Wahram III, IV, 24, 6–8.
62 P.O. Skjærvø and H. Humbach, *The Sassanian Inscription of Paikuli*, Wiesbaden, 1983, p. 44 (Parthian: line 18).
63 S. Mori contends that the Paikuli inscription is basically relating the traditional Near Eastern story of how a king achieves supremacy with the aid of the gods in the epic form. He also believes that the early Islamic texts, such as Al-Tabarī are of little use for the history of the Sasanian period, "The narrative structure of the Paikuli Inscription," *Orient*, vol. 30–31, 1995, pp. 182–193. I wonder if then we should again rely solely on the Greco-Roman sources if our historical inscriptions and the Sasanian royal chronicle are of little use for understanding Sasanian history!
64 Paikuli, Skjærvø, *op. cit.*, p. 44: line 18.
65 A.Sh. Shahbazi, "Narse's Relief at Naqš-i Rustam," *Archäologische Mitteilungen aus Iran*, vol. 16, 1983, pp. 255–268.
66 Lactantius, *de mortibus persecutorum*, 9, 6–8 provides an insight into Galerius' invasion via Armenia and his capture of Narseh's belongings, Dodgeon and Lieu, *op. cit.*, p. 125.
67 Petrus Patricuius, *frag. 14, FGH IV*, p. 189, Dodgeon and Lieu, *op. cit.*, p. 133.
68 Buzandaran Patmut'iwnk', *The Epic Histories Attributed to P'awstos Buzand*, translated and Commentary by N.G. Garsoïan, Cambridge, 1989, Epic Histories IV.50,59.
69 Armazd, Anahīt, and Vahagn, who are Ohrmazd, Anahid, and Wahram. This fact demonstrates that the Armenians did not see these deities as specifically Iranian, Agathangelos, pp. 51–53. These deities are also equated with Zeus, Artemis, and Heracles.
70 J.R. Russell, *Zoroastrianism in Armenia*, Harvard Iranian Series, Cambridge, Massachusetts, 1987.
71 Meskewiyeh, 1369; 135.
72 *Šahrestānīhā-i Ērānšahr*, 43, ed. T. Daryaee, Costa Mesa, 2002.
73 R.N. Frye, "The Sasanian System of Walls for Defense," *Studies in Memory of Gaston Wiet*, ed. M. Rosen-Ayalon, Jerusalem, 1977 (reprinted) *Islamic Iran and Central Asia (7th-12th Centuries)*, Variorum Reprints, London, 1979, pp. 8–11; and H. Mahamedi, "Wall as a System of Frontier Defense during the Sasanid Period," *Mēnōg ī Xrad: The Spirit of Wisdom, Essays in Memory of Ahmad Tafazzolī*, ed. T. Daryaee and M. Omidsalar, Mazda Publishers, Costa Mesa, 2004, pp. 156–158.
74 Al-Tabarī, p. 56.
75 R. Hoyland, *op. cit.*, p. 28.
76 Ammianus Marcellinus, Book XVII.5.1.
77 Ammianus Marcellinus XX.7.9.
78 *Die Chronik von Arbela* 1985, 85.

79 Ammianus Marcellinus XVII.5.1.
80 M. Azarnoush, *The Sasanian Manor House at Hājīābād, Iran*, Casa Editrice Le Lettere, Fierenze, 1994, p. 14.
81 Shabuhr II's Persepolis inscription, Ps-I.3, M. Back, *Die Sassanidischen Staatsinschriften*, E.J. Brill, Leiden, 1978, pp. 490–492.
82 Ammianus Marcellinus, XXIII.6.14.
83 Tabarī 1999, 65.
84 N. Schindel, *Sylloge Nummorum Sasanidarum, Shapur II.-Kawad* I, 3/1 and 3/2, Verlag der Österreichischen Akademie der Wissenschaften, Wien, 2004, 26.
85 Ammianus Marcellinus XVIII.9.
86 Libanius, *Selected Orations*, vol. I, translated by A.F. Norman, Cambridge University Press, London 1969 (reprint 2003), xviii.254–255.
87 G.W. Bowersock, *Julian the Apostate*, Harvard University Press, Cambridge, Massachusetts, 1978, pp. 123–124.
88 Libanius xviii.263.
89 Ammianus Marcellinus XXV.3.6 : Libanius xviii.269–270.
90 Eutropius, *Breviarium* X.16.
91 Ammianus Marcellinus XXV.7.13.
92 Ammianus Marcellinus XXV.7.9.
93 For Shabuhr II's wars see Winter and Dignas, *op. cit.*, pp. 51–54; Chronicon Paschale 554.
94 Ammianus Marcellinus xxiii.3.5; xxiv.7.8.
95 Ammianus Marcellinus xxv.7.12.
96 Buzandaran Patmut'iwnk', Epic Histories V.vii.
97 Epic Histories IV.lv.
98 Epic Histories IV.lviii.
99 Ammianus Marcellinus xxvii.12.15.
100 Garsoïan 1997; 90–91.
101 Epic Histories IV.xliv.
102 Garsoïan 1997; 91.
103 R.N. Frye, "Iran under the Sasanians," *The Cambridge History of Iran*, vol. 3(1), ed. E. Yarshater, Cambridge University Press, Massachusetts, 1983, p. 132.
104 M. Back, *op. cit.*, pp. 490–491.
105 The building of Kermānšah associated with Wahram IV, Nöldeke, *op. cit.*, p. 102, ff. 2.
106 Tabarī has Ardashir II killing many of the grandees and the nobility; Shabuhr III is killed by the same noble families (Arabic *ahl al-buyūtāt*), and Wahram IV is killed by an unnamed group, Nöldeke, *op. cit.*, pp. 100–103, which was probably the court and nobility or the army.
107 Tabarī, pp. 68–69.
108 Nöldeke, *op. cit.*, p. 103, ff.1.
109 For Maruthas' mission to Persia and Yazdgerd's killing of some Zoroastrian priests see Socrates Scholasticus, Chapter VIII.7.9.

110 Labourt, *Le Christianisme dans l'empire perse*, pp. 87–109; Asmussen, "Christians in Iran," *The Cambridge History of Iran*, ed. E. Yarshater, Vol. 3(2), 1983, pp. 940.

111 Agathias Scholasticus, *The Histories*, Book IV.26.8. For the treatment of the Sasanians by Agathias see A. Cameron, "Agathias on the Sassanians," *Dumberton Oaks Papers*, vol. 22–23, 1969–1970, pp. 126–127.

112 B. Gheiby, *Ayādgār ī Zarērān*, Pahlavi Literature Series, Nemudar Publication, Bielefeld, 1999, p. 21(64); for its occurrance in the Dēnkard (DkM, 600.12) see M. Shaki, "Observations on the Ayādgār ī Zarrēn," *Archiv Orientální*, vol. 54, 1986, p. 265.

113 Procopius, I.ii.1–10.

114 Cyril of Scythopolis Vit. Euthym 10 (18.5–19.9) in G. Greatrex and S.N.C. Lieu, *The Roman Eastern Frontier and the Persian Wars*, Part II (AD 363–630), Routledge, London and New York, 2002, p. 37.

115 Conf. Peroz (AMS IV.258–259); Socrates Scholasticus *HE* VII.18 (363.2–365.24), Greatrex and Lieu, pp. 38–39.

116 Nöldeke, *op. cit.*, p. 136.

117 *Zand ī Wahman Yasn: A Zoroastrian Apocalypse*, edited and translated by C. Cereti, Istituto Italiano per il medio ed Estremo Oriente, 1995, p. 152.

118 Priscus, frg. 41.1.1–3–27, Greatrex and Lieu, *op. cit.*, p. 57.

119 For the inscription of Mihr-Narseh see, Back, *op. cit.*, p. 498; L. Bier, "Notes on Mihr Narseh's Bridge near Firuzabad," *Archäologische Mitteilungen aus Iran*, Vol. 19, 1986, 263–268; for Mihr-Narseh's commitment to Zoroastrianism and service to fire-temples, namely those of Ardāwahišt and Abzōn-Ardashir see *Madigān ī Hazār Dādestān*, edited and translated by A. Perikhanian, *The Book of a Thousand Judgments*, Mazda Publishers, Costa Mesa, 1997, A39.11–17; A40.3–5.

120 Elishē, *History of Vardan and the Armenian War*, Translated and Commentary by Robert W. Thomson, Harvard University Press, Cambridge, Massachusetts, 1982, pp. 77–80. *The History of Łazar P'arpets'i* also covers these events, translated and commentary by Robert W. Thomson, Occasional Papers and Proceedings. Columbia University, Program in Armenian Studies, Georgia, 1991.

121 Elishē, pp. 178–179.

122 T. Daryaee, "National History or Keyanid History? The Nature of Sasanid Zoroastrian Historiography," *Iranian Studies*, vol. 28, nos. 3–4, 1995, pp. 129–141.

123 *The Chronicle of Pseudo-Joshua the Stylite*, translated with note and introduction by F. Trombley and J.W. Watt, Liverpool University, Press, 2000, pp. 9–10.

124 T. Daryaee, "Ardašīr Mowbed-e Mowbedān: Yek Tashih dar Matn-e Bundahiš," *Iranshenasi*, 2001, pp. 145–146.

125 For the fifth century relations see Winter and Dignas, op. cit., pp. 54–57; *The Chronicle of Joshua the Stylite*, p. 9–10.

126 Łazar P'arpets'i, 136.
127 Sebeos reports that seven of Peroz's sons were killed with him, Chapter 8.67, p. 5.
128 For Peroz's campaign in the east see Procopius, *History of the Wars*, Book I.i–iv.
129 Nöldeke, *op. cit.*, p. 151, ff. 1.
130 For a detailed study of the administrative seals and the functionaries see R. Gyselen, *La geographie administrative de l'Empire sassanides*, Paris, 1989.
131 Procopius, *History of the Wars*, Book I.v.1–2. Also Agathias, *The Histories*, "He was even reputed to have made a law that wives should be held in common," Book 4.7, p. 130.
132 H. Gaube in his essay has suggested that Mazdak was a fictional character, "Mazdak: Historical Reality or Invention?," *Studia Iranica*, vol. 11, 1982, pp. 111–122.
133 P. Crone, "Kavād's Heresy and Mazdak's Revolt," *Iran*, vol. 29, 1992, p. 30. On an ostracon found at Erk-kala from Turkmenia it is written: "He gave a doubtful oath, but a *mowbed* should not tell lies, and he died ..." A.B. Nititin, "Middle Persian Ostraca from South Turkmenistan," *East and West*, vol. 42, no. 1, 1992, pp. 105–106.
134 Agathias, *The Histories*, Book 4.28, p. 131.
135 M.J. Kister, "Al-Hīra, some notes on its relations with Arabia," *Arabica*, vol. xi, 1967, pp. 143–169.
136 M. Shaki, "An Appraisal of Encyclopaedia Iranica, vols. II and III,"*Archiv Orientálni*, Vol. 59, p. 406; and a review of the evidence T. Daryaee, "Modafe' Darvīšān va Dāvar dar Zamān-e Sasanīān," *Tafazzolī Memorial Volume*, ed. A. Ashraf Sadeghi, Sokhan Publishers, Tehran, 2001, pp. 179–188.
137 F. Gurnet, "Deux notes à propos du monnayage de Khusro II," *Revue belge de Numismatique*, 140, 1994, p. 36–37.
138 Z. Rubin, "The Reforms of Khusrō Anūshirwān," in *The Byzantine and Early Islamic Near East, States, Resources and Armies*, vol. III, ed. A. Cameron, Princeton, 1995, pp. 227–296.
139 Sebeos, Chapter 9.70, p. 10.
140 Procopius, 1.7.1.
141 Zachariah of Mytilene. *HE* VII.3 (22.15–22), Greatrex and Lieu, *op. cit.*, p. 63.
142 Theophanes A.M. 5996 (145.24–146.15), Greatrex and Lieu, *op. cit.*, p. 67.
143 Procopius, I.14.34–55, Greatrex and Lieu, *op. cit.*, pp. 89–91.
144 J.C. Wilkinson, "The Julanda of Oman," *The Journal of Oman Studies*, vol. I, 1975, pp. 98–99.
145 E.H. Schafer, "Iranian Merchants in T'ang Dynasty Tales," *University of California Publications in Semitic Philology*, vol. 11, 1951, pp. 403–422.
146 For information on Kāwūs and his discontent with Khusro's attempt to seize the throne see Z. Mara'šī, *Tārīkh-e Tabarestān va Rōyān va Māzandarān*,

ed. B. Dorn, *Geschicte von Tabristan, Rujan und Masanderan*, St. Petersburg, 1850, reprint Gostareh Publishers, Tehran, 1363, pp. 201–206.

147 *Shahnameh*, translated by R. Levy, p. 321.

148 *Shahnameh*, p. 321.

149 For the function of the *dehgāns* see A. Tafazzolī, *Sasanian Society*, Bibliotheca Persica Press, New York, 2000, pp. 38–58.

150 R.N. Frye, "The Sasanian System of Walls for Defense," *Studies in Memory of Gaston Wiet*, Jerusalem, 1977, pp. 7–15.

151 T. Daryaee, "Mind, Body, and the Cosmos: The Game of Chess and Backgammon in Ancient Persia," *Iranian Studies*, vol. 34, no. 4, 2001, pp. 218–312.

152 Agathias actually portrays Khusro's encounter with the philosophers quite negatively, *The Histories*, Book 2.3.

153 On the Persian military tactics and capabilities see *Maurice's Strategikon*, Handbook of Byzantine Military Strategy, translated by G.T. Dennis, University of Pennsylvania Press, Philadelphia, 1984, pp. 113–115. Also for the Iranian material see A. Tafazzolī, "Un chapitre du Dēnkard sur les guerriers," *Au carrefour des religions: Mélanges offerts á Philippe Gignoux*, Res Orientales VII, Peeters, Leuven, 1995, pp. 297–302. An old but useful treatment of Persian military tactics is by K. Inostrantsev, *Motal'ātī dar-bare-ye Sasanīān*, BTNK, Tehran, 1348, pp.49–89.

154 Greatrex and Lieu, *op. cit.*, pp. 96–97.

155 Procopius, II.2–3.

156 Malalas 18.87 (405.65–479.23–480.5), and other notices Greatrex and Lieu, *op. cit.*, pp. 103–107.

157 Theophanes (of Byzantium) 1 (*FHG* IV.270), Greatrex and Lieu, *op. cit.*, pp. 135–136.

158 Theophanes (Byzantium) 4 (FHG IV.271), Greatrex and Lieu, *op. cit.*, p. 150.

159 For the sixth century relations see Winter and Dignas, *op. cit.*, pp. 57–65.

160 These coins may be his and not that of Khusro II if we are to accept *Bundahišn*'s account, bestowing these titles to Khusro I.

161 Theophylact Simocatta, Book iii.17.1

162 Sebeos, Chapter 10.73, p. 14.

163 Theophylact Simocatta, Book iv.1.1.

164 Theophylact Simocatta, Book iv.9–10.

165 Theophylact Simocatta, Book iv.12.8. For a different version of the content of the letter sent by Khusro to Maurice see Sebeos, Chapter 11.76, pp. 18–19.

166 It is known that he has coins with the year 6, but Paruck states that he had also seen a year 10 coin which may be correct, since every time Khusro II defeated his enemies, changes took place on his coins, see T. Daryaee, "Religio-Political Propaganda on the Coins of Xusro II," *American Journal of Numismatics*, vol. 7, 1997, 141–154

167 *Narratio de rebus Armeniae*, 109–13 (p. 41), Greatrex and Lieu, *op. cit.*, pp. 186–187.

168 M. Morony, "Syria Under the Persians 610–629," *Proceedings of the Second Symposium on the History of Bilād al-Shām During the Early Islamic Period up to 40 AH/640 AD*, ed. M.A. Bakhit, Amman, 1987, pp. 87–95.

169 R. Altheim-Stiehl, "The Sasanians in Egypt – Some Evidence of Historical Interest," *Bulletin de la société d'archéologie Copte*, vol. 31, 1992, p. 87, 92; on the papyrological evidence see E. Venetis, "The Sassanid Occupation of Egypt (7th Cent. AD) According to Some Pahlavi Papyri Abstracts," *Greco-Arabica*, vols. 9–10, 2004, pp. 403–412.

170 Antiochus Strategos, in F.C. Conybeare, "Antiochus Strategos' Account of the Sack of Jerusalem in AD 614," in *English Historical Review*, vol. 25, 1910, pp. 502–517. Also see *Chronicon Paschale*, for the events of 614, p. 156.

171 For events in Byzantinum see A.N. Stratos, *Byzantium in the Seventh Century*, vol. I, Amsterdam, 1968.

172 Theophanes A.M. 6114, 307.19–308.25; Movsēs Daskhuranst'i II.10 (130.3–132.5), Greatrex and Lieu, *op. cit.*, pp. 200–2003, and for other sources see N. Garsoïan, "Byzantium and the Sasanians," *The Cambridge History of Iran*, ed. E. Yarshater, Vol. 3(1), Cambridge University Press, 1983, p. 592.

173 J.M. Fiey, "The Last Byzantine Campaign into Persia and Its Influence on the Attitude of the Local Populations Towards the Muslim Conquerors 7–16 H./628 AD," *Proceedings of the Second Symposium on the History of Bilād al-Shām During the Early Islamic Period up to 40 AH/640 AD*, ed. M.A. Bakhit, Amman, 1987, p. 97.

174 Some sources state that Khusro II had fallen ill in Ctesiphon and was dying, Theophanes A.M. 6118 (325.10–327.16), Greatrex and Lieu, *op. cit.*, p. 223.

175 For the latest study see A. Soudavar, *The Aura of the Kings: Legitimacy and Divine Sanction in Iranian Kingship*, Mazda Publishers, Costa Mesa, 2003.

176 There are illusions to his opulence in the a short Middle Persian text, *Māh Frawardīn Rōz ī Hordād*, passage 27, translated by S. Kiyā, where eighteen amazing things were beheld by Khusro.

177 According to Sebeos, Chapter 46.149, p. 115 after the capture of Jerusalem, Khusro assembled the Christian bishops in his court and presided over their disputation.

178 Sebeos, Chapter 13.85, p. 29.

179 For a treatment of Kavad II and his career see H.M. Malek, "The Coinage of the Sasanian King Kavād II (AD 628)," *The Numismatic Chronicle*, vol. 155, 1995, pp. 119–129.

180 *Chronicon anyonymum ad a.d. 1234 pertinens*, 100, Greatrex and Lieu, *op. cit.*, p. 225.

181 *Chronicon 724*, 147.18–24, Greatrex and Lieu, *op. cit.*, p. 226.

182 Sebeos, Chapter 40.129, p. 88.

183 *Chronicle of Seert*, 93, PO 13.556, Greatrex and Lieu, *op. cit.*, p. 227.

184 H.M. Malek and V. Sarkhos Curtis, "History and Coinage of the Sasanian Queen Bōrān (AD 629–631)," *The Numismatic Chronicle*, vol. 158, 1998, p. 113–129.

185 T. Daryaee, "The Coinage of Queen Bōrān and its Significance in Sasanian Imperial Ideology," *Bulletin of the Asia Institute*, vol. 13, 1999, pp. 77–83.

186 For a detailed study of Queen Bōrān see H. Emrani, *The Political Life of Queen Bōrān: Her Rise to Power and Factors that Legitimized her Rule*, MA Thesis, California State University, Fullerton, 2005.

187 For the seventh century relations see Winter and Dignas, *op. cit.*, pp. 67–71; *The Khuzistan Chronicle*, 29, Greatrex and Lieu, *op. cit.*, p. 237.

188 For this period in Sasanian history see, T. Daryaee, *Fall of the Sasanian Empire and the end of Late Antiquity: Continuity and Change in the Province of Persis*, PhD Thesis, UCLA, 1999.

189 For the importance of the *dehqāns* in the late Sasanian and early Islamic period see, A. Tafazzolī, *Sasanian Society*, Ehsan Yarshater Distinguished Lecture Series, Bibliotheca Persica Press, New York, 2000, pp. 38–58.

190 For a chronology of events and rulers see T. Daryaee, *Soghūt-e Sasanīān (The Fall of Sasanians)*, Nashr-e Tarīkh-e Irān, 2004, pp. 59–79.

191 Sebeos, Chapter 42.136, p. 98.

192 J. Harmatta, "The middle Persian-Chinese Bilingual Inscription from Hsian and the Chinese-Sasanian Relations," *La Persia nel Medioevo*, Accademia Nazionale dei Lincei, Roma, 1971, p. 374.

193 A. Forte, "On the Identity of Aluohan (616–710) A Persian Aristocrat at the Chinese Court," *La Persia e l'Asia Centrale da Alessandro al X secolo*, Accademia Nazionale dei Lincei, Roma, 1996, p. 190.

194 C. Guocan, "Tang Qianling shirenxiang ji qi xianming de yanjiu," *Wenwu jikan*, vol. 2, 1980, p. 1988; Forte, *ibid.*, p. 191.

195 The classical work on Chinese-Persian relations in this period is that of B. Laufer, *Sino-Iranica: Chinese Contributions to the History of Civilization in Ancient Iran, with Special Reference to the History of Cultivated Plants and Products*, Field Museum of Natural History, Publication 201, Anthropological Series, vol. 15, no. 3, Chicago, 1919; also see E.H. Schafer, *The Golden Peaches of Samarkand, A Study of T'ang Exotics*, University of California Press, 1963, pp. 10–25; For a more general treatment see J. Gernet, *A History of Chinese Civilization*, Cambridge University Press, 1982, pp. 282–287. The latest work is by M. Compareti, "The Last Sasanians in China," *Eurasian Studies*, vol. II, no. 2, 2003, pp. 197–213.

196 C.G. Cereti, "Again on Wahram ī Warzāwand," *La Persia e l'Asia Centrale da Alessandro al X secolo*, Accademia Nazionale dei Lincei, Roma, 1996, pp. 629–639.

197 Harmatta, *ibid.*, p. 375; Forte, *op. cit.*, pp. 193–194.
198 C.E. Bosworth, "The Heritage of Rulership in Early Islamic Iran and the Search for Dynastic Connections with the Past," *Iranian Studies*, vol. xi, 1978, pp. 7–34.

CHAPTER 2: THE SOCIETY OF *IRANSHAHR*

1 A. Bausani, *I Persiani*, Florence, 1962.
2 For the city building program of the Sasanians see N.V. Pigulevskaïa, *Les villes de l'état iranien aux époques parthe et sassanide*, Paris, 1963.
3 G. Gnoli, *The Idea of Iran: An Essay on its Origin*, Istituto Italiao per il Medio ed Estremo Oriente, Rome, 1989, p. 148.
4 *Ibid.*, p. 131.
5 S.N.C. Lieu, "Captives, Refugees, and Exiles: A Study of Cross-Frontier Civilian Movements and Contacts between Rome and Persia from Valerian to Jovian," *The Defense of the Roman and Byzantine East, Proceedings of a colloquium held at the University of Sheffield in April 1986*, ed. P. Freeman and D. Kennedy, part ii, British Institute of Archaeology at Ankara, Monograph No. 8, BAR International Series 297, 1986, pp. 473–508.
6 Ibn Balxī, *Fārsnāme*, ed. Le Strange and Nicholson, Cambridge University Press, 1921, p.168.
7 See C. Cereti, *Zand ī Wahman Yasn, A Zoroastrian Apocalypse*, Istituto Italiano per il Medio ed Estremo Oriente, Rome 1995, 7.9 and commentary, p. 206.
8 A. de Jong, "Sub Specie Maiestatis: Reflections on Sasanian Court Rituals," *Zoroastrian Ritual in Context*, ed. M. Stausberg, Brill, Leiden, 2004, p. 356.
9 *Ibid.*, p. 358.
10 F.M. Kotwal and Ph.G. Kreyenbroek with contributions by J.R. Russell, *The Hērbedestān and Nērangestān*, vol. I, II, Studia Iranica – Cahier 10, Paris, 1992–95. See also Modi, 335 ff.
11 R. Gyselen, "Note de glyptique sassanide les cachets personnels de l'ohrmazd-mogbed," *Études irano-aryennes offertes á Gilbert Lazard*, ed. C.-H de Fouchécour and Ph.Gignoux, Association pour l'avancement des études iraniennes, Paris, 1989, p .186.
12 Ph. Kreyenbroek, "On the Concept of Spiritual Authority in Zoroastrianism," *Jerusalem Studies in Arabic and Islam*, vol. 17, 1994, pp. 1–15.
13 The *Šāyest nē-Šāyest* states that whenever a *zarduxšttom* dies abroad a heretic is born, Chapter IX, p. 111, edited and translated by K. Mazdāpour, Cultural Studies and Research Institute, Tehran, 1369.
14 *Šāyest Nē-Šāyest*, p. 95.
15 *Šāyest Nē-Šāyest*, p. 181.

16 *Mēnō-ye Xrad*, chapter 30, edited and translated by A. Tafazzolī, Tus Publishers, Tehran, 1364, p. 48.
17 A.B. Nikitin, "Middle Persian Ostraca from South Turkmenistan," *East and West*, vol. 42, no. 1, 1992, pp. 105–107.
18 *Husraw ud Rēdag*, passage 9, see D. Monchi-Zadeh, "Khusrov ut Rētak," *Monumentum Georg Morgenstierne*, vol. II, E.J. Brill, 1982, p. 64.
19 In a short text named *Gizistag Abāliš*, one day the main character of the text is hungry and thirsty and goes to a fire-temple (*ātaxš-kādag*) to receive help and to perform his prayer, H.F. Chacha, *Gajastak Abalish*, Bombay, 1936.
20 Sh. Shaked, *Wisdom of the Sasanian Sages*, 1979
21 M. Shaki, "The Filet of Nobility," *Bulletin of the Asia Institute*, vol. 4.
22 For a review of the material in regard to asceticism in the Zoroastrian tradition see T. Daryaee, "Sasanian Persia," *Iranian Studies*, 1998, pp. 444–445.
23 *Mēnōg ī Xrad*, chapter 58, p. 77.
24 A. Tafazzolī "Un chapitre du Dēnkard sur les guerriers," *Au carrefour des religions: Mélanges offerts á Philippe Gignoux*, Res Orientales VII, Peeters, Leuven, 1995, pp. 297–302.
25 Al-Tabarī, 1999, pp. 262.
26 Al-Tabarī, 1999, pp. 262–263. Shahbazi has noted that by comparing the list of weapons in al-Tabarī and that of the Wīdēwdād 14.9 we can see that this text may have gone through changes in the Sasanian period, since the list is very similar, Sh. A. Shahbazi, "Army," *Encyclopaedia Iranica*, vol. II, 1987, p. 497.
27 Shahbazi, *ibid.*, p. 497. See Procopius
28 Ammianus Mercelinus, 25.1.14, Shahbazi, *ibid.*, p. 497.
29 Al-Tabarī, 1999, p. 36.
30 Al-Tabarī, 1999, p. 118.
31 Maurice's Strategicon, also K. Inostrantsev, "Fūnūn-e jangī-ye sāsānī," in *Motale'atī darbāre-ye sāsānīyān (Etudes sassanides)*, Tehran, 1348, pp. 49–89.
32 V.F. Piacentini, "Ardashīr ī Pāpakān and the wars against the Arabs: Working hypothesis on the Sasanian hold of the Gulf," *Proceedings of the Seminar for Arabian Studies*, vol. 15, 1985, pp. 57–85.
33 Al-Tabari, 1999, p. 240.
34 Ibn Hišam, *Sīrat rasūl Allāh*, translated by A. Guillaume, Karachi, 1955, pp. 41–43.
35 A. Tafazzolī, "A List of Trades and Crafts in the Sasanian Period," *Archaeologische Mitteilungen aus Iran*, vol. 7, 1974, pp. 191–196. *Dēnkard VIII* supplies a short section of navigation which is supposed to have been part of the eighteenth Nask of the lost Avesta (Sakātom). See Ch. A'zamī-Sansari, "Sanadī az ayyīn-e nāvbarī dar asr-e sāsānī," Mehr o dād o bahār, ed. A.K. Balazadeh, Tehran, 1377, pp. 33–37.

36 M. Grignaschi, "Quelques specimens de la litterature sassanide conserves dans les bibliotheques d'Istanbul," *Journal Asiatique*, 1966, p. 1ff. p. 24, p. 42n. 76; Shahbazi, *Encyclopaedia* p. 498.
37 Al-Tabarī, pp. 96–97.
38 *Mēnō-ye Xrad*, Chapter 30, p. 48.
39 M. Shaki, "Class System III. In the Parthian and Sasanian Period," *Encyclopaedia Iranica*, p. 654.
40 *Mēnō-ye Xrad*, Chapter 31, pp. 48–49.
41 In the Islamic sources which are based on royal documents, the warriors were sometimes placed above the priests, see Miskawayhi, *Tajarib al-Umam* (Experience of Nations), edited and translated into Persian by A. Emami, Soroush Press, Tehran, 1980, p. 120.
42 R. Foltz, "When Was Central Asia Zoroastrian?," *The Mankind Quarterly*, Vol. XXXVIII, No. 3, 1998, pp. 189–200.
43 R.N. Frye, "The Fate of Zoroastrians in Eastern Iran," *Au Carrefour des Réligions: Mélanges offerts à Philippe Gignoux*, ed. R. Gyselen, Peeters, Leuven, 1995, pp. 67–68.
44 *Madīyān ī Hazār Dādestān*, pt. 1, p.3. M. Shaki, "Class System III. In the Parthian and Sasanian Period," *Encyclopaedia Iranica*, p. 654.
45 *Husraw ud Rēdag*, passage 62, pp. 76–77.
46 *Husraw ud Rēdag*, passage 62, pp. 76–77.
47 For cooking see J. Amouzegār, "Cooking," *Encyclopaedia Iranica* and her further comments in Persian "Namūnah-hā'ī az honar-e khwalīgarī dar farhang-e kohan-e Irān," Kelk, vols. 85–88, April-July 1997, pp. 162–166. The mention of *xwahlīgar* also appears in the Middle Persian text *Sūr Āfrīn*, passage 18.
48 *Husraw ud Rēdag*, passage 63, p. 77.
49 V. Sarkhosh Curtis, "Minstrels in Ancient Iran," *The Art and Archaeology of Ancient Persia, New Light on the Parthian and Sasanian Empires*, eds. V. Sarkhosh Curtis, *et al.*, I.B.Tauris Publishers, London and New York, 1998, pp. 182–187.
50 *Bundahišn*, Chapter IX, Bahār's edition, Tūs Publication, Tehran, xxxx under the sub-heading "On the Manner of Voices," p. 93.
51 For the Manichaean material see Ch.J. Brunner, "Liturgical Chant and Hymnody among the Manicheans of Central Asia," *Zeitschrift der Deutschen Morgenländischen Gesellschaft*, vol. 130, no. 2, 1980, pp. 342–368.
52 A. de Jong, *Ibid.*, p. 358.
53 *Husraw ud Rēdag*, passage 58, p. 75.
54 Ph. Gignoux, "Matériaux pour une histoire du vin dans l'iran ancien," *Matériaux pour l'histoire économique du monde iranien*, ed. R. Gyselen and M. Szuppe, Paris, 1999, pp. 43–44.
55 Ph. Gignoux
56 D.N. MacKenzie, "Shapur's Shooting," *Bulletin of the School of Oriental and African Studies*, vol. 41, 1978, pp. 499–511.

57 A. Sh. Shahbazi, "Studies in Sasanian Prosopography: III Barm-i Dilak: Symbolism of Offering Flowers," *The Art and Archaeology of Ancient Persia*, ed. V.S. Curtis et. al, I.B.Tauris, 1998, pp. 58–66.
58 For these titles under their heading in *Encyclopaedia Iranica* see, T. Daryaee, "Sasanian Persia," *Iranian Studies*, 1998, pp. 453–456.
59 A. Tafazzoli, *Sasanian Society*, Bibliotheca Persica Press, New York, 2000, pp. 21–22.
60 Tafazzoli, *ibid.*, p. 30.
61 Tafazzoli, *ibid.*, p. 23 and 29.
62 *Handarz ī Adurbād ī Mahrspandān*, passage 58 and 129; Tafazzoli, *ibid.*, p. 27.
63 *Husraw ud Rēdag*, passage 10, p. 64.
64 *Abar Ēwēbag Nāmag Nibēsišnīh*, pp. 141–143.
65 For the latest edition of these letters see D. Weber, *Ostraca, Papyri und Pergamente*, Corpus Inscriptionum Iranicarum, Part III Pahlavi Inscriptions, London, 1992.
66 Tafazzoli, *op. cit.*, pp. 31–33.
67 Tafazzoli, *op. cit.*, p. 33.
68 *Mādayān ī Hazār Dādestān*, pt. 2, p. 34; Shaki, "Documents," p. 459.
69 M. Shaki, "Documents," p. 459.
70 *Mādayān ī Hazār Dādestān*, pt. 2, p. 38; Shaki, "Documents," p. 459.
71 M. Shaki, "Commerce iii," *Encyclopaedia Iranica*,
72 *Mādayān ī Hazār Dādestān*, pt. 1, p. 78.
73 *Mādayān ī Hazār Dādestān*, pt. 2, p. 13; Shaki, "Documents," p. 459.
74 Tafazzoli, p. 34.
75 R.N. Frye, "The Persepolis Middle Persian Inscriptions from the time of Shapur II," *Acta Orientalia*, vol. xxx, 1966, p. 84; Back, *op. cit.*, p.
76 G. Le Strange, *The Lands of the Eastern Caliphate*, Barnes and Noble, New York, 1966, p. 203.
77 The Classic work on Christians of the Sasanian empire is now J.M. Fiey, *Communautés syriaques en Iran et Irak des origines à 1532*, London, 1979.
78 R. Gyselen, *La Géographie administrative de l'empire Sassanide, Les témoignages sigillographiques*, Res Orientales I, E. Peeters, Leuven, 1989, p. 72.
79 For a collection of stories see S. Brock and S. Harvey, "Persian Martyrs," *Holy Women of the Syrian Orient*, 1998, pp. 67.
80 A. Forte, "Edict of 638 Allowing the Diffusion of Christianity in China," in P. Pelliot, *L'Inscription nestorienne de Si-Ngan-Fou*, edited with Supplements by A. Forte, Scuola di Studi sull'Asia Orientale, Kyoto and Collège de France, Institut des Hautes Éudes Chionises, Paris, 1996, pp. 353–355 and pp. 361–362.
81 T. Daryaee, "Dīdgāhhā-ye mowbedān va šāhanšāhī-ye Sāsānī darbare-ye Iranšahr," *Nāme-ye Irān-e Bāstān, The International Journal of Ancient Iranian Studies*, vol. 3, no. 2, 2003–2004, pp. 19–28.
82 For the study of concept of driyōšīh see G. Itō, "From the Dēnkard," *Monumentum H.S. Nyberg*, vol. I, E.J. Brill, Leiden, 1975, pp. 423–434.

83 Ardā Wirāz Nāmag; 41.16; for a perliminary treatment of the poor see; Shaki, "Darwish," *Encyclopaedia Iranica*; and T. Daryaee, "Modāfe' darwišān wa dāvar," *Taffazoli Memorial Volume*, Tehran, 1380, pp. 179–189.
84 M. Shaki, "Class System iii. Parthian and Sasanian Period," *Encyclopaedia Iranica*, p. 73.
85 Sh. Shaked, *Dēnkard*, pp. 58–59.
86 The Pahlavi Texts, ed. J. Asana, p. 71; Shaki, "Drīst-Dēnān," *Ma'ārif*, p. 29.
87 *Pahlavi Vendidad*, 3.41; *Ardā Wirāz Nāmag*, 33.19. (See also *Dēnkard* Madan II.723 and West translation, p. 78.)
88 Shaki, Mazdak, ff.142.
89 For the influence of this institution on the *Waqf*, see M. Macuch, "Sasanidische Institutionen in früh-Islamischer Zeit," *Transtion Periods in Iranian History*, L'association pour l'avancement des études iraniennes, Paris, pp. 178–179.
90 See *Gizistag Abāliš*, Question 3.
91 M. Macuch, "Barda and Bardadārī ii," *Encyclopaedia Iranica*; M. Shaki, "Class System," *Encyclopaedia Iranica*, www.iranica.com
92 For a good introduction to women in the Sasanian period see J. Rose, "Three Queens, Two Wives, and a Goddess: Roles and Images of Women in Sasanian Iran," *Women in the Medival Islamic World*, ed. G. Hambly, 1998, pp. 29–54.
93 A. de Jong, "Women and ritual in Medieval Zoroastrianism," *Ātaš-e Dorun (The Fire Within), J.A. Sourushian Memorial Volume*, ed. C. Cereti, 2003, p. 147.
94 *Ibid.*, p. 150.
95 A. de Jong, "Jeh the Primal Whore? Observations on Zoroastrian Misogyny," *Female Stereotypes in Religious Traditions*, eds. R. Kloppenborg and W.J. Hanegraaff, Studies in the History of Religions, vol. 66, Leiden, 1995, pp. 15–41.
96 Bahār, pp. 83–84.
97 Note the modern Persian idiom, "*bē sar o pā*," meaning "without head-cover and foot cover."
98 *Ardā Wirāz Nāmag*, 45.2–4, p. 213.
99 Until recently there were small huts which exist in Kermān in Zoroastrian villages which suggest the existence of *dašt~nest~n.*
100 For references see M. Shaki, "Drīst-Dēnān," *Ma'ārif*, pp. 42–43.
101 M. Shaki, "Sasanian Matrimonial Relations," *Archív Orientalní*, vol. 39, 1971, pp. 322–345.
102 *Mādayān ī Hazār Dādestān*, p. 105; Shaki, p. 445.
103 M. Shaki, "The Concept of Obligated Successorship in the Mādiyān ī Hazār Dādestān," *Hommages et Opera Minor Monumentum H.S. Nyberg*, Acta Iranica, vol. ii, E.J. Brill, Leiden, 1975, p. 229.
104 *Riwāyat ī Ēmēd ī Ašawahištān*, Chapter 7; *Sad-dar Nasr*, Chapter 92.

105 *The Pahlavi Rivāyat of Ādurfarnbag*, Chapter 14.

106 M. Shaki, "Pahlavica," *A Green Leaf: Papers in Honour of Prof. J. Asmussen*, Acta Iranica 28, Leiden, 1988, pp. 96–98; *ibid.*, "Family Law," *Encyclopaedia Iranica*, vol. IX, Bibliotheca Persica, New York, 1999, p. 185.

107 *Rivāyat ī Ēmēd ī Ašawahištān*, Chapter 30; Shaki, *ibid.*, "Family Law," p. 185.

108 Shaki, *op. cit.*, "Divorce," p. 445.

109 Shaki, *op. cit.*, "Divorce," p. 444.

110 *Mādyān ī Hazār Dādestān*; pt. 1, p. 33; M. Shaki, "The Sasanian Matrimonial Relations," *Archiv Orientalni*, vol. 39, 1971, p. 337; Shaki, *op. cit.*, "Family Law," p. 187.

111 *Mādyān ī Hazār Dādestān*, pt. 1, p. 73; *Nērangestān*, fol. 7r) Shaki, *op. cit.*, "Family Law," p. 188.

112 *Rivāyat ī Ēmēd ī Ašawahīštān*, Chapter 42; *Mādayān ī Hazār Dādestān*, pt. 1, p. 73 *Šāyest nē-Šāyest*, I, p. 2); Shaki, "Family Law," p. 189.

113 *Nērangestān*, fol. 6v; Shaki, *op. cit.*, "Family Law," p. 189.

114 *Husraw ud Rēdag*, passage 96, pp. 81–82.

115 *Andarz ī Anōšag Ruwān Ādūrbād ī Maharsapandān*, passage 50.

116 *Andarz ī Anōšag Ruwān Ādūrbād ī Maharsapandān*, passage 111.

117 *Fragments*, passage 9, p. 249.

118 *Handarz ī Anōšag Ruwān Ādurbād Mārspandān*, passage 11.

119 *Fragment*, p. 11, p.290.

120 *Wāžag ē-Čand ī Ādurbād ī Mārspandān*, passage 48.

121 *Handarz ī Anōšag Ruwān Ādurbād Mārspandān*, passage 152.

122 *Mēno-ye Xrad*, chapter 7, p. 22.

123 The relevant texts have been collected in Persian by B. Gheybi, "Došnā-e Zardosht," *Khorde Maqālāt*, Part 5, No. 38, pp. 335–353.

124 With some modifications see Sanjana, *The Dēnkard*, edited and translated by D.P. Sanjana, vol. xvi, Kegan Paul, trench, Trubner and Co., London, 1917, p. 30. Modern Parsi commentators also have considered the more ambiguous attestations of sodomy as concerning homosexual activity.

125 *Ardā Wirāz Nāmag*, Text p. 24, p. 202.

126 *Ardā Wirāz Nāmag*, Text p. 44, p. 213.

127 For a collection of texts and discussion of homosexuality see B. Gheiby, "Došnām-e Zardosht," *Khorde Maqālāt*, Part 5, No. 38, Nemudar Publications, Bielefeld, 2000, pp. 335–353.

128 See E.W. West, "The meaning of Khvētūk-das," *Pahlavi Texts*, Part II, Oxford University Press, 1882, pp. 389–430. Contra see D.P. Sanjana, Sanjana, D.P. "The Alleged Practice of Consanguineous Marriages in Ancient Iran," *The Collected Works of the Late Dastur Darab Peshotan Sanjana*, British India Press, Bombay, 1932, pp. 462–499.

129 J.P. de Menasce, *Le troisième livre du Dēnkart*, Paris, 1973, pp. 85–86. All the evidence for this practice has been assembled by O. Bucci, "Il matrimonio fra consanguinei (khvētūdās) nella tradizione giuridica

delle genti iraniche," *Apollinaris*, vol. 51, 1978, pp. 291–319. Also see the important work by R.N. Frye, "Zoroastrian Incest," *Orientalia Iosephi Tucci Memoriae Dicata*, eds. G. Gnoli and L. Lanciotti, Istituto Italiano per il Medio ed Estremo Oriente, Roma, 1985, pp. 445–455.

130 J. de Menasce, "La conqête de l'iranisme et la récupération des mages hellénisés," *Annuaire de l'École Partique de Hautes Études*, 1956–1957, 7; Gnoli, *op. cit.*, p. 172.

131 *Madīyāh ī Hazār Dādestān*, A15.2, p. 273; Shaki, *op. cit.*, "Family Law," p. 187.

132 *Madīyāh ī Hazār Dādestān*, 73.1–2.

133 *Ayādgār ī Zarlran*, edited and translated into Persian by B. Gheybi, Nemudar Press, Bielefeld, 1999, transctiption p. 9, tranlsation p. 27, Middle Persian text p. 16.

134 R. Kent, *Old Persian Grammar, Text, Lexicon*, American Oriental Society, New Haven, Connecticut, Column III 32.2.70–78, p. 124.

135 P.O. Skjærvø, *The Sasanian Inscription of Paikuli*, passage 58, p. 54.

136 The Zoroastrian priest ruled that bathhouses that were in open air would be better since the sun would cleanse the pollution. Until recently in Yazd this type of bath was also known, K. Mazdapur, "Garmabe-ye bastani-ye Iran (Ancient Iranian Bathhouses)," *Farhang*, vol. 9, no. 3, 1996, p. 319.

137 *RHA*, Question 19, pp. 145–146.

138 H.-P. Schmidt, "The Incorruptibility of the Sinner's Corpse," *Studien zur Indologie und Iranistik*, vol. 19, 1994, pp. 247–268.

139 Sh. Meskūb, *Sōg ī Sīyāwaš*, Khwārazmī Publishers, Tehran, 1350 (Dēnkard XXXIII.11 p. 27.

140 *Tārīx-e Buxārā*, p. 28.

141 *Athār al-Baghīya*, E. Sachau, 235, pp. 10–11.

142 Ancient Art from the Shumei Collection, The Metropolitan Museum of Art, 1996, pp. 142–143. For further comments see J. Lerner, "Central Asians in Sixth-Century China: A Zoroastrian Funerary Rite," *Iranica Antiqua*, Vol. 30, 1995, pp. 179–190.

143 J. K. Choksy, *Purity and Pollution in Zoroastrianism: Triumph Over Evil*, Texas University Press, Austin, 1989.

CHAPTER 3: RELIGIONS OF THE EMPIRE: ZOROASTRIANS, MANICHAEANS, JEWS AND CHRISTIANS

1 It may be possible to see the royal insignia of the Sasanians which is shown on their coins and other places on a coin of Autophradates I, which suggests a connection or borrowing. See D. Sellwood, "Minor States in Southern Iran," *The Cambridge History of Iran*, ed. E. Yarshater, vol. 3(1), pp. 299–321; see plate 10, pict. 5.

2 M. Back, *Die Sassanidischen Staatsinschriften*, Acta Iranica 18, E.J. Brill, Leiden, 1978, p. 281.

3 M. Shaki, "The Dēnkard Account of the History of the Zoroastrian Scriptures," *Archív Orientalní*, vol. 49, 1981, p. 115.

4 For contemporary material relating Ardashir promoting Zoroastrianism see M. Walburg, *Die fruehen sasanidischen Koenige als Vertreter un Foerderer der zarathustrischen religion*, Frankfurt-Bern, 1982.

5 *Nāme-ye Tansar*, ed. M. Minovi, Kharazmi Publishers, Tehran, 1311; M. Boyce, *The Letter of Tansar*, Rome, 1965.

6 S. Adhami, "A Question of Legitimacy: The Case of Ardašir I (Dēnkard IV)," *Indo-Iranian Journal*, vol. 46, 2003, pp. 226–227.

7 For points of tension between the Zoroastrian Church and the Sasanian State see Ph. Gignoux, "Church-State Relations in the Sasanian Period," *Monarchies and Socio-Religious Traditions in the Ancient Near East*, ed. H.I.H Prince T. Mikasa, Wiesbaden, 1984, pp. 72–80.

8 M. Macuch, "The Talmudic Expression "Servant of the Fire" in the Light of Pahlavi Legal Sources," *Jerusalem Studies in Arabic and Islam*, vol. 26, 2002, p. 125.

9 A. Hintze, "The Avesta in the Parthian Period," in *Das Partherreich und seine Zeugnisse*, Franz Steiner Verlag Stuttgart, 1998, pp. 157–158.

10 The Cult of Mithra/Mihr in Persia was also popular, most probably as a mystery cult which is mentioned in textual and iconographic sources. For the cult itself see C. Colpe, "Mithra-Verehrung, Mithras-Kult und die Existenz iranischer Myserien," *Mithraic Studies*, vol. II, Manchester, 1975, pp. 378–405. For convincing argument in regard to the existence of the cult of Mithra/Mihr see P. Callieri, "On the Diffusion of Mithra Images in Saanian Iran: New Evidence from a Seal in the British Museum," *East and West*, vol. 40, nos. 1–4, 1990, pp. 88–89.

11 For this interrelation see A. Henrichs, "Mani and the Babylonian Baptists: A Historical Confrontation," pp. 23–59.

12 For the text and translation see, D.N. MacKenzie, "Mani's Shabuhragān," *Bulletin of the School of Oriental and African Studies*, 1979, pp. 500–534; "Mani's Shabuhragān II," *Bulletin of the School of Oriental and African Studies*, 1979, pp. 288–310.

13 For the English reader one can find translations of many texts and fragments of the Manichaean religion in specific categories in Klimkite, *The Silk Road*.

14 J. Neusner, "How Much Iranian in Jewish Babylonia?," *Journal of the American Oriental Society*, vol. 95, no. 2, 1975, p. 189.

15 B. Sarkārāti, "Akhbār-e Tārīkhī dar Āthār ī Mānavī: Mānī wa Šāpūr," *Sāyehā-ye Šekār Šode*, Našr Qatre, Tehran, 1378, p. 185.

16 B. Sarkārāti, "Akhbār-e Tārīkhī dar Āthār ī Mānavī: Mānī wa Bahrām," *Sāyehā-ye Šekār Šode*, Našr Qatre, Tehran, 1378, p. 204.

17 "W.B. Henning, "Mani's Last Journey," *Bulletin of the School of Oriental and African Studies*, vol. x, part 4, 1942, pp. 948–949.

18 W.B. Henning, "Mani's Last Journey," *Bulletin of the School of Oriental and African Studies*, vol. x, part 4, 1942, pp. 946–950; Sarkārāti, *ibid.*, pp. 206–207.

19 For the subject of Persian interest in biography which was very much a characteristic of the Persian historical tradition see A. Momigliano, "Persian Historiography, Greek Historiography, and Jewish Historiography," *The Classical Foundations of Modern Historiography*, University of California Press, Berkeley, Los Angeles, London, 1990, pp. 5–28.

20 For a challenge to this old view and a fresh look at the state of Zoroastrianism in the Sasanian period see Sh. Shaked, *Dualism in Transformation: Varieties of Religion in Sasanian Iran,* Jordan Lectures in Comparative Religion, School of Oriental and African Studies, University of London, 1994; and a critical response by M. Boyce, "On the Orthodoxy of Sasanian Zoroastrianism," *Bulletin of the School of Oriental and African Studies*, vol. lix, part 1, 1996, pp. 11–28.

21 Ph. Huyse, "Kerdir and the first Sasanians," *Proceedings of the Third European Conference of Iranian Studies*, ed. N. Sims-Williams, Part 1, Dr. Ludwig Reichert Verlag, Wiesbaden, 1998, p. 118.

22 D.N. MacKenzie, *The Sasanian Rock Reliefs at Naqsh-i Rustam*, Iranische Denkmäler, 1989, paragraph 17, p. 59.

23 For a review of literature on this word see W. Sundermann who interprets the word as magi-codex see, "Review of H. Humbach and P.O. Skjærvø, The Sassanian Inscription of Paikuli," *Kratylos, Kritisches Berichts und Rezensionsorgan für Indogermanische und Allgemeine Sprachwissenschaft*, vol. 28, 1993 [1994], p. 88.

24 The best translation of this difficult passage in the *Dēnkard* is by M. Shaki, "The Dēnkard Account of the History of the Zoroastrian Scriptures," *Archiv Orientalni*, vol. 49, 1981, pp. 114–125.

25 KZ 9–10, Back, pp. 414–415.

26 T.D. Barnes, "Constantine and the Christians of Persia," *The Journal of Roman Studies*, vol. lxxv, 1985, pp. 131–132.

27 S.P. Brock, "Christians in the Sasanian Empire: A Case of Divided Loyalties," *Studies in Church History*, vol. 18, 1982, p. 8.

28 For Shabuhr I's incursion into Syria and its effect on the Christianization of Ērānšahr and the persecution of the Christians in the fourth century see the conclusions reached by M.L. Chaumont, *La Christianisation de l'empire iranien des origins aux grandes persecutions du IVe siècle*, Peeters, Louven, 1988, pp. 157–160.

29 *Šahrestānīhā ī Ērānšahr*, passages 10, 47.

30 J. Neusner, "Jews in Iran," *The Cambridge History of Iran*, vol. 3(2), ed. E. Yarshater, Cambridge University Press, 1983, p. 915.

31 S. Munk, *Notice sur Rabbi Saadia Gaon et sa version arabe d'saïe et sur une version persane manuscrite de la Bibliothèque Royale*, Paris, 1838; Sh. Shaked, "Middle Persian Translations of the Bible," *Encyclopaedia Iranica*, vol. iv, Routledge and Kegan Paul, London and New York, 1990, p. 207.

32 Shaked, *ibid.*, p. 206.
33 M. Rostovtzeff, *Drua Europos and its Art*, Clarendon Press, Oxford, 1938, pp. 112–113.
34 Neusner, *op. cit.*, p. 890.
35 N. Sims-Williams, "Sogdian Translations of the Bible," *Encyclopaedia Iranica*, vol. iv, Routledge and Kegan Paul, New York and London, 1990, p. 207.
36 A. Netzer, "Some Notes on the Characterization of Cyrus the Great in the Jewish and Judeo-Persian Writings," *Acta Iranica, Hommage Universel*, E.J. Brill, 1974, p. 35.
37 J. P. Asmussen, "Judeo-Persian Translations of the Bible," *Encyclopaedia Iranica*, vol. iv, Routledge and Kegan Paul, New York and London, 1990, p. 268.
38 For an excellent study of Kerdir's journey see P.O. Skjærvø, "Kirdir's Vision: Translation and Analysis," *Archaeologische Mitteilungen aus Iran*, vol. 16, 1983, pp. 269–306.
39 F. Grenet, "Pour une nouvelle visite à la "vision de Kerdir,"" *Studia Asiatica*, vol. 3, no. 1–2, 2002, p. 6.
40 Grenet, p. 18.
41 M. Schwartz, "Kerdir's Clairvoyants: Extra-Iranian and Gathic Persepectives," p. 6. I would like to thank M. Schwartz for giving me the unpublished manuscript.
42 F. Vahman, *Ardā Wiraz Nāmag, The Iranian 'Divina Commedia'*," Curzon Press, London and Malmo, 1986, p. 85.
43 *Zand ī Wahman Yasn*, edited and translated by M.T. Rashid Mohassel, Tehran, 1370, p. 2; Carlo Cereti, *Zand ī Wahman Yasn*, Rome, 1995, 3.6.
44 S.H. Nyberg, *Religionen des Alten Iran*, Osnabrück, Otto Zeller, 1966. In the preface to the 1966 edition of the book, Nyberg discusses the Nazi reaction to his work in 1939, especially W. Wüst, in *Archiv für Religionswissenschaft*, vol. xxxvi, 1939–1940, pp. 248–249. At that time he was denounced by an array of people, from Nazi Orientalists to W.B. Henning, the great Middle Iranian scholar who had fled Nazi Germany. For a study of the various reactions see J.R. Russell, "Kartīr and Mānī: a shamanistic model of their conflict," *Iranica Varia: Papers in honor of Professor Ehsan Yarshater*, E.J. Brill, Leiden, 1990, pp. 180–193. For a recent survey of this type of journey in Iran see, Ph. Gignoux, "'Corps osseux et ême osseuse': essai sur le chamanisme dans l'Iran ancient," *Journal Asiatique*, vol. 267, 1979, pp. 41–79.
45 An excellent article dealing with this issue is that of W. Hinz, "*Mani and Kardēr*," *La Persia nel Medievo*, Accademia Nazionale dei Lincei, Roma, 1971, pp. 485–499; also P.O. Skjærvø, "Iranian Elements in Manichaeism," *Au Carrefour des Religions. Mélanges offerts à Philippe Gignoux*, Res Orientales VII, 1995, pp. 263–284.
46 Paikuli, pargraph 19, p. 35.

47 *Čīdag ī Andarz ī Pōryōtkēšān*, passage IX.

48 On this concept see Sh. Shaked, "From Iran to Islam: Notes on Some Themes in Transmission," *Jerusalem Studies in Arabic and Islam*, vol. 4, 1984, pp. 39–40. Similar notions are present in the Persian literature, for example see *Nāme-ye Tansar*, p. 53; *Šāhnāme*, Moscow Edition, vol. viii, lns. 558–561.

49 The Classical work on Zurvan is by R.C. Zaehner's *Zurvan, A Zoroastrian Dilemma*, Biblio and Tannen, New York, 1955 (reprint 1972).

50 Sh. Shaked, "The Myth of Zurvan: Cosmogony and Eschatology," *Messiah and Christos, Studies in the Jewish Origins of Christianity Presented to David Flusser on the Occasion of His Seventy-Fifth Birthday*, ed. I. Gruenwald, *et al.*, J.C.B. Mohr (Paul Siebeck), Tübingen, 1992, pp. 229–240.

51 Ammianus Marcellinus, XVII. 5,1f.

52 H. Scharfe, "Sacred Kingship, Warlords, and Nobility," in *Ritual, State and History in South India, Essays in Honour of J.C. Heesterman*, ed. A.W. Van den Hoek, *et. al.*, E.J. Brill, Leiden, New York, Cologne, p. 312.

53 M. Shaki, "The Dēnkard Account of the History of the Zoroastrian Scriptures," *Archív Orientálni*, vol. 49, 1981, pp. 117–119.

54 M. Shaki, "Some Basic Tenets of the Eclectic Metaphysics of the Dēnkart," *Archív Orientálni*, vol. 38, 1970, pp. 277–312.

55 Sh. Shaked, "First Man, First King, Notes on Semitic-Iranian Syncretism and Iranian Mythological Transformations," *Gilgul, Essays on Transformation, Revolution and Permanence in the History of Religions Dedicated to R.J. Zwi Werblowsky*, eds. Sh. Shaked, *et. al.*, E.J. Brill, Leiden, 1987, pp. 238–256; T. Daryaee, "The Sect of Gayomartiya," *J.A. Sourushian Memorial Volume*, ed. C. Cereti, (forthcoming 2000); Daryaee, "Clay king or Mountain king," *Hanns-Peter Schmidt Festshcrift*, ed. S. Adhami, Mazda Publishers, 2003, pp. 339–349.

56 Shaked, *ibid.*, pp. 246–247, although I would assign more influence to the early Islamic period, still Jewish influence should not be denied.

57 Shaki, Dēnkard Account, 1981, p. 117–119.

58 *Ardā Wiraz Nā*mag, Edited and Translated by F. Vahman, Curzon Press, London and Malmo, 1986, text, p. 79, translation, p. 191.

59 *The Supplementary Texts to the Šāyest nē-Šāyest*, edited and translated by F.M.P. Kotwal, Kobenhavn, 1969, XIII.17, pp. 46–47.

60 *Šāyest nē Šāyest*, Cultural and Research Institute, Tehran, 1990, edited and translated by K. Mazdapour, chapter 15.16–17. It is curious then that when it came to hell, the Zoroastrian tradition holds it to be dark, cold and full of stench, where no one burns.

61 M. Boyce, "On Mithra, Lord of Fire," Monumentum H.S. Nyberg, vol. I, E.J. Brill, Leiden, 1975, pp. 71–72.

62 M. Schwartz, "Saugand Xurdan, 'To take an oath' not *'to drink sulpher'," *Études irano-aryennes offertes à Gilbert Lazard*, ed. C.-H. de Fouchécour and Ph. Gignoux, Paris, 1989, pp. 293–296.

63 Sh. Shaked, "Esoteric Trends in Zoroastrianism," *Proceedings of the Israel Academy of Sciences and Humanities*, vol. 3, 1969, pp. 175–222. Others have objected that there is nothing esoteric or mystic in the Zoroastrian religion, but one may argue with the definition of esotericism and mysticism and what it meant, as James Russell argues, being part of every religion, "On Mysticism and Esotericism among the Zoroastrians," *Iranian Studies*, vol. 26, nos. 1–2, 1993, pp. 73–74. If Wīrāz partakes in the drinking of the drink which gives him visions into the netherworld, or Kerdir is able to do this by going through the proper initiation to see the gods and heaven and hell, one would be hard pressed to deny any esoteric or mystical trends in Zoroastrianism. Probably only the very righteous and exemplary Zoroastrians were given the opportunity to make this journey.

64 M. Shaki, "The Social Doctrine of Mazdak in the Light of Middle Persian Evidence," *Archív Orientální*, vol. 46, 1978, p. 306.

65 P. Crone, "Kawād's Heresy and Mazdak's Revolt", *Iran*, vol 29, 1991, p. 25.

66 *Wāzag-ē Čand ī Adurbād ī Māraspandān*, passage 6.

67 A. Bausani, "Two Unsuccessful Prophets: Mani and Mazdak," *Religion in Iran. From Zoroaster to Baha'ullah*, Bibliotheca Persica Press, New York, 2000, p. 101.

68 M. Shaki, "Drist-Dēnān," *Ma'ārif*, for the best general study of Mazdak and the history of his movement see E. Yarshater, "Mazdakism," *The Cambridge History of Iran*, vol. III (2), Cambridge, Massachusets, 1983, pp. 991–1024; also see P. Crone, "Kavad's Heresy and Mazdak's Revolt," Iran, vol. 29, 1991, pp. 21–42; M. Morony, "Mazdak," *The Encylcopaedia of Islam*, vol. vi, 1991, pp. 449–452.

69 Dēnkard III 653–654 as translated by Shaki, "The Social Doctrine of Mazdak," pp. 294–295.

70 *Ibid.*, p. 295.

71 *Ibid.*, p. 298.

72 *Ibid.*, 299.

73 *Wāzag-ē Čand ī Adurbād ī Māraspandān*, passage 13.

74 M. Shaki, "The Cosmological and Cosmological Teachings of Mazdak," *Papers in Honour of Professor Mary Boyce*, Acta Iranica 25, E.J. Brill, Leiden, 1985, pp. 527–543.

75 Shaki, "Social Doctrine," *op. cit.*, p. 297.

76 M. Shaki, "A Signal Catalogue of Sasanian Seals and Bullae," *Archív Orientální*, vol. 57, 1989, pp. 167–168; T. Daryaee, "Modafe' Darvīšān va Dādvar," Yādnāme-ye Doktor Ahmad-e Tafazzolī, Sokhan Publishers, 1379, pp. 179–188.

77 M. Macuch, "Sasanidische Institutionen in früh-Islamischer Zeit," *Transition Periods in Iranian History*, L'Association pour l'avancement de études iraniennes, Paris, 1987, pp. 178–179; Macuch, "Charitable Foundations. i. In the Sasanian Period," *Encyclopaedia Iranica*, 1991, pp. 380–382.

78 *Zand ī Wahman Yasn*, edited and translated by C. Cereti, chapter II, pp. 133–134, p. 150.

79 Shaki, "The Dēnkard Account," pp. 118–121.

80 T. Daryaee, "Sasanian Persia," *Iranian Studies*, vol. 31, no. 3–4, 1998, p. 442.

81 For the three schools of thought or legal schools see, K. Mazdapur, "Chāštehā, Se Nahle-ye Feghhī dar Rōzegār-e Sasanī," *Yād-e Bahār*, Tehran, 1376, pp. 383–412.

82 See the comments by Mazdāpur in *Šāyest nē Šāyest, A Pahlawī Text*, 1990, p. 86.

83 Mazdāpur, *ibid.*, p. 93; *Bundahiš*, edited and translated by M. Bahār, Tūs Publishers, 1369, p. 134; Pahlavi Vendidad, Fragard I.15.

84 As to the possibility of a hierarchy, such as the pope and the archbishops, Kreyenbroeck has shown that it may be quite unlikely that a rigid system existed, "On the Concept of Spiritual Authority in Zoroastrianism," *Jerusalem Studies in Arabic and Islam*, vol. 17, 1994, pp. 1–15. I tend to think that indeed there was not a hierarchy as a whole, but rather each group had their own teacher and leader, like Mazdak, Sēn, and the priests at Ray whose leader was called the "great priest."

85 M.M. Malayeri, *Farhang-e Iranī-ye Pēš az Islam wa Asar-e ān dar Tamaddun-e Islāmī wa Adabīyāt-e Arabī*, Tus Publishers, Tehran, 1374, p. 52; Arabic texts mention other centers of priestly activity and theological disscussion in the Islamic period, such as the *Qla'ye jas* located at Arrajan, i.e. Weh-az-amid-kawad, at the eastern border of Persis, *ibid.*, p. 54.

86 B.T. Anklesaria, *Pahlavi Vendidād*, Bombay, 1949, chapter I.15.

87 M. Molé, "Le Problème des sectes Zoroastriennes dans les livres Pehlevis," *Oriens*, vol. 13–14, 1960–1961, pp. 12–14.

88 Sh. Shaked, *Dualism in Transformation, Varieties of Religion in Sasanian Iran*, Jordan Lectures 1991, School of Oriental and African Studies, University of London, 1994, p. 97.

89 T. Daryaee, "Apocalypse Now: Zoroastrian Reflections on the Early Islamic Centuries," *Medieval Encounters*, vol. 4, no. 3, 1998, pp. 188–202.

90 *Andarz ī Dānāgān ō Māzdēsnān*, passage 2.

91 *Wāzag-ē Čand ī Adurbād ī Māraspandān*, passage 72.

92 *Husraw ud Rēdag*, passage 9.

93 R. Gyselen, *Sceaux magiques en Iran sassanide*, Studia Iranica, cahier 17, Paris, 1995.

94 K.E. Kanga, "King Faridun and a Few of His Amulets and Charms," *K.R. Cama Memorial Volume, Essays on Iranian Subjects in Honor of Mr. Kharshedji Rustamji Cama On the Occasion of his seventieth birth-day*, ed. J.J. Modi, Bombay, Fort Printing Press, Bombay, 1900, pp. 141–145.

95 E. Pirart, *Kayān Yasn, l'origine avestique des dynasties mythiques d'Iran*, Barcelona, Editorial Ausa, 1992, p. 7.

96 M. Molé, *La légende de Zoroastre*, Paris, 1967; J. Amuzegar and A. Tafazzolī, *Osture-ye Zendegī-ye Zartošt*, Našr Āvīšan, Tehran, 1372, pp. 55–110.

97 *Dēnkard VII*, vii.36.
98 P. Callieri, "In the Land of the Magi. Demons and Magic in the Everyday Life of Pre-Islamic Iran," *Démons et merveilles d'orient*, ed. R. Gyselen, Res Orientales XIII, Peeters, Leuven, 2001. p. 24.
99 J. Naveh and Sh. Shaked, *Amulets and Magic Bowls, Aramaic Incantations of Late Antiquity*, The Magnes Press, The Hebrew University, Jerusalem, 1998, p. 13; M. Morony, "Magic and Society in Late Sasanian Iraq," presented at a symposium on *Prayer, Magic, and the Stars in the Ancient and Late Antique World*, March 3–5, 2000 at the University of Washington, Seattle. I should like to thank Professor Morony for giving me an unpublished draft of the article.
100 For seal amulets and their Mediterranean and Near Eastern influence on the Sasanian period see, M. Magistro, "Alcuni Aspetti della Glittica Sacro-Magica Sasanide: Il 'Cavaliere Nimbato,'" *Studia Iranica*, vol. 29, 2000, pp. 167–194.
101 M. Bahār, *op. cit.*, pp. 120–121.
102 For a complete list of demons in the Zoroastrian tradition see A. Christensen, *Essai sur la démonolgie iranienne*, DVS, Historisk-filologiske meddeleleser, XXVIII/1, København, 1941.
103 P.O. Skjærvø, "A Seal-Amulet of the Sasanian Era: Imagery and Topology, the Inscription, and Technical Comments," *Bulletin of the Asia Institute*, vol. 6, p. 50.
104 Sh. Shaked, "The Pahlavi Amulet and Sasanian Courts of Law," *Bulletin of the Asia Institute*, vol. 7, p. 166.
105 *Dēnkard VII*, translated by W. E. West, in Pahlavi Texts, part V, Motilal Banarsidass Publishers, Delhi, 1897 (reprint 1994), chapter I.12.
106 *Ibid.*, IV.36.
107 *Ibid.*, IV.42.
108 *Ibid.*, IV.45. What is interesting here is that their bodies are buried and this would bring pollution to the earth which is a sin in the Zoroastrian religion. The passage, however, goes on to tell us that demons were not to be present in the bodily form.
109 *Tārīkh-e Bukhāra*, p. 28.
110 *Ancient Art from the Shumei Family Collection*, The Metropolitan Museum of Art, New York, 1996, P. 144.
111 A. Bērūnī, *Athār al-Baghiya*, ed. E. Sachau, Leipzig, 1878, p. 235.

CHAPTER 4: LANGUAGES AND TEXTUAL REMAINS OF THE CITIZENS

1 For a survey of Fahlavīyāt and Bābā-Tāher's poetry see, *Bābā-Tāher-Nāme*, ed. P. Azkā'ī, Tūs Publishers, Tehran, 1375.
2 *Zabān-e Fārsī dar Āzarbāyejān*, ed. I. Afshar, Tehran, 1368.

3 The late Y.M. Nawabī who was a native of the region has done much work on Shirazi Persian, see his *Opera Minora*, ed. M. Tavoossi, Navid Publications, Shiraz, 1998.

4 *Qur'an-e Quds*, ed. A. Ravāghī, 2 vols., Tehran, 1377.

5 P. O. Skjærvø, "Thematic and linguistic parallels in the Achaemenian and Sassanian inscriptions," *Papers in Honour of Professor Mary Boyce*, Acta Iranica 25, E.J. Brill, Leiden, 1985, pp. 593–603; P. Huyse, "Noch einmal zu Parallelen zwischen Achaemeniden-und Sāsanideninschriften," *AMI*, vol. 23, 1990, pp. 177–183.

6 S. Mori, "The Narrative Structure of the Paikuli Inscription," *Orient*, vol. xxx–xxxi, 1995, pp. 182–193. Skjærvø does not deny the total historicity of these inscriptions but still holds the same view as Mori in that here we have the terms of the presentation of the material, "conflation of epic tales and historical accounts," *ibid.*, "Royalty in Early Iranian Literature," *Proceedings of the Third European Conference of Iranian Studies*, Part 1, Old and Middle Iranian Studies, ed. N. Sims-Williams, Dr. Ludwig Reichert Verlag, Wiesbaden, 1998, p. 106.

7 As translted by R.N. Frye, *The History of Ancient Iran*, appendix 4, p. 372.

8 D.N. MacKenzie, "Shapur's Shooting," *The Bulletin of the School of Oriental and Africa Studies*, vol. 41, 1978, p. 503; R. Bašāš Kanzaq, "Katibe-ye Hājjīābād dar Arse-ye Tārīkh wa Ostūre," Zabān, *Katibe wa Motūn-e Kohan*, Sāzmān-e Mirath-e Farhangī, 1375, pp. 43–56.

9 P.O. Skjærvø, p. 54.

10 *Ibid.*, p. 66.

11 For the latest work on the knowledge of the Sasanians about the Achaemenids see A. Sh. Shahbazi, "Early Sasanians' Claim to Achaemenid Heritage," *Nāme-ye Irān-e Bāstān, The International Journal of Ancient Iranian Studies*, vol. 1, no. 1, 2001, pp. 61–74.

12 W.B. Henning, "The Inscription of Firuzabad," *Asia Major*, vol. 4, 1954, p. 101.

13 F. de Blois, "The Middle Persian Inscription from Constantinople: Sasanian or Post-Sasanian," *Studia Iranica*, vol. 19, 1990, pp. 20–16.

14 E.W. West, "The Pahlavi Inscriptions at Kanheri," *Indian Antiquary*, 1880, pp. 265–268.

15 J. Harmatta, "The middle Persian-Chinese Bilingual Inscription from Hsian and the Chinese-Sāsānian Relations," *La Persia nel Medioevo*, Roma, 1971, pp. 363–376.

16 For a complete list see A. Tafazzolī, *Tārīx-e Adabiyāt-e Irān Pēš az Islām*, *Soxan* Publishers, 1376, pp. 102–104.

17 O. Hansen, *Die mittelpersischen Papyri*, Abh. PAW, Berlin, 1938; D. Weber, *Ostraca, Papyri und Pergamente*, Corpus Inscriptionum Iranicarum, London, 1992; E. Venetis, "The Sasanian occupation of Egypt (7th cent. AD) according to some Pahlavi papyri abstracts," *Graeco-Arabica*, vol. 9, 2001 (forthcoming).

18 For a survey of Middle Persian literature see E. West, "Pahlavi Literature," *Grundriss der Iranischen Philologie*, II/2, pp. 75–129 J.C. Tavadia, *Die mittelpersiche Sprache und Literature der Zarathustrier*, Leipzig, 1956; M. Boyce, "Middle Persian Literature," *Handbuch der Orientalistik, Iranistik*, Literatur, Lieferung 1, E.J. Brill, Leiden/Cologne, 1968, pp. 32–66; A. Tafazzolī, *Tārīx-e Adabiyāt-e Irān Pēš az Islām*, Soxan Publishers, 1376; C.G. Cereti, *La letteratura Pahlavi. Introduzione ai testi con riferimenti alla storia degli studi e alla tradizione manoscritta*, Mimesis, Milan, 2001.

19 B. Utas, "Non-Religious Book Pahlavi Literature as a Source on the History of Central Asia," *Studies in the Sources on the History of Pre-Islamic Central Asia*, ed. J. Harmatta, Akadémiai Kiadó, Budapest, 1979, pp. 119–128.

20 The latest translation is in Persian by the late M. Bahār, *Bundahiš-e Farnbag-e Dādagī*, Tūs Publishers, Tehran, 1369. For the English version see B.T. Anklesaria, *Zand-Ākāsīh, Iranian or Greater Bundahišn*, Bombay 1956. One should note that the Indian version of this text has some ommissions and additions which are interesting in terms of animal classification and ethnography, see R. Behzādī, *Bundahiš-e Hindī*, Tehran, 1368.

21 The only complete translation exists in English by D.D.P. Sanjana, *The Dēnkard*, Kegan Paul, Trench, Trübner and Co., London, 1916.

22 For a survey of literature and content on the Dēnkard see, Ph. Gignoux, "La composition du Dēnkard et le contenu du livre V," *Tafazzoli Memorial Volume*, ed. A.A. Sadeghi, Sokhan Publishers, Tehran, 2001, pp. 29–38.

23 J. de Menasce, *Le Troisième Livre du Dēnkard*, Travaux de l'Institut d'Etudes Iraniennes de l'Université de Paris III no. 5, Paris, 1973.

24 *Dēnkard*, Madan edition 470.7; Similar notions are present in the Persian literature. For example see *Nāme-ye Tansar*, p. 53; *Šāhnāme*, Moscow Edition, vol. viii, lns. 558–561.

25 E.W. West *Pahlavi Texts*, Part V, Oxford University Press, 1892 (reprint by Motilal Banarsidass Publishers, Delhi, 1994); J. Amuzegār and A. Tafazzolī, *Dēnkard V*, Cahiers de Studia Iranica, Peeters, Luven, 2001.

26 Sh. Shaked, *Wisdom of the Sasanian Sages*, Caravan Press, Boulder, Colorado, 1979.

27 M. Molé, *La Légende de Zoroastre selon les textes pehlevis*, Paris, 1967; and J. Āmuzegār and A. Tafazzolī, *Ostūre-ye Zendegī-ye Zartošt*, Tehran, 1376.

28 For Books eight and nine, see E.W. West, *Pahlavi Texts*, Part IV, Oxford University Press, 1892 (reprint by Motilal Banarsidass Publishers, Delhi, 1994).

29 M.T. Rashid, *Gozīdehāye Zāsdpram*, Mohassel, Tehran, 1366; Ph. Gignoux and A. Tafazzolī, *Anthologie de Zādspram*, Studia Iranica, Cahier 13, Paris, 1993.

30 E.W. West and A. Tafazzolī, *Mēnō-ye Xrad*, Tus Publishers, Tehran, 1364.

31 Tafazzoli, *Adabīyāt*, pp. 153–155.

32 M. Navābī, *Manzūme-ye Draxt-e Āsūrīk*, Tehran, 1346; C.J. Brunner, "The Fable of the Babylonian Tree," *Journal of Near Eastern Studies*, vol. xxxix, 1980, pp. 191–202; 291–302.

33 J.P. de Menasce, *Škand-Gumānīk Vičār*, Fribourg-Suisse, 1945.

34 H.F. *Chacha, Gajastak Abalish*, Bombay, 1936; and in Persian, I.Mirzā-ye Nāzir, *Matīkān ī Gujastak Abālīš*, Hērmand Publishers, Tehran, 1375.

35 F. Vahman, *Ardā Wirāz Nāmag, The Iranian 'Divina Commedia'*, Curzon Press, London and Malmo, 1986.

36 T. Daryaee, "Kerdīr's Naqsh-i Rajab Inscription," *Nāme-ye Irān-e Bāstān, The International Journal of Ancient Iranian Studies*, vol. 1, no. 1, 2001, pp. 3–10.

37 G. Messina, *Ayātkār ī Zāmāspīk*, Roma,1939.

38 Shaked, *Wisdom of the Sasanian Sages*, Caravan Press, Boulder, Colorado, 1979.

39 M. Grignaschi, "Quelques spécimens de la literature sassanide," *Journal Asiatique*, 1966, pp. 16–45.

40 G. Gnoli in many studies has emphasized Sīstān as the location of Zoroaster's ministry, see his two-book length study, *Zoroaster's Time and Homeland*, IsMEO, Napoli, 1980; *idem.*,"Zoroaster in History," Bibliotheca Persica, 2000.

41 T. Daryaee, *Šahrestānīhā ī Ērānšahr*, Mazda Publishers, Costa Mesa, 2002.

42 D. Monchi-Zadeh, *Die Geschichte Zarēr's*, Acta Universitatis Upsaliensis, Uppsala, 1981; and for the Persian translation see, B. Gheiby, *Ayādgār ī Zarērān*, Nemudar Publications, Bielefeld, 1999.

43 E.K. Antia, *Kārnāmak-I Artakhshīr Pāpakān*, Bombay, 1900; S. Hedāyat, *Kārnāme-ye ardašīr ī bābakān*, Amir Kabir Publishers, Tehran, 1332.

44 A. Perikhanian, *The Book of A Thousand Judgment*, Mazda Publishers, Costa Mesa, 2000.

45 J.C. Tavadia, *Šāyest nē-Šāyest, A Pahlavi Text on Religious Customs*, de Gruyter and Com.B.H., Hamburg, 1930. The Persian translation is by K. Mazdapour, *Šāyest nā-Šāyest*, Cultural Studies and Research Institute, Tehran, 1990.

46 A. Panaino, *La Novella Degli Scacchi e Della Tavola Reale*, Mimesis, Milano, 1999; T. Daryaee, "Mind, Body, and the Cosmos: The Game of Chess and Backgammon in Ancient Persia," *Iranian Studies*, 2002, pp. 281–313.

47 J.C. Tavadia, "Sūr Saxvan: Or a Dinner Speech in Middle Persian," *Journal of the K.R. Cama Oriental Institute*, vol. 29, 1935, pp. 1–99.

48 S.H. Nyberg and B. Utas, *Frahang ī Pahlavīk*, Wiesbaden, 1988.

49 H. Jamaspji Asa and M. Haug, *An Old Pahlavi-Pazand Glossary*, Bombay and London, 1870. H. Reichelt, *Der Frahang I Oīm*, WZKM, Wien, 1900.

50 S. Brock and S. Harvey, "Persian Martyrs," *Holy Women of the Syrian Orient*, 1998, pp. 63–99.

51 F.C. Andreas and K. Barr, *Bruchstücke einer Pehlevi-Übersetzung der Psalmen* SPAW, Phil.-hist. Kl., 1933.

52 D.N. MacKenzie, "Mani's Šāburagan," *The Bulletin of the School of Oriental and African Studies*, XLII, 1979, and XLIII, 1980, and in Persian N. Omrānī, *Šāpuragān*, Aštād Publishers, Tehran, 1379.

53 R.L. Khānīkī and R. Bashāš, *Sang Negāre-ye Lāx-Mazār*, Mīrās-e Farhangī, Tehran, 1373.

54 V. Minorsky, "Vīs u Rāmīn, a Parthian Romance," *Bulletin of the School of Oriental and African Studies*, vol. XI, 1946, pp. 741–763; XII, 1947, pp. 20–35; XVI, 1954, pp. 91–92.

55 See the many articles of Henning reprinted in *W.B. Henning – Selected Papers*, Acta Iranica, vols. V and VI, E.J. Brill, Leiden, 1977.

56 M. Boyce, *The Manichaean hymn-cycles in Parthian*, Oxford, 1954, and her *A Reader in Manichaean Middle Persian and Parthian*, Tehran-Liege, Acta Iranica 9, 1975 and for a survey her "The Manicaean Literature in Middle Iranian," *Handbuch der Orientalistik, Iranistik II*, Literature I, Leiden, 1968, pp. 67–76.

57 W. Sundermann, *Mitteliranische manichäisches Texte kirchengeschichtlichen Inhalts*, Berliner Turfantexte XI, Berlin, 1981; *idem., Ein manichäisch-soghdisches Parabelbuch*, 1985; *idem., Der Sermon vom Licht-Nous: eine Lehrschrift des östlichen Manichäismus, Edition der parthischen und soghdischen Version*, 1992; *idem., Der Sermon von der Seele: eine Lehrschrift des östlichen Manichäismus: Edition der parthischen und soghdischen Version*, with an introduction by Peter Zierne, Die türkischen Fragmente des Sermons von der Seele. c1997.

58 W.B. Henning, "Sogdian Tales," *Bulletin of the Schools of Oriental and Africa Stud*ies, vol. XI, 1946, pp. 713–740.

59 M. Schwartz, *Studies in the texts of the Christian Sogdians*, Ph.D. dissertation of the University of California, Berkeley, California, 1967; N. Sims-Williams, *Christian Sogdian MS C2. Sogdian and English. The Christian Sogdian Manuscript C2*, translated and with commentary, Berlin, 1985.

60 D.N. MacKenzie, *The "Sūtra of the Causes and Effects of Actions" in Sogdian*, London, 1970. For a survey of these texts see J. Dresden, "Sogdian Language and Literature," *The Cambridge History of Iran*, vol. 3(2), Cambridge, 1983, pp. 1222–1224.

61 N. Sims-Williams, in "The Sogdian Fragments of the British Library," *The Indo-Iranian Journal*, vol. 18, 1976, pp. 43–82.

62 R.E. Emmerick, *The Book of Zambasta*, London, 1968.

63 H.W. Bailey, *Khotanese Texts*, 6 vols., Cambridge, 1945–1967.

64 E. Benveniste, "Inscriptions de Bactriane," *Journal Asiatique*, 1961, pp. 133–152; I. Gershevitch, "Bactrian Inscriptions and Manuscripts," *Indogermanische Forschungen*, LXXI, 1967, pp. 27–57.

65 N. Sims-William, *Bactrian Documents, Legal and Economic Documents*, vol. I, Oxford University Press, 2000.

66 W.B. Henning, "The Choresmian Documents," *Asia Major*, vol. XI, 1965, pp. 66–79; *ibid.*, *A fragment of a Khwarezmian dictionary*, ed. By D.N. MacKenzie, Tehran University Press, 1971.

67 M. Shaki, "Some Tenants of the Eclectic Metaphysics of the Dēnkard," *Archiv Orientalni*, vol. 38, 1970, pp. 277–312.

68 T. Daryaee, "The Zoroastrian Sect of Gayomartiya," *Arbab Jamsheed Sourushian Memorial Volume*, ed. C. Cereti, 2003, pp.131–137.

69 M. Shaki, "The Dēnkard Account of the History of the Zoroastrian Scriptures," *Archiv Orientální*, 1981, vol. 49, p. 119.

70 *Ibid.*, p. 123. H.W. Bailey, *Zoroastrian Problems in the Ninth-Century Books*, Oxford, 1971, p. 86.

71 *Ibid.*, p. 81.

72 Bailey, *ibid.*, pp. 81–82; 87–92; M. Shaki, "Some Basic Tenents of the Eclectic Metaphysics of the Dēnkart," *Archiv Orientální*, vol. 38, 1970, pp. 277–312.

73 The evidence has been gathered by the impressive work of D. Gutas, *Greek Thought, Arabic Culture, The Graeco-Arabic Translation Movement in Baghdad and Early 'Abbāsid Society (2nd-4th/8th-10th centuries)*, Routledge, New York, 1998, p. 26. Also see the excellent article by J. Walker, "The Limits of Late Antiquity: Philosophy between Rome and Iran," *The Ancient World*, vol. 33, 2002, pp. 45–69.

74 Baiely, *op. cit.*, p. 86.

75 B. Utas, "Chess I. The History of Chess in Persia," *Encyclopaedia Iranica*, ed. E. Yarshater, vol. v, 1992, p. 395.

76 On the board games and their significance for the Sasanian period see, T. Daryaee, "Chess, Backgammon and the Cosmos in Ancient Persia," *Iranian Studies*, vol. 33, 2002, pp. 281–313.

77 F. de Blois, *Burzōy's Voyage to India and the Origin of the Book of Kalīlah wa Dimnah*, London, 1990.

78 *Dāstānh -ye Bīdpāy*, translated by M.b.A. al-Buxārī, ed. by P.N. Xānlarī and M. Rošan, Xārazmī Publishers, Tehran, 1369.

79 D.N. MacKenzie, "Zoroastrian astrology in the Bundahišn," *Bulletin of the School of Oriental and African Studies*, vol. XXVII, part 3, 1964, p. 171f.

80 S. Hedāyat, *Kārnāme-ye ardašīr ī bābakān*, Amir Kabir Publishers, Tehran, 1332, pp. 170–171; S.H. Nyberg, *A Manual of Pahlavi*, Otto Harrasowitz, p. 2.

81 See the Middle Persian text D. Monchi-Zadeh, "Xusrōv ut Rētak," Monumentom Morgenstierne, vol. II, Acta Iranica, vol. 22, pp. 47–91; and more generally see W. Knauth, *Das altiranische Fürstenideal von Xenophon bis Ferdousi*, nach d. antiken u. einheim, Steiner, Wiesbade, 1975.

82 For a list of Middle Persian words used for Syriac, Greek, and Arabic terms see Rezā'ī Bāgh-Bīdī "Sassanian Neologisms and Their Influence on Dari Persian," *Nāme-ye farhangestān*, vol. 15, No. 3, pp. 148–149.

CHAPTER 5: THE ECONOMY AND ADMINISTRATION OF *IRANSHAHR*

1 M. Morony, "Continuity and Change in the Administrative Geography of Late Sasanian and Early Islamic al-'Iraq," *IRAN*, Journal of the British Institute of Persian Studies, vol. XX, 1982, p. 1.

2 R. Gyselen, "Les données de géographie administrative dans le shahrestānīhā-ī Ērān," *Studia Iranica*, tome 17, fasc. 2, 1988, p. 206.

3 R. Gyselen, *La Géographie administrative de l'empire Sassanide, Les témoignages sigillographiques*, Paris, 1989, and also her *Nouveaux matériaux pour la géographie historique de l'empire Sassanide: Sceaux administratifs de la collection Ahmad Saeedi*, Paris, 2002.

4 J. Marquart, *Ērānshahr nach der Geographie des Ps. Moses Xorenac'i*, Weidmannsche Buchhandlung, Berlin, 1901, p. 16.

5 Abu Manṣūr Abd al-Malik ibn Muhammad ibn Isma'il al-Tha'alibi, *Gharar Axbar al-mulâk al-Fars wa Sayrhum*, ed. H. Zotenberg, Paris, 1990, p. 393.

6 Gignoux basically disagrees with this division, "Le Spāhbed des Sassanides," *Jerusalem Studies in Arabic and Islam*, 13, 1990, pp.1–14. Gignoux has now changed his position.

7 G. Kreyenbroek, "The Zoroastrian Priesthood," *Transition Periods in Iranian History*, Actes du symposium de Fribourg-en-Brisgau (22–24 Mai 1985), Istituto Italiano per il Medio ed Estremo Oriente, p. 152.

8 F. Gurnet, "Deux notes á propos du monnayage de Khusro II," *Revue belge de Numismatique*, tome CXL, 1994, pp. 36–37.

9 KR certainly stands for Kermān where it appears on the mint GNCKR, which has been proposed to stand for ganj Kerman "treasury of Kermān," see M.I. Mochiri, Garmikirmān: A Sasanian and Early Islamic Mint in Kirmān Province, *NC*, 145, 1985, pp. 109–122.

10 Gurnet, *op. cit.*, p. 37.

11 G. Ostrogorsky, *History of the Byzantine State*, Rutgers University Press, Revised Edition, New Brunswick, New Jersey, 1969, pp. 97–98; J. F. Haldon, *Byzantium in the Seventh Century*, Cambridge, 1990, p. 35.

12 V. Lukonin, "Administrative division of Parthian and Sasanian Period," *The Cambridge History of Iran*, ed. E. Yarshater, Cambridge University Press, Cambridge, 1995, p. 701.

13 *Madīyān ī Hazār Dādestān* 100.4–5.

14 Lukonin believes that the *rustag* was a rural district and its villages were the *deh*, p. 727; Piacentini states that *rustāq* indicated a lesser administrative area with a rural character (though more rarely it might also have designated a village or a small rural area including one or more villages), V. F. Piacentini, "Madīna/Shahr, Qarya? Deh, Nāhiya/Rustāq The City as Political-Administrative Institution: the Continuity of a Sasanian Model," *Jerusalem Studies in Arabic and Islam*, vol. 17, 1994, p. 92.

15 F. De Blois, "The Middle-Persian Inscription From Constantinople: Sasanian or post-Sasanian," *Studia Iranica*, Tome 19, 1990, Fasc. 2, pp. 209–218.
16 Piacentini, *op. cit.*, p. 96.
17 Dīnāwarī, *Axbār at-Ṭiwāl*, p. 228; Morony, 1984, *op. cit.*, p. 129; others believe that a *Ṭassūj* was divided into rasōtāq, and the rasōtāq into *Ṭassūj*, R.N. Frye, *The Golden Age of Persia*, p. 10.
18 *Tārīx Bala'mī*, pp. 874–875.
19 Bal'amī says that a letter from Ardawān, the last Parthian king to Ardaxšīr states that: "you are a man from the *rusta* of Staxr, your father Babak was a man from the *rusta*, it was not large enough for you to come to a *shahr*, that according to him you would take over Staxr," p. 880; Ṭabarī (I, 814) states that Ardaxšīr was from the *qarya* of Tīrūdeh, belonging to the *rustāq* of Khīr, in the *kūra* of Istakhr of the *balad* of Fars.
20 *Tārīx Qom*, ed. S.J. Moddares, Tūs Publication, Tehran, 1982, p. 23.
21 N. Adontz, *Armenia in the Period of Justinian, The Political Conditions Based on the Naxarar System*, Calouste Gulbenkian Foundation, Lisbon, 1970, p. 238.
22 Lukonin, *op. cit.*, p. 727.
23 *Madīgān ī Hazār Dādestān* 100.5–7.
24 *Madīgān ī Hazār Dādestān* 100.5–7.
25 M. Morony, *Iraq After the Muslim Conquest*, Princeton University Press, Princeton, New Jersey, 1984, p. 129.
26 W.B. Henning, "A New Parthian Inscription," *Journal of the Royal Asiatic Society of Great Britain and Ireland*, parts 3 and 4, 1953, p. 134.
27 R.N. Frye, "Notes on the early Sassanian State and Church," *Estratto de Studi Orientalistici in onore di Giorgio Levi ella Vida*, vol. 1, Roma, Istituto per l'oriente, Viale D. Lubin, 2, 1956, pp. 331 and 335.
28 This *kadag-xwadāy* is not an ordinary "master of the house" and must have been of a noble house to be positioned before the shahrab. I owe this suggestion to Hanns-Peter Schmidt.
29 H. Humbach and P.O. Skjærvø *The Sassanian Inscription of Paikuli*, Dr. Ludwig Reichert Verlag, Wiesbaden, 1983, paragraph 32.
30 Back, *op. cit.*, p. 483.
31 R.N. Frye, "The Persepolis Middle Persian Inscriptions from the Time of Shapur II," *Acta Orientalia*, XXX, 1966, p. 85.
32 Gyselen, *La géographie*, 1989, p. 28.
33 R.N. Frye, *op. cit.*, 1966, p.85.
34 A.B. Nikitin, "Middle Persian Ostraca from South Turkmenistan," *East and West*, IsMEO, vol. 42, No. 1, March 1992, pp. 105.
35 M. Shaki, "Dād," *Encyclopaedia Iranica*, vol. VI, 1994, p. 544.
36 W. B. Henning, "Notes on the Inscription of Šāpūr," *Professor Jackson Memorial Volume*, p. 53; F. Grenet, "Observations sur les titres de Kirdīr," *Studia Iranica*, tome 19, 1990, fasc. 1, p. 94.
37 R. Gyselen, "Note de glyptique sassanide les cachets personnels de

l'ohrmazd-mogbed," *études irano-aryennes offertes á Gilbert Lazard*, ed. C.-H de Fouchécour and Ph. Gignoux, Association pour l'avancement des études iraniennes, Paris, 1989, p. 186.

38 *Madīyān ī Hazār Dādestān* 26.15.

39 R. Gyselen, "Les sceaux des mages de l'Iran sassanide," *Au carrefour des religions Mélanges offerts á Philippe Gignoux*, ed. R. Gyselen, Res Orientales, vol. VII, Groupe pour l'Žtude de la civilisation du moyen-orient, Bures-sur-Yvette, 1995, p. 123.

40 M. Morony, "Mobadh," *Encyclopaedia of Islam*, Leiden, 1987, p. 576.

41 Agathias, *The Histories*, II.26.5.

42 S. Shaked, "Administrative Functions of Priests in the Sasanian Period," *Proceedings of the First European Conference of Iranian Studies*, Rome, 1990, p. 268.

43 N. G. Garsoïan, *History of Ancient and Medieval Armenia*, Chapter III "The Marzpanate (428–652)," ed. R. Hovannisian, 1984, unpublished manuscript, p. 4.

44 Ełishe, *History of Vardan and the Armenian War*, Harvard University Press, Cambridge, Massachusetts, London, England, 1982, p. 60.

45 *Vichitakiha-i Zadsparam*, Bombay, 1964, XXXIII.5, p. 87; Ph. Gignoux and A. Tafazzoli, *Anthologie de Zādspram*, Association pour l'avancement des Études Iraniennes, Paris, 1993, pp. 114–115.

46 M. Shaki, "Dādwar, Dādwarīh," *Encyclopaedia Iranica*, vol. VI, 1994, p. 557.

47 J. de Menasce, "Le protecteur des pauvres dans l'Iran sasanide," *Mélanges Henri Massé*, Tehran 1963, p. 283.

48 *Pahlavi Rivayats* 196; *Sad-dar Nasr* XXII.3.

49 *Ardā Wirāz Nāmag*, XIX.15.

50 J. de Menasce, *op. cit.*, pp. 282–287.

51 Ph. Gignoux, "Problémes d'interprétation historique et philologique des titres et noms propres sasanides," *Acta Antiqua Academiae Scientiarum Hungaricae*, XXIV, vol. 1–4, 1976, p. 105.

52 Gyselen, *op. cit.*, 1989, p. 31.

53 *Ibid.*, p. 59.

54 S. Shaked, "Some Legal and Administrative Terms," *Monumentum H.S. Nyberg II*, Acta Iranica, E.J. Brill, Leiden, 1975, p. 215.

55 Shaked believes that the title was a complimentary one, designating the mowbeds of Fars in particular, *ibid.*, pp. 215–216.

56 N.G. Garsoian, "Protecteur des pauvres," *Revue des études arméniennes*, tome XV, 1981, p. 24; J.R. Russell, "Advocacy of the Poor: The Maligned Sasanian Order," *Journal of the K.R. Cama Oriental Institute*, Bombay, 1986, p. 136.

57 For *driyōš* see W. Sundermann, "Commendatio pauperum," *Altorientalische Forschungen*, IV, Akademie-Verlag, Berlin, 1976, pp. 179–191; also M. Shaki, "An Appraisal of Encyclopaedia Iranica, vols II, and III," *Archív Orientalní*, 59, 1991, p. 406.

58 S. Shaked, *The Wisdom of the Sasanian Sages*, Westview Press, Boulder, Colorado, 1979, p. 57; see also passage 23, p. 13; passage 35, p. 15; passage 91, p. 37.

59 J.P. de Menasce, *Feux et fondations pieuses dans le droit sassanide*, Paris, 1964, pp. 59–62; M. Macuch, "Sasanidische Institutionen in Früh-Islamischer Zeit," *Transition Periods in Iranian History*, L'association pour l'avancement des études iraniennes, 1987, pp. 178–179.

60 Frye, *op. cit.*, 1973, pp. 84–85.

61 Gyselen, *La géographie administrative de l'empire sassanide*, p. 33.

62 *Pahlavi Texts*, ed. J.M. Jamasp-Asana, 1913, p. 157; J.C. Tavadia, "Sūr Saxvan, A Dinner Speech in Middle Persian," *Journal of Cama Oriental Institute*, vol. 29, 1935, 42f. and 63f.

63 *Tansar-nāme*, ed. M. Minovī, Tehran, 1932, p. 57 and 143.

64 M.L. Chaumont, "Andarzbad," *Encyclopaedia Iranica*, vol. II, 1987, p. 22.

65 Shabuhr I, Ka'ba-ye Zardošt, line 33, Chaumont, *op. cit.*, p. 22.

66 *History of Łazar P'arpec'i*, Scholars Press, Atlanta Georgia, 1991, 88.50 and 98.

67 *Zādspram*, p. 88.

68 A. Périkhanian, "Notes sur le lexique iranien et arménien," *Revue des Études Arméniennes*, Nouvelle série, Tome V, Paris, 1968, p. 21.

69 *Madīyān ī Hazār Dādestān* 110.148.

70 *Muruj al-dhahab*, p. 240; it should be mentioned that due to the corrupt nature of the pasage *qāḍi al-quḍat* may stand for *mowbedān mowbed.*

71 For the complete list of his responsibilities see M. Shaki, "Dādwar, Dādwarīh," *Encyclopaedia Iranica*, vol. VI. 1984, p. 558.

72 *Madīyān ī Hazār Dādestān* A5.11

73 Frye, *op. cit.*, 1973, p. 63.

74 Gyselen, *op. cit.*, 1989, p. 112.

75 Gyselen, *op. cit.*, pp. 35–36.

76 R.C. Zaehner, "Nāmak-nipēsīšnih," *Bulletin of the School of Oriental and African Studies*, vol. 9, 1937–1939, pp. 93–109.

77 Tafazzolī, Sasanian Society, p. 27. For further observation on the *dibīrān* see the chapter on Society in this book.

78 R. Gyselen, "Economy IV. In the Sasanian Period," *Encyclopaedia Iranica*, ed. E. Yarshater, 1997, pp. 104–105.

79 Wenke, 1987, p. 255; for Iraq see Adamns, 1965, 73.

80 R.N. Frye, "Feudalism in Iran," *Jerusalem Studies in Arabic and Islam*, vol. 9, 1987, p. 14.

81 de Menasce and Macuch, 1993, p. 649.

82 Wenke, 1987, p. 255.

83 J. de Menasce, "Textes pehlevis sur les Qanats," *Acta Orientalia*, vol. 30, 1966, reprint in Études Iraniennes, Studia Iranica Cahier, p. 146.

84 R.J. Wenke, "Western Iran in the Partho-Sasanian Period: The Imperial Transformation," ed. F. Hole, *The Archaeology of Western Iran, Settlement*

and Society from Prehistory to the Islamic Conquest, Smithsonian Institution Press, Washington, D.C., and London, 1987, p. 253.

85 Wenke, 1987, p. 255.

86 *Ibid.*, p. 253.

87 Wenke, 1987, p. 262.

88 For a good discussion of this building activity during this period see N.V. Pigulevskaïa, *Les villes de l'état iranien aux époques parthe et sassanide*, Paris, 1963.

89 *A Catalogue of the Provincial Capitals of the Ērānshahr*, J. Markwart, ed. G. Messina, Pontificio Istituto Biblico, Rome, 1931; T. Daryaee, *The Shahrestānīhā ī Ērānshahr*, Mazda Publishers, Costa Mesa, 2002.

90 For example, Weh-Ardaxšīr: Ardashir-xwarrah; Ērān-Xwarrah-Shabuhr; Bishabuhr; Weh-Andīog-Shabuhr.

91 The building of these cities have been ascribed to Ardaxšīr I: Wahišt-Ardešīr; Rām-Ardešīr; Rām-Mehrz-Ardešīr; Būd-Ardašīr; Batn-Ardašīr; Anša-Ardašīr; Bahman-Ardašīr; Ardašīr-Xorrah; Mēlī-Ardašīr; Harmšīr; Hujastan-Wājār (this would be Wāzār, since he mentions that this city was the center of the traders and businessmen); Beh-Ardašīr, *Kitab ta'rīkh sinī mulūk al-arḍ wa'l-anbiyā'*, ed. S.H. Taqizadeh, Berlin, 1921, p. 44.

92 R.McC. Adams, *Land Behind Baghdad: A History of Settlement on the Diyalal Plain,* Chicago, Chicago University Press, 1965, pp. 115–116.

93 Wenke, p. 256.

94 J.A. Neely, "Sasanian and Early Islamic Water-Control and Irrigations Systems on the Deh Luran Plain, Iran," ed. T.E. Downing and M. Gibson, *Irrigation's Impact on Society*, University of Arizona Press, Tuscon, 1974, p. 30.

95 Neely, Ibid., p. 39.

96 M. Morony, "Land Use and Settlement Patterns in Late Sasanian and Early Islamic Iraq," *The Byzantine and Early Islamic Near East, Land Use and Settlement Patterns*, eds. G.R.D. King and A. Cameron, vol. II, The Darwin Press, Princeton, New Jersey, 1994, p. 227.

97 Wenke, 1987, p. 259.

98 Gnoli, *op. cit.*, p. 131.

99 Gnoli, *op. cit.*, 157.

100 M. Morony, "Landholding in Seventh-Century Iraq: Late Sasanian and Early Islamic Patterns," *The Islamic Middle East, 700–1900: Studies in Economic and Social History*, ed. A.L. Udovitch, The Darwin Press, Princeton, New Jersey, 1981, p. 164.

101 A. Williamson, "Persian Gulf Commerce in the Sassanian Period and the First Two Centuries of Islam," *Bāstān Chenāsī wa Honar-e Iran*," vol. 9–10, 1972, pp. 97–109: M. Kervran, "Forteresses, entrepôts et commerce: une historie à suivre depuis les rois sassanides jusqu' aux princes d'ormuz," *Itinéraires d'orient, hommages à claude cahen*, eds. R. Curiel and R. Gyselen, Res Orientales, vol. VI, 1994, pp. 325–350.

102 Dinawarī, p. 44; Hoyland, *Arabia and the Arabs from the Bronze Age to the coming of Islam*, Routledge, New York and London, 2001, pp. 27–28.

103 S.M. Awtab, *Kitāb ansāb al-ʿarab*, Bibliothèque Nationale, Ms. Arabe 5019, 271r.; Hoyland, *ibid.*, p. 28.

104 V.F. Piacentini, "Ardashīr I Pāpakān and the wars against the Arabs: Working hypothesis on the Sasanian hold on the Gulf," *Proceedings of the Seminar for Arabian Studies*, vol. 15, London, 1985, pp. 57–78.

105 R. Boucharlat and J.F. Salles, "The History and Archaeology of the Gulf from 5th century BC to the 7th century AD: a review of the evidence," *Proceedings of the Seminar for Arab Studies*, vol. 11, London, 1981, p. 66.

106 V.F. Piacentini, *Merchants-Merchandise and Miliatry Power in the Persian Gulf (Sūriyān/Shahriyāj-Sīrāf)*, Atti Della Academia Nazionale Dei Lincei, Roma, 1992, p. 117.

107 Boucharlat and Salles, *op. cit.*, p. 66,

108 B. de Cardi, "A Sasanian Outpost in Northern Oman," *Antiquity*, vol. XLVI, no. 184, 1972, p. 306.

109 Boucharlat and Salles, *op. cit.*, p. 71; R. Ghirshman, "The Island of Kharg," *Iranian Oil Operating Companies*, 1960, p. 10.

110 For Sasanian presence in Eastern Africa see "Kilwa: a Preliminary Report," *Azania, The Journal of the British Institute of History and Archaeology of East Africa*, vol. I, 1996, p. 7.

111 Istakhrī, Masalik wa Mamalik, ed. I. Afšār, p. 113.

112 For Sasanian presence at Sīrāf see D. Whitehouse and A. Williamson, "Sasanian Maritime Trade," *Iran*, vol. XI, 1973, p. 35; D. Huff, "Archaeology IV. Sasanian," *Encyclopaedia Iranica*, 1989, p. 303: N.M. Lowick, *The Coins and Monumental Inscriptions*, The British Institute of Persian Studies, Siraf XV, 1985, pp. 11–16.

113 D. Whitehouse, "Maritime Trade in the Arabian Sea: The 9th and 10th Centuries AD," *South Asian Archaeology*, ed. M. Taddei, vol. 2, 1977,p. 868.

114 J. Kröger, "Sasanian Iran and India: Questions of Interaction," *South Asian Archaeology*, ed. H. Härtel, 1979, p. 447.

115 *Kosma aigyptiou monachou Christianika topographi. The Christian Topography of Cosmas, An Egyptian Monk*, The Kakluyt Society, Burt Franklin, New York, p. 365.

116 B. Senior, "Some new coins from Sind," Oriental Numismatic Society, No. 149, Summer 1996, p. 6. I would like to thank William B. Warden for bringing this fact to my attention and pictures of other similar coins found in the Sind area.

117 H.M. al-Naboodah, "The Commercial activity of Bahrain and Oman in the early Middle Ages," *Proceedings of the Seminar for Arabian Studies*, vol. 22, London, 1992, p. 81.

118 B. Spuler, "Trade in the Eastern Islamic Countries in the Early Centuries," *Islam and the Trade in Asia*, 1970, p. 14.

119 J. C. Wilkinson, "Sūhār in the Early Islamic Period: The Written Evidence," *South Asian Archaeology*, 1973, ed. E. Taeddi, vol. 2, p. 888.

120 B. de Cardi, "A Sasanian Outpost in Northern Oman," *Antiquity*, vol. XLVI, no. 184, Dec. 1972, p. 308; D.T. Potts, "A Sasanian Lead Horse from North Eastern Arabia," *Iranica Antiqua*, vol. XXVIII, 1993, p. 197.

121 D. Whitehouse, "Maritime Trade in the Arabian Sea: The 9th and 10th Centuries AD," *South Asian Archaeology*, ed. M. Taddei, vol. 2, 1977, pp. 874–879.

122 B. de Cardi, "The British Archaeological Expedition to Qatar 1973–1974," *Antiquity*, vol. XLVIII, No. 191, Sept. 1974, p. 199.

123 B. de Cardi, "Archaeological Survey in N. Trucial States," *East and West*, IsMEO' vol. 21, No. 3–4, Sept.-Dec. 1971, pp. 260, 268.

124 Spuler, *ibid.*, pp. 81–82.

125 For Persians in China see E.H. Schafter, "Iranian Merchants in T'ang Dynasty Tales," *University of California Publications in Semitic Philology*, vol. xi, 1951, pp. 403–422.

126 D. Whitehouse, "Chinese Stoneware from Siraf: The Earliest Finds," *South Asian Archaeology*, 1971, pp. 241–243.

127 Ammianus Marcellinus, XXIII, 6, 11.

128 Procopius, I.xx.12.

129 H. Nai, "A Survery of Sasanian Silver Coins Found in China," *K'ao Ku 'Hsüeh Pao*, No. 1, 1974, pp. 93, 107.

130 Nai, *ibid.*, p. 95; P.D. Curtin, *Cross-Cultural Trade in World History*, Cambridge University Press, Cambridge, 1984, p. 101.

131 H. Nai, *Studies in Chinese Archaeology*, The Institute of Arcaheological Academia Sinica, Peking, 1961, p. 171.

132 F. Thierry, "Sur les monnaies sassanides trouvées en chine," *Circulations des monnaies, des marchandises et des biens*, ed. R. Gyselen, Res Orientales, vol. V, Bures-sur-Yvette, 1993, see map on p. 90.

133 J.E. Cribb, "Far East," *A Survey of Numismaic Research*, 1978–1984, eds. M. Price, E. Besly, D. Macdowall, M. Jones, and A. Oddy, vol. II, London, 1986, p. 814.

134 R.C. Houston, "A Note on Two Coin Hoards Reported in Kao Ku," *The American Numismatic Society Museum Notes*, vol. 20, 1975, pp. 158–159.

135 M. Morony, "Land Use and Settlement Patterns in Late Sasanian and Early Islamic Iraq," *The Byzantine and Early Islamic Near East, Land Use and Settlement Patterns*, eds. G.R.D. King and A. Cameron, vol. II, The Darwin Press, Princeton, New Jersey, 1994, p. 227.

136 N.N. Chegini and A.V. Nikitin, "Sasanian Iran – Economy, Society, Arts and Crafts," *History of Civilizations of Central Asia*, vol. III, ed. B.A. Litvinsky et. al., UNESCO Publishing, Paris, 1996, p. 43.

137 One can view the Sasanian influence on silk cloth patterns as far as Egypt, see O.P. Harper, *The Royal Hunter*, New York, 1978.

138 Thierry, pp. 125–128.

139 B.I. Marshak and N.N. Negmatov, "Sogdiana," *History of Civlizations of Central Asia*, vol. III, ed. B.A. Litvinsky et. al., UNESCO Publishing, Paris, 1996, P. 234.

140 M. Morony, "Trade and Exchange: The Sasanian World to Islam," *The Late Antiquity and Early Islam Workshop, Trade and Exchange AD. 565–770*, unpublished draft, p. 7.
141 Procopius, *The History of the Wars*, London and New York, 1914, pp. 480–481; Morony, Trade, p. 11.
142 Morony, Trade, p. 11.
143 Menander Protector in Constantine Porphyrogenitus, *Excerpta de legationibus*, ed. C. de Boor, i, 180.
144 Morony, Trade, p. 12.
145 R. Göbl was one of the first scholars to classify the seals and sealings based on typology, *Der Sāsānidische Siegelkanon*, Braunschweig, 1973.
146 R.N. Frye, "Sassanian Clay Sealings in the Baghdad Museum," *Sumer*, vol. 26, 1970, p. 240; "Methodology in Iranian History," *Neue Methodologie in der Iranistik*, ed. R.N. Frye, Otto Harrassowitz, Wiesbaden, 1974, p. 68; R. Gyselen, *La géographie administrative de l'empire sassanide, les témoignages siglloraphiques*, Centre National pour la Recherce Scientifique et de l'Associaton pour l'Avancement des Etudes Iraniennes, Paris, 1989.
147 Ph. Gignoux, "Sceaux chértiens d'époque sasanide," *Iranica Antiqua*, vol. XV, 1980, pp. 299–314. For a through bibliography see Ph. Gignoux and R. Gyselen, *Sceaux sasanides de diverses collections privées*, Éditions Peeters, Leuven, 1982; *Ibid.*, *Bulles et sceax sassanides de diverses collections*, Studia Iranica – Cahier 4, Association pour l'avanement des études iraniennes, Paris, 1987.
148 V.G. Lukonin, pp. 742–743.
149 R.N. Frye, "Sasanian Seal Inscriptions," *Beiträge zur Alten Geschichte und deren Nachleben, Festschrift für Franz Altheim zum 6.10.1968*, eds. R. Stiehl und H.E. Stier, Zweiter Band, Walter de Gruyter and Co., Berlin, 1970, pp. 79, 84.
150 R.N. Frye, "Commerce III. In the Parthian and Sasanian Periods," *Encyclopaedia Iranica*, ed. E. Yarshater, vol. VI, Mazda Publishers, Costa Mesa, p. 62.
151 N.V. Peegulevskaya, "Economic Relations in Iran during the IV–VI Centuries AD.," *Journal of the K.R. Cama Oriental Institute*, No. 38, 1956, p. 67.
152 J.K. Choksy, "Loan and Sales Contracts in Ancient and Early Medieval Iran," *Indo-Iranian Journal*, vol. 31, 1988, p. 210.
153 *Dēnkard*, Madan edition,, 757.10 translated by Tafazzolī, "A List of Trades and Crafts in the Sassanian Period," *Archaeologische Mitteilungen aus Iran*, vol. 7, 1974, p. 192.
154 Tafazzolī, *ibid.*, pp. 193–196.
155 Tafazzolzī, *op. cit.*, p. 192.
156 ŠKZ 35; Back, *op. cit.*, p. 366.
157 Tafazzolī, *op. cit.*, p. 195.
158 *Mēnōg ī Xrad*, pp. 48–49.
159 ŠKZ 5/4/10, Back, p. 293.

160 R.C. Blockley, "Subsidies and Diplomacy: Rome and Persian in Late Antiquity," *Phoenix*, vol. 39, no. 1, 1985, pp. 63–64.

161 *Ibid.*, p. 67.

162 *Ibid.*, p. 68.

163 *Ibid.*, p. 70–71.

164 Wenke states that the widespread use of bronze coinage in the Susania plain, 1987, p. 271.

165 R. Göbl, "Sasanian Numismatics," *The Cambridge History of Iran*, ed. E. Yarshater, vol. 3(2), 1983, p. 332.

166 C. Reider, "Legend Variations of the Coins of Ardashir the Great," *Oriental Numismatic Society*, No. 147, Winter 1996, pp. 10–11.

167 T. Daryaee, "The Persian Gulf Trade in Late Antiquity," *Journal of World History*, vol. 14, no. 1, 2003, pp. 1–16.

168 Cowell and Lowick, "Silver from the Panjhīr," Khurasan, Bates' notes given to me by M. Bates.

169 See Holst, Samanid.bib, who holds for wood-fuel supplies, Emily Savage-Smith made comment that lack of fuel at the mine site would have made smelting more expensive there rather than transport of ore elsewhere to be smelted.

170 Agapius, Kitāb al-'Unwan, Pat. Or. VIII, 1911.

171 B. Laufer, *Sino-Iranica*, p. 515.

172 R.J. Forbes, op. cit., pp. 409 ff.

173 *Kārnāmg ī Ardaxšīr ī Pābagān*, Nyberg's edition in his reader, 6.7, 1964.

174 M. Maczek, estimates that Persia contains thirteen million tons of iron, "Der Erzbergbau im Iran," p. 198.

175 H.E. Wulff, *The Traditional Crafts of Persia*, The Massachusetts Institute of Technology, 1966, p. 7.

176 S. Parhām, "Tārīkh-e khoan-e farš-bāfī-e Fars," (The ancient history of carpet weaving in Fars), *AYANDEH*, vol. 7, No. 4, 1981, pp. 262–263.

177 Wulff, Ibid., p. 213.

178 M. Shaki saw this passage as a fabrication based on the Christian monastic model, "Darvīš," *Encyclopaedia Iranica*, while M.-L. Chaumont saw genunie Zoroastrian ascetism, "Vestiges d'un courant ascétique dans le zoroastrisme sassanide d'apres le Vie livre du Dēnkart," *Revue de l'histoire des religions*, CLVI, no. 1, 1959, pp. 1–24; also my comments "Sasanian Persia," *Iranian Studies*, vol. 31, Nos. 3–4, 1998, pp. 444–445.

179 *Mēnōg ī Xrad*, , 1364, p. 18.

180 Morony, *Landholding*, p. 146.

181 Morony, *Landholding*, p. 150.

182 Morony, *Landholding*, p. 163.

183 Z. Rubin, "Reforms of Khusro Anūshirwān," *The Byzantine and Early Islamic Near East, States, Resources and Armies*, vol. III, ed. A. Cameron, Darwin Press, Princeton, New Jersey, 1995, p. 291.

184 Rubin, *ibid.*, p. 293–294.

Bibliography

JOURNALS AND REFERENCE WORKS

AAH	*Acta Antiqua Academiae Scientiarum Hungaricae*
Aas	*Artibus Asiae*
AION	*Annali dell'Istiuto Universitario Orientale di Napoli*
AMI	*Archäologische Mitteilungen aus Iran*
AOH	*Acta Orientalia Academiae Scientiarum Hungaricae*
ArO	*Archív Orientalní*
BSOAS	*Bulletin of the School of Oriental and African Studies*
CHI	*The Cambridge History of Iran*
EIr	*Encyclopaedia Iranica*, ed. E. Yarshater
EW	*East and West*
Farh	*Farhang*
GIrPH	*Grundriss der iranischen Philologie*, ed. B. Geiger and E. Kuhn, Strassburg 1895–1901
Hdo	*Handbuch der Orientalistik*, ed. B. Spuler, Leiden-Cologne
IIJ	*Indo-Iranian Journal*
IrAnt	*Iranica Antiqua*
JA	*Journal Asiatique*
JAOS	*Journal of the American Oriental Society*
JCOI	*Journal of the K.R. Cama Oriental Institute*
JSAI	*Jerusalem Studies in Arabic and Islam*
NFar	*Nāme-ye Farhangestān*
NIB	*Nāme-ye Irān-e Bāstān*
NS	*Numismatic Chronicle*
RSO	*Rivista degli Studi Orientali*
StIr	*Studia Iranica*
TAVO	*Tübinger Atlas des Vorderen Orients*
ZDMG	*Zeitschrift der Deutschen Morgenländischen Gesellschaft*

PRIMARY TEXTUAL SOURCES

An invaluable collection of primary sources for the Sasanian–Roman relations and more is gathered by M.H. Dodgeon and S.N.C. Lieu *The Roman Eastern Frontier and the Persian Wars (AD 226–363), A Documentary History*, Routledge, London and New York, 1991. This is followed by G. Greatrex and S.N.C. Lieu, *The Roman Eastern Frontier and the Persian Wars (AD 363–630)*, Part II, Routledge, London and New York, 2002. Also see the recent work of B. Dignas and E. Winter, *Rome and Persia in Late Antiquity*, Cambridge University Press, 2007 (English Version).

Arabic Sources

Agapius, *Kitāb al-'Unwān*, Pat. Or. VIII, 1911.

Bērūnī, A. *Athār al-Baghīya*, 'an al-qurūnal-akhāliah, E. Sachau, as Chronologie orientalischer Völker, Leipzig, 1878.

Grignaschi, M. "Quelques spécimens de la littérature sassanide conserves dans les bibliothéques d'Istanbul," *Journal Asiatique*, vol. 254, 1966, 1–142. A collection of speeches attributed to Ardaxšīr, Xusrō I and others in Arabic.

Ibn Hišam, 'A.M. *Sīrat rasūl Allāh*, translated by A. Guillaume, The Life of Muhammad,Karachi, 1955.

Iṣfahānī, H.H. *Kitab ta'rīkh sinī mulūk al-arḍ wa'l-anbiyā'*, ed. S.H. Taqizadeh, Berlin, 1921. The Persian translation under the same title, Amir Kabir Publishers, Tehran, 1367.

Ibn Miskawiya, A.A. *Tajarib al-Umam* (Experience of Nations), edited and translated into Persian by A. Emami, Soroush Press, Tehran, 1980.

al-Tabarī, M.J. *Ta'rīkh al-rusul wa-al-mulūk*, ed. M.J. de Goeje, Leiden, 1879–1901. The English translation with copious notation is by C.E. Bosworth, *The History of al-Tabarī, vol. V, The Sāsānids, the Byzantines, the Lakmids, and Yemen*, State University of New York Press, 1999.

al-Tha'alibi, A.M.A.M.M.I. *Gharar Axbar al-mulâk al-Fars wa Sayrhum*, ed. H.Zotenberg, Paris, 1990.

Armenian Sources

Agathangełos, *History of the Armenians*, translation and commentary by R.W. Thomson, State University of New York Press, Albany, 1976.

Buzandaran Patmut'iwnk', *The Epic Histories Attributed to P'awstos Buzand*, translation and commentary by N.G. Garsoïan, Cambridge, 1989.

Elishē, *History of Vardan and the Armenian War*, translation and commentary by R.W.Thomson, Harvard University Press, Cambridge, Massachusetts, 1982.

Łazar P'arpets'i, *The History of Łazar P'arpets'i*, translation and commentary by R.W.Thomson, Occasional Papers and Proceedings. Columbia University, Program in Armenian Studies, Georgia, 1991.

Sebeos, *The Armenian History attributed to Sebeos*, translation and notes by R.W. Thomson, historical commentary by J. Howard-Johnston, assistance from T. Greenwood, 2 vols., Liverpool University Press, Liverpool, 1999.

Coptic Sources

The Kephalaia of the Teacher, ed. I. Gardner, E.J. Brill, Leiden, 1995.

Greek and Latin Sources

Agathias Scholasticus, *Agathias: The Histories*, translated by J.D.C. Frendo, 1975.

Ammianus Marcellinus, *The Surviving Books of the History*, edited and translated by J.C. Rolfe, Cambridge, Massachussets, 1937–1939.

Antiochus Strategos, in F.C. Conybeare, "Antiochus Strategos' Account of the Sack of Jerusalem in AD 614," in *English Historical Review*, vol. 25, 1910, pp. 502–517.

Chronicon Paschale, translated by M. Whitby and M. Whitby, Liverpool University Press, 1989.

Dio Cassius, *Dio's Roman History*, translated by E. Cary, Loeb Classical, Cambridge University Press, 1969.

Eutropius, *Breviarium*, translated with an introduction and commentary by H.W. Bird, Liverpool University Press, 1993.

Evagrius Scholasticus, *The Ecclesiastical History of Evagrius Scholasticus*, translated with an introduction by M. Whitby, Liverpool University Press, 2000.

Herodian, translated by C.R. Whittaker, Loeb, Cambridge University Press, 1970.

Kosma aigyptiou monachou Christianika topographi, The Christian Topography of Cosmas, An Egyptian Monk, The Kakluyt Society, Burt Franklin, New York.

Libanius, *Selected Orations*, vol. I, translated by A.F. Norman, Cambridge University Press, London, 1969 (reprint 2003).

Maurice's Strategikon, Handbook of Byzantine Military Strategy, translated by G.T. Dennis, University of Pennsylvania Press, Philadelphia, 1984.

Menander Protector, *The History of Menander the Guardsman*, translated by R.C. Blockley, Liverpool, Francis Cairns, 1985.

Procopius: History of the Wars, translated by H.B. Dewing, London Cambridge, Massochusetts, William Heinemann – Harvard University Press, 1954–1992.

Theophylact Simocatta, edited and translated by M. Whitby and M. Whitby, Liverpool University Press, 1986.

Middle Persian Sources

Abar Ēwēnag ī Nāmag-nibēsišnīh, translated into English by R.C. Zaehner, "Nāmaknipēsīšnih," *Bulletin of the School of Oriental and African Studies*, vol. 9, 1937–1939, pp. 93–109.

Abar Madan ī Wahrām ī Warzāwand, edited and translated into English by M.F. Kanga, in *All India Oriental Conference*, 12, iii, pp. 687–691; into Persian by S. Oriān, *Motūn-e Pahlavī*, Tehran, 1371, pp. 190–191.

Andarz ī Anōšag Ruwān Ādūrbād ī Maharsapandān, contained in Pahlavi Texts, edited and translated by J.M. Jamasp-Asana, Bombay, 1897–1913; into Persian by S. Oriān, National Library of Iran, Tehran, 1992.

Ardā Wirāz Nāmag, *The Iranian 'Divina Commedia'*, edited and translated by F. Vahman, Curzon Press, London and Malmo, 1986.

Ayādgār ī Zarērān, edited and translated in German by D. Monchi-Zadeh, Uppsala, 1981; into Persian by B. Gheiby, Pahlavi Literature Series, Nemudar Publication, Bielefeld, 1999.

Bundahiš, edited and translated by B.T. Anklesaria, *Zand ī Akāsīh*, Bombay, 1956; into Persian by M. Bahār, *Bondahēš*, Tūs Publishers, 1369.

Bundahiš-e Hindī (Indian Bundahišn), R. Behzādī, *Bundahiš-e Hindī*, Tehran, 1368.

Čīdag Andarz ī Pōryōtkēšān, edited and translated into English by M.F. Kanga, *Cītak Handarz I Pōryōtkēšān: A Pahlavi Text*, Bombay, 1960; into Persian by by S. Oriān, *Motūn-e Pahlavī*, Tehran, 1371, pp. 86–93.

Dēnkard, Sanjana, *The Dēnkard*, edited and translated by D.P. Sanjana, vol. xvi, Kegan Paul, Trench, Trubner and Co., London, 1917 provides a complete but outdated translation. Also W. West, *Pahlavi Texts*, The Sacred Books of the East, Oxford, 1880; for Book three, J.P. de Menasce, *Dēnkart III*, Paris, Librairie Klincksieck, 1974; Book five, J. Amuzegār and A. Tafazzolī, *Dēnkard V*, Cahiers de Studia Iranica, Peeters, Luven, 2001. *Dēnkard V*, Studia Iranica – Chaier xx, 2001; Book six, Sh. Shaked, *Wisdom of the Sasanian Sages*, Caraban Books, 1979; Book Seven, M. Molé, *La légende de Zoroastre*, Paris, 1967.

Draxt ī Āsūrīg, *Manzūme-ye Draxt-e Āsūrīk*, edited and translated into Persian by M. Navabi, Tehran, 1346; into English by C.J. Brunner, "The Babylonian Tree, A Western Middle Iranian Verse Text," *Special Supplement to the Grapevine*, Selected Texts from PreIslamic Iran.

Fragment, contained in *Pahlavi Texts*, edited and translated by J.M. Jamasp-Asana, Bombay, 1897–1913; into Persian by S. Oriān, *Motūn-e Pahlavī*, Tehran, 1371, pp. 111, 121–122.

Farhang ī Ōīm-ēwag, edited and translated into English by H. Jamaspji Asa and M. Haug, *An Old Pahlavi-Pazand Glossary*, Bombay and London, 1870; into German by H. Reichelt, *Der Frahang I Oīm*, Wien, 1900.

Frahang ī Pahlavīg, edited by S.H. Nyberg and B. Utas, *Frahang ī Pahlavīk*, Wiesbaden, 1988.

Gajastak Abalish, H.G. Chacha, Bombay, 1936, translated into Persian by I. Mirzā-ye Nāzir, *Matīkān ī Gujastak Abālīš*, Hērmand Publishers, Tehran, 1375.

Jāmāsp Nāmag, edited and translated into Italian by G. Messina, *Ayātkār ī Zāmāspīk*, Roma, 1939.

Husraw ud Rēdag, edited and translated into English by D. Monchi-Zadeh, "Xusrōv ut Rētak," Monumentom Morgenstierne, vol. II, Acta Iranica 22, Leiden, 1982, pp. 47–91. C.J. Brunner, "Khusraw, Son of Kawad, and A. Page, A Middle Iranian 'Didactic' Text," *Special Supplement to the Grapevine*, Selected Texts from Pre-Islamic Iran.

Kārnāme-ye ardašīr ī bābakān, edited and translated into English by E.K. Antia, Bombay, 1900; into Persian by S. Hedāyat, Amir Kabir Publishers, Tehran, 1332. Also B. Farahwašī, Tehran, 1354.

Madigān ī Hazār Dādestān, edited and translated by A. Perikhanian, *The Book of a Thousand Judgments*, Mazda Publishers, Costa Mesa, 1997; M. Macuch, *Das sasanidische Rechtsbuch "Mātakdān i Hazār Dātistān,"* Teil II, Wiesbaden, 1981; *ibid., Rechtskasuistik und Gerichtspraxis zu Begin des siebenten Jahrhunderts in Iran*, Wiesbaden, 1993.

Māh Frawardīn Rōz ī Hordād, edited and translated by M.F. Kanga, Bombay, 1946; into Persian by S. Kiyā, Iran Kūde 16, and S. Oriān, *Motūn-e Pahlavī*, Tehran, 1371, pp. 141–145.

Mēnō-ye Xrad, translated into English by E. West, Stuttgart-London, 1871; into Persian by A. Tafazzolī, Tus Publishers, Tehran, 1364.

The Pahlavi Rivāyat of Ādurfarnbag and Farnbag-Srōš, edited and translated by B.T. Anklesaria, 2 vols., Bombay, 1969.

Pahlavi Vendidād, edited and translated by B.T. Anklesaria, Bombay, 1949.

Rivāyat ī Ēmēd ī Ašawahištān, edited and translated N. Safa-Isfehani, *Rivāya-I Hēmīt-I Ašawahistān, A Study in Zoroastrian Law*, Harvard Iranian Series, 1980.

Šahrestānīhā ī Ērānšahr, A Catalogue of the Provincial Capitals of the Ērānšahr, J. Markwart, ed. G. Messina, Pontificio Istituto Biblico, Rome, 1931, and T. Daryaee, *Šahrestānīhā ī Ērānšahr, A Middle Persian Text on Geography, Epic and History*, Mazda Publishers, Costa Mesa, 2002.

Šāyest nē Šāyest, edited and translated into English by J.C. Tavadia, Hamburg, 1930; into Persian by K. Mazdapour, Cultural and Research Institute, Tehran, 1990.

The Supplementary Texts to the Šāyest Nē-Šāyest, edited and translated by F.M.P.Kotwal, Kobenhavn, 1969.

Sūr ī Saxwan, J.C. Tavadia, "Sūr Saxvan: Or a Dinner Speech in Middle Persian," *Journal of the K.R. Cama Oriental Institute*, vol. 29, 1935, pp. 1–99.

Wāžag ē-Čand ī Ādurbād ī Mārspandān, Contained in Pahlavi Texts, edited and translated by J.M. Jamasp-Asana, Bombay, 1897–1913; into Persian by S. Oriān, *Motūn-e Pahlavī*, Tehran, 1371, pp. 176–184.

Wizādagīha ī Zadspram, edited and translated into English by B.T. Ankelsaria, *Vichitakiha-i Zadsparam*, Bombay, 1964; into French by Ph.

Gignoux and A. Tafazzolī, *Anthologie de Zādspram*, Studia Iranica, Cahier 13, Paris, 1993; into Persian by M.T. Rashid, *Gozīdehāye Zāspram*, Mohassel, Tehran, 1366.

Wizārišn Čatrang ud Nahišn Nēw-Ardaxšīr, Panaino, *La novella degli scacchi e della tavola reale*, Mimesis, Milano, 1999. Translated into English by C.J. Brunner, "The Middle Persian Explanation of Chess and Invention of Backgammon," *The Journal of Ancient Near Eastern Society of Columbia University*, vol. 10, 1978, pp. 45–53. T. Daryaee, "Mind, Body and the Cosmos: The Game of Chess and Backgammon in Ancient Persia," *Iranian Studies*, vol. 35, no. 4, 2002, pp. 281–312.

Zand ī Wahman Yasn: A Zoroastrian Apocalypse, edited and translated into English by C. Cereti, Istituto Italiano per il medio ed Estremo Oriente, 1995. Translated into Persian as *Zand ī Wahman Yasn*, M.T. Rashid Mohassel, Tehran, 1370.

Persian Sources

Ibn Balxī, *Fārsnāme*, ed. Le Strange and Nicholson, Cambridge University Press, 1921.

Dāstānhā-ye Bīdpāy, translated by M. b. A. al-Buxārī, ed. by P.N. Xānlarī and M. Rošan, Xārazmī Publishers, Tehran, 1369.

Istaxrī, *Masalik wa Mamalik*, ed. I. Afšār, Tehran, 1340.

Mara'šī Z. *Tārīkh-ē Tabarestān va Rōyān va Māzandarān*, ed. B. Dorn, *Geschicte von Tabristan, Rujan und Masanderan*, St. Petersburg, 1850, reprint Gostareh Publishers, Tehran, 1363.

Nāma-ye Tansar, ed. M. Mīnoī, Tehran, 1352. English translation by M. Boyce, *The Letter of Tansar*, Rome, 1968.

Naršaxī, A.B.M. *Tārīkh-e Buxārā*, Tehran, 1972.

Qur'an-e Quds, ed. A. Ravāghī, 2 vols., Tehran, 1377.

Šāhnāme, Moscow Edition, vol. viii, lns. 558–561.

Tārīx Qom, ed. S.J. Moddares, Tūs Publication, Tehran, 1982.

Syriac Sources

Kawerau, P. *Die Chronik von Arbela*, Peeters, Louvan, 1985.

The Chronicle of Pseudo-Joshua the Stylite, translated with note and introduction by F.F. Trombley and J.W. Watt, Liverpool University, Press, 2000.

SECONDARY SOURCES

Afshar, I. *Zabān-e Fārsī dar Āzarbāyejān*, Tehran, 1368.

Alram, M. *Iranische Personennamenbuch, Nomia Propria Iranica in Nummis*, vol. 4, Vienna, 1986.

——. "The Beginning of Sasanian Coinage," *Bulletin of the Asia Institute*, vol. 13, 1999, pp. 67–76.

Altheim-Stiehl, R. "The Sasanians in Egypt — Some Evidence of Historical Interest," *Bulletin de la société d'archéologie Copte*, vol. 31, 1992, pp. 87–96.

Amuzegar, J. and Tafazzolī, A. *Osture-ye Zendegī-ye Zartošt*, Našr Āvīšan, Tehran, 1372.

——. "Namūnah-hā'ī az honar-e khwalīgarī dar farhang-e kohan-e Irān," Kelk, vols. 85–88, April-July 1997, pp. 162–166.

Ancient Art from the Shumei Family Collection, The Metropolitan Museum of Art, New York, 1996.

Adontz, N. *Armenia in the Period of Justinian, The Political Conditions Based on the Naxarar System*, Calouste Gulbenkian Foundation, Lisbon, 1970.

Andreas, F.C. and Barr, K. *Bruchstücke einer Pehlevi-Übersetzung der Psalmen* SPAW, Phil.-hist. Kl., 1933.

Asmussen, J.P. "Christians in Iran," *The Cambridge History of Iran*, ed. E. Yarshater, vol. 3(2), 1983, pp. 924–948.

——. "Judeo-Persian Translations of the Bible," *Encyclopaedia Iranica*,' vol. iv, Routledge and Kegan Paul, New York and London, 1990, pp. 208–209.

Azarnoush, M. *The Sasanian Manor House at Hājīābād, Iran*, Casa Editrice Le Lettere, Fierenze, 1994.

Bābā-Tāher-Nāme, ed. P. Azkā'ī, Tūs Publishers, Tehran, 1375.

Back, M. *Die Sassanidischen Staatsinschriften, Studien zur Orthographie und Phonologie des Mittelpersischen der Inschriften zusammen mit einem etymologischen Index des mittelpersischen Wortgutes und einem Textcorpus der behandelten Inschriften*, Acta Iranica 18, E.J. Brill, Leiden, 1978.

Bailey, H.W. *Zoroastrian Problems in the Ninth-Century Books*, Oxford, 1971.

Barnes, T.D. "Constantine and the Christians of Persia," *The Journal of Roman Studies*, vol. 75, 1985, pp. 126–136.

Bašāš, K.R. and Khānīkī R.L. *Sang Negāre-ye Lāx-Mazār*, Mīrās-e Farhangī, Tehran, 1373.

——. "Katibe-ye Hājjīābād dar Arse-ye Tārīkh wa Ostōre," Zabān, *Katibe wa Motōn-e Kohan*, Sāzmān-e Mirath-e Farhangī, 1375, pp. 43–56.

Bausani, "Two Unsuccessful Prophets: Mani and Mazdak," *Religion in Iran. From Zoroaster to Baha'ullah*, Bibliotheca Persica Press, New York, 2000, p. 80–110.

Benveniste, E. "Inscriptions de Bactriane," *Journal Asiatique*, 1961, pp. 133–152.

Bier, L. *The 'Sasanian' Palace near Sarvistan*, New York, 1979.

——. "Notes on Mihr Narseh's Bridge near Firuzabad," *Archäologische Mitteilungen aus Iran*, vol. 19, 1986, pp. 263–268.

Blockley, R.C. "Subsidies and Diplomacy: Rome and Persian in Late Antiquity," *Phoenix*, vol. 39, no. 1, 1985, pp. 62–74.

de Blois, F. "The Middle Persian Inscription from Constantinople: Sasanian or Post-Sasanian," *Studia Iranica*, vol. 19, 1990, pp. 209–218.

——. *Burzōy's Voyage to India and the Origin of the Book of Kalīlah wa Dimnah*, Curzon Press, London, 1990.

Bosworth, C.E. "The Heritage of Rulership in Early Islamic Iran and the Search for Dynastic Connections with the Past," *Iranian Studies*, vol. xi, 1978, pp. 7–34.

Boucharlat R. and Salles, J.F. "The History and Archaeology of the Gulf from 5th century BC. to the 7th century AD: a review of the evidence," *Proceedings of the Seminar for Arab Studies*, vol. 11, London, 1981, p. 65–94.

Bowersock, G.W. *Julian the Apostate*, Harvard University Press, Cambridge, Massachusetts, 1978.

Boyce, M. "The Manicaean Literature in Middle Iranian," *Handbuch der Orientalistik, Iranistik II*, Literature I, Leiden, 1968, pp. 67–76.

——. "Middle Persian Literature," *Handbuch der Orientalistik, Iranistik*, Literatur, Lieferung 1, E.J. Brill, Leiden/Cologne, 1968, pp. 32–66.

——. *The Manichaean hymn-cycles in Parthian*, Oxford, 1954, and her *A Reader in Manichaean Middle Persian and Parthian*, Tehran-Liege, Acta Iranica 9, 1975.

——. "On Mithra, Lord of Fire," Monumentum H.S. Nyberg, vol. I, E.J. Brill, Leiden, 1975, pp. 69–76.

——. M. *Zoroastrianism, Its Antiquity and Constant Vigour*, Columbia Lectures on Iranian Studies, Mazda Publishers, Costa Mesa, California, 1992.

——. "On the Orthodoxy of Sasanian Zoroastrianism," *Bulletin of the School of Oriental and African Studies*, vol. lix, part 1, 1996, pp. 11–28.

Brock, S. "Christians in the Sasanian Empire: A Case of Divided Loyalties," *Studies in Church History*, vol. 18, 1982, pp. 1–19.

—— and Harvey, S. "Persian Martyrs," *Holy Women of the Syrian Orient*, University of California Press, 1998.

P. Callieri, "On the Diffusion of Mithra Images in Saanian Iran: New Evidence from a Seal in the British Museum," *East and West*, vol. 40, nos. 1–4, 1990, pp. 79–98.

——. "In the Land of the Magi. Demons and Magic in the Everyday Life of Pre-Islamic Iran," *Démons et merveilles d'orient*, ed. R. Gyselen, Res Orientales XIII, Peeters, Leuven, 2001, pp. 11–36.

Cameron, A. "Agathias on the Sassanians," *Dumberton Oaks Papers*, vol. 22–23, 1969–1970, pp. 67–183.

de Cardi, B. "Archaeological Survey in N. Trucial States," *East and West*, IsMEO' vol. 21, No. 3–4, Sept.-Dec. 1971, pp. 225–290.

——. "A Sasanian Outpost in Northern Oman," *Antiquity*, vol. XLVI, No. 184, Dec. 1972, pp. 305–309.

——. "The British Archaeological Expedition to Qatar 1973–1974," *Antiquity*, vol. XLVIII, No. 191, Sept. 1974, pp. 196–200.

Cereti, C. "Again on Wahrām ī Warzāwand," *La Persia e l'Asia Centrale da Alessandro al X secolo*, Accademia Nazionale dei Lincei, Roma, 1996, pp. 629–639.

——. *La letteratura Pahlavi. Introduzione ai testi con riferimenti alla storia degli studi e alla tradizione manoscritta*, Mimesis, Milan, 2001.

Chaumont, M.L. "Le culte de Anāhitā à Stakhr et les premiers Sassanides," *Revue de l'Histoire des Religions*, vol. 153, 1958, pp. 154–175.

——. "Vestiges d'un courant ascétique dans le zoroastrisme sassanide d'apres le Vie livre du Dēnkart," *Revue de l'histoire des religions*, CLVI, no. 1, 1959, pp. 1–24.

——. "Le culte de la déesse Anāhitā (Anahit) dans la religion des monarques d'Iran et d'Arménie au Ier siècle de notre ère," *Journal Asiatique*, vol. 253, 1965, pp. 168–171.

——. *La Christianisation de l'empire iranien des origins aux grandes persecutions du IVe siècle*, Peeters, Louven, 1988.

Chegini, N.N. and Nikitin, A.V. "Sasanian Iran – Economy, Society, Arts and Crafts," *History of Civilizations of Central Asia*, vol. III, ed. B.A. Litvinsky *et al.*, UNESCO Publishing, Paris, 1996, pp. 45–76.

Choksy, J.K. *Purity and Pollution in Zoroastrianism: Triumph Over Evil*, Texas University Press, Austin, 1989.

——. "A Sasanian Monarch, His Queen, Crown Prince and Dieties: The Coinage of Wahram II," *American Journal of Numismatics*, vol I, 1989, pp. 117–137.

——. "Loan and Sales Contracts in Ancient and Early Medieval Iran," *Indo-Iranian Journal*, vol. 31, 1988, pp. 191–218.

Christensen, A. *Essai sur la démonolgie iranienne*, DVS, Historisk-filologiske meddeleleser, XXVIII/1, Copenhagen, 1941.

——. *L'Iran sous les Sassanides*, Copenhagen, 1944.

C. Colpe, "Mithra-Verehrung, Mithras-Kult und die Existenz iranischer Myserien," *Mithraic Studies*, vol. II, Manchester, 1975, pp. 378–405.

M. Compareti, "The Last Sasanians in China," *Eurasian Studies*, vol. II, no. 2, 2003, pp. 197–213.

Cribb, J.E. "Far East," *A Survey of Numismaic Research*, 1978–1984, eds. M. Price, E. Besly, D. Macdowall, M. Jones, and A. Oddy, vol. II, London, 1986, pp. 81–85.

Crone, P. "Kawād's Heresy and Mazdak's Revolt," *Iran*, vol. 29, 1991, pp. 21–42.

Curtin, P.D. *Cross-Cultural Trade in World History*, Cambridge University Press, Cambridge, 1984.

Daryaee, T. "National History or Keyanid History? The Nature of Sasanid Zoroastrian Historiography," *Iranian Studies*, vol. 28, nos. 3–4, 1995, pp. 129–141.

——. "Religio-Political Propeganda on the Coins of Xusro II," *American Journal of Numismatics*, vol. 7, 1997, pp. 141–154.

——. "Apocalypse Now: Zoroastrian Reflections on the Early Islamic Centuries," *Medieval Encounters*, vol. 4, no. 3, 1998, pp. 188–202.

——. "Sasanian Persia," *Iranian Studies*, vol. 31, nos. 3–4, 1998, pp. 431–462.

——. "Middle Iranian Sources for the Study of Early Islamic History," *Bulletin of the Middle East Medievalists*, vol. xx, no. 2, 1998, pp. 36–39.

——. *Fall of the Sāsānian Empire and the end of Late Antiquity: Continuity and Change in the Province of Persis*, Ph.D. Thesis, UCLA, 1999.

——. "Source for the Economic History of Late Sāsānian Fārs," *Matériaux pour l'histoire économique du monde iranien*, eds. R. Gyselen, M. Szuppe, Studia Iranica, Cahier 21, 1999, pp.131–149.

——. "Laghab-e Pahlavī-ye 'ihr az yazdān' va Šāhanšāhī-ye Sāsānī," *Nāme-ye Farhangestān*, vol. 4, No. 4, 2000, pp. 28–32.

——. "Modafe' Darvīšān va Dāvar dar Zamān-e Sāsānīān," *Tafazzolī Memorial Volume*, ed. A. Ashraf Sadeghi, Sokhan Publishers, Tehran, 2001, pp. 179–189.

——. "Kerdīr's Naqsh-i Rajab Inscription," *Nāme-ye Irān-e Bāstān, The International Journal of Ancient Iranian Studies*, vol. 1, no. 1, 2001, pp. 3–10.

——. "Zed-e Zandīyūn," *Ma'ārif*, vol. XVIII, no. 2, 2001, pp. 51–57.

——. "Mind, Body, and the Cosmos: Chess, Backgammon in Ancient Persia," *Iranian Studies*, vol. 35, no. 4, 2002, pp. 281–312.

——. "Ardašīr Mowbed-e Mowbedān: Yek Tashih dar Matn-e Bundahiš," *Iranshenasi*, 2002, pp. 145–147.

——. "The Coinage of Queen Bōrān and its Significance in Sasanian Imperial Ideology," *Bulletin of the Asia Institute*, vol. 13, 1999 (2002), pp. 1–6.

——. "Memory and History: The Construction of the Past in Late Antique Persia," *Nāme-ye Irān-e Bāstān, The International Journal of Ancient Iranian Studies*, vol. 1, no. 2, 2002, pp. 1–14.

——. "Notes on Early Sasanian Titulature," *Journal of the Society for Ancient Numismatics*, vol. 21, 2002, pp. 41–44.

——. "Clay king or Mountain king," *Paitimāna, Essays in Iranian, Indo-European, and Indian Studies in Honor of Hanns-Peter*, ed. S. Adhami, Mazda Publishers, Costa Mesa, 2003, pp. 339–349.

——. "The Sect of Gayomartiya," *Ātaš-e Dorun (The Fire Within), J.A. Sourushian Memorial Volume*, ed. C. Cereti, 2003, pp. 131–137.

——. "History, Epic, and Numismatics: On the Title of Yazdgird I (Rāmšahr)," *Journal of the American Numismatic Society*, vol. 14, 2002 (2003), pp. 89–95.

——. "The Ideal King in the Sasanian World: Ardaxšīr ī Pābagān or Xusrō Anōšag-ruwān?," *Nāme-ye Irān-e Bāstān, The International Journal of Ancient Iranian Studies*, vol. 3, no. 1, 2003, pp. 33–45.

——. "Dīdgāhhā-ye mowbedān va šāhanšāhī-ye Sāsānī darbare-ye Ērānšahr," *Nāme-ye Irān-e Bāstān, The International Journal of Ancient Iranian Studies*, vol. 3, no. 2, 2003–2004, pp. 19–28.

——. *Soghūt-e Sāsānīān (The Fall of Sasanians)*, Nashr-e Tarīkh-e Irān, 2004.

——. *Mēnōg ī Xrad: The Spirit of Wisdom, Essays in Memory of Ahmad Tafazzolī*, ed. T. Daryaee and M. Omidsalar, Mazda Publishers, Costa Mesa, 2004.

Dodgeon, M.H. and Lieu, S.N.C., *The Roman Eastern Frontier and the Persian Wars, A Documentary History*, Routledge, London and New York, 1991.

Dresden, J. "Sogdian Language and Literature," *The Cambridge History of Iran*, vol. 3(2), Cambridge, 1983, pp. 1222–1224.

Elton, H. *Frontiers of the Roman Empire*, Indiana University Press, Bloomington and Indianapolis, 1996.

Emmerick, R.E. *The Book of Zambasta*, London, 1968. H.W. Bailey, *Khotanese Texts*, 6 vols., Cambridge, 1945–1967.

——. "Khotanese and Tumshuqese," *Compendium Linguarum Iranicarum*, ed. R. Schmitt, Dr. Ludwig Reichert Verlad, Wiesbaden, 1989, pp. 204–229.

Emrani, H. *The Political Life of Queen Bōrān: Her Rise to Power and Factors that Legitimized her Rule*, MA Thesis, California State University, Fullerton, 2005.

Fiey, J.M. *Communautés syriaques en Iran et Irak des origines à 1532*, London, 1979.

——. "The Last Byzantine Campaign into Persia and Its Influence on the Attitude of the Local Populations Towards the Muslim Conquerors 7–16 H./628 AD," *Proceedings of the Second Symposium on the History of Bilād al-Shām During the Early Islamic Period up to 40 AH./640 AD*, ed. M.A. Bakhit, Amman, 1987, pp. 97–110.

Foltz, R. "When Was Central Asia Zoroastrian?," *The Mankind Quarterly*, vol. XXXVIII, no. 3, 1998, pp. 189–200.

Forte, A. "On the Identity of Aluohan (616–710) A Persian Aristocrat at the Chinese Court," *La Persia e l'Asia Centrale da Alessandro al X secolo*, Accademia Nazionale dei Lincei, Roma, 1996, pp. 187–197.

——. "Edict of 638 Allowing the Diffusion of Christianity in China," in P. Pelliot, *L'Inscription nesotrienne de Si-Ngan-Fou*, edited with Supplements by A. Forte, Scuola di Studi sull'Asia Orientale, Kyoto and Collège de France, Institut des Hautes Éudes Chionises, Paris, 1996.

Frye, R.N. "Notes on the early Sassanian State and Church," *Studi Orientalistici in onore di Giorgio Levi Della Vida*, Rome, 1956, pp. 314–335.

——. "The Persepolis Middle Persian Inscriptions from the time of Shapur II," *Acta Orientalia*, vol. xxx, 1966, pp. 83–93.

——. "Sasanian Seal Inscriptions," *Beiträge zur Alten Geschichte und deren Nachleben, Festschrift für Franz Altheim zum 6.10.1968*, eds. R. Stiehl and H.E. Stier, Zweiter Band, Walter de Gruyter and Co., Berlin, 1970, pp. 77–84.

——. "Sassanian Clay Sealings in the Baghdad Museum," *Sumer*, vol. 26, 1970, pp. 237–240.

——. R.N. "Methodology in Iranian History," *Neue Methodologie in der Iranistik*, ed. R.N. Frye, Otto Harrassowitz, Wiesbaden, 1974, p. 57–69.

——. "The Sasanian System of Walls for Defense," *Studies in Memory of Gaston Wiet*, Jerusalem, 1977, pp. 7–15.

——. *The History of Ancient Iran*, C.H. Beck'sche Verlagsbuchhandlung, Munich, 1983.

——. "The Political History of Iran Under the Sasanians," *The Cambridge History of Iran*, ed. E. Yarshater, vol. 3(1), 1983, pp. 116–180.

——. "Commerce III. In the Parthian and Sasanian Periods," *Encyclopaedia Iranica*, ed. E. Yarshater, vol. VI, Mazda Publishers, Costa Mesa, pp. 61–64.

——. "Zoroastrian Incest," *Orientalia Iosephi Tucci Memoriae Dicata*, eds. G. Gnoli and L. Lanciotti, Istituto Italiano per il Medio ed Estremo Oriente, Rome, 1985, pp. 445–455.

——. "The Fate of Zoroastrians in Eastern Iran," *Au Carrefour des Réligions: Mélanges offerts à Philippe Gignoux*, ed. R. Gyselen, Peeters, Leuven, 1995, pp. 67–68.

Gariboldi, A. "Astral Symbology on Iranian Coinage," *East and West*, vol. 54, 2004, pp. 31–53.

Garsoïan, N., "Protecteur des pauvres," *Revue des études arméniennes*, vol. XV, 1981, pp. 20–34.

——. "Byzantium and the Sasanians," *The Cambridge History of Iran*, ed. E. Yarshater, vol. 3(1), Cambridge University Press, 1983, pp. 568–593.

——. "The Aršakuni Dynasty (AD 12–[180?]–428), *Armenian People from Ancient to Modern Times*, vol. I, ed. R.G. Hovannisian, St. Martin's Press, New York, 2004, pp. 63–94.

Gaube, H. "Kavād's Heresy and Mazdak's Revolt," *Studia Iranica*, vol. 11, 1982, pp. 111–122.

Gernet, J. *A History of Chinese Civilization*, Cambridge University Press, 1982.

Gershevitch, I. "Bactrian Inscriptions and Manuscripts," *Indogermanische Forschungen*, LXXI, 1967, pp. 27–57.

Gheybi, B. "Došnām-e Zardušt," *Khorde Maqālāt*, Part 5, no. 38, pp. 335–353.

Ghirshman, R. *Bīchāpour*, 2 vols., Paris, 1956.

——. "The Island of Kharg," *Iranian Oil Operating Companies*, Tehran, 1960.

Gignoux, Ph. "Problémes d'interprétation historique et philologique des titres et noms propres sasanides," *Acta Antiqua Academiae Scientiarum Hungaricae*, XXIV, vol. 1–4, 1976.

——. "'Corps osseux et âme osseuse': essai sur le chamanisme dans l'Iran ancient," *Journal Asiatique*, vol. 267, 1979, pp. 41–79.

——. "Sceaux chértiens d'époque sasanide," *Iranica Antiqua*, vol. XV, 1980, pp. 299–314.

——. T and R. Gyselen, *Sceaux sasanides de diverses collections privées*, Éditions Peeters, Leuven, 1982.

——. *Bulles et sceax sassanides de diverses collections*, Studia Iranica – Cahier 4, Association pour l'avanement des études iraniennes, Paris, 1987.

——. "Les quatre régions administratives de l'Iran sasanide et la symboliques des nombres trois et quatre," *Annali dell'Istiuto Universitario Orientale di Napoli*, 44, 1984, pp. 555–572.

——. "Le Spāhbed des Sassanides," *Jerusalem Studies in Arabic and Islam*, 13, 1990, pp. 1–14.

——. *Les Quatre inscription du mage Kirdīr*, textes et concordances, Association pour l'avancement des études iraniennes, Leuven, 1991.

——. "Matériaux pour une histoire du vin dans l'iran ancien," *Matériaux pour l'histoire économique due monde iranien*, ed. R. Gyselen and M. Szuppe, Paris, 1999, pp. 43–44.

——. "La composition du Dēnkard el le contenu du livre V," *Tafazzoli Memorial Volume*, ed. A.A. Sadeghi, Sokhan Publishers, Tehran, 2001, pp. 29–38.

Gnoli, G. *Zoroaster's Time and Homeland*, IsMEO, Napoli, 1980.

——. *The Idea of Iran, an Essay on Its Origin*, Serie Orientale Roma LXII, Rome, 1989.

Göbl, R. *Sasanidische Numismatik*, Klinkhardt and Biermann, Braunschweig, 1968.

——. *Der Sāsānidische Siegelkanon*, Braunschweig, 1973.

——. "Sasanian Numismatics," *The Cambridge History of Iran*, ed. E. Yarshater, vol. 3(2), 1983, pp. 322–342.

Grenet, F. "Observations sur les titres de Kirdīr," *Studia Iranica*, vol. 19, 1990, fasc. 1, pp. 87–94.

——. "Pour une nouvelle visite à la "vision de Kerdīr"," *Studia Asiatica*, vol. 3, no. 1–2, 2002, pp. 5–27.

Gunter, A.C. and Jett, P. *Ancient Iranian Metalwork in the Arthur M. Sackler Gallery andthe Freer Gallery of Art*, Smithsonian Institution, Washington, DC, 1992.

Guocan, C. "Tang Qianling shirenxiang ji qi xianming de yanjiu," *Wenwu jikan*, vol. 2, 1980, p. 198b8.

Gurnet, F. "Deux notes à propos du monnayage de Xusrō II," *Revue belge de Numismatique*, 140, 1994, pp. 25–41.

Gutas, D. *Greek Thought, Arabic Culture, The Graeco-Arabic Translation Movement in Baghdad and Early 'Abbāsid Society (2nd–4th/8th–10th centuries)*, Routledge, New York, 1998.

Gyselen, R. "Les données de géographie administrative dans le šahrestānīhā-ī Ērān," *Studia Iranica*, tome 17, fasc. 2, 1988, pp. 191–206.

——. *La géographie administrative de l'empire sassanide, les témoignages siglloraphiques*, Centre National pour la Recherce Scientifique et de l'Associaton pour l'Avancement des Etudes Iraniennes, Paris, 1989.

——. "Note de glyptique sassanide les cachets personnels de l'Ohrmazd-mogbed," *Études irano-aryennes offertes á Gilbert Lazard*, ed. C.-H de Fouchécour and Ph. Gignoux, Association pour l'avancement des études iraniennes, Paris, 1989, pp. 185–192.

——. "Economy IV. In the Sasanian Period," *Encyclopaedia Iranica*, ed. E. Yarshater, vol. VIII, Costa Mesa, 1997, pp. 104–107.

——. "Les sceaux des mages de l'Iran sassanide," *Au carrefour des religions Mélanges offerts á Philippe Gignoux*, ed. R. Gyselen, Res Orientales, vol. VII, Groupe pour l'étude de la civilisation du moyen-orient, Bures-sur-Yvette, 1995, pp. 121–150

——. *Sceaux magiques en Iran sassanide*, Studia Iranica, cahier 17, Paris, 1995.

——. *Démons et merveilles d'orient*, ed. R. Gyselen, Res Orientales XIII, Peeters, Leuven, 2001.

——. *Nouveaux matériaux pour la géographie historique de l'empire Sassanide: Sceaux administratifs de la collection Ahmad Saeedi*, Paris, 2002.

Haldon, J.F. *Byzantium in the Seventh Century*, Cambridge, 1990.

Hansen, O. *Die mittelpersischen Papyri der Papyrussammlung der Staatlischen Museen zu Berlin*, Verlag der Akademie der Wissenschaften, Berlin, 1938.

Harmatta, J. "The middle Persian-Chinese Bilingual Inscription from Hsian and the Chinese-Sasanian Relations," *La Persia nel Medioevo*, Accademia Nazionale dei Lincei, Roma, 1971, pp. 363–376.

Harper, P.O. *The Royal Hunter, Art of the Sasanian Empire*, The Asia Society, New York, 1978.

Henning, W.B. "Mani's Last Journey," *Bulletin of the School of Oriental and African Studies*, vol. x, part 4, 1942, pp. 941–953.

——. "Sogdian Tales," *Bulletin of the Schools of Oriental and Africa Studies*, vol. XI, 1946, pp. 713–740.

——. "A New Parthian Inscription," *Journal of the Royal Asiatic Society of GreatBritain and Ireland*, parts 3 and 4, 1953, pp. 132–136.

——. "The Inscription of Firuzabad," *Asia Major*, vol. 4, 1954, p. 98–102.

——. "Notes on the Great Inscription of Šāpūr I," *Professor Jackson Memorial Volume*, Bombay, 1954, pp. 25–29.

——. "The Choresmian Documents," *Asia Major*, vol. XI, 1965, pp. 66–79.

——. *A fragment of a Khwarezmian dictionary*, ed. By D.N. MacKenzie, Tehran University Press, 1971.

——. *W.B. Henning — Selected Papers*, Acta Iranica, vols. V and VI, E.J. Brill, Leiden, 1977.

Henrichs, A. "Mani and the Babylonian Baptists: A Historical Confrontation," *Harvard Studies in Classical Philology*, vol. 77, 1973, pp. 23–59.

Herrmann, G. *The Iranian Revival*, Elsevier-Phaidon, 1977.

——. "Shapur I in the East: Reflections from his Voctory Reliefs," *The Arts and Archaeology of Ancient Persia, New Light on the Parthian and Sasanian Empires*, eds. V.S. Curtin, R. Hillenbrand, and J.M. Rogers, I.B.Tauris, 1998, pp. 38–51.

Herzfeld, E. *Iran in the Ancient East*, Hacker Art Books, New York, reprint 1988.

Hinz, W. *Altiranische Funde und Forschungen*, Walter de Gruyter and Co., Berlin, 1969.

——. "Mani and Kardēr," *La Persia nel Medievo*, Accademia Nazionale dei Lincei, Roma, 1971, pp. 485–499.

Hintze, A. "The Avesta in the Parthian Period," in *Das Partherreich und seine Zeugnisse*, Franz Steiner Verlag, Stuttgart, 1998, pp. 147–162.

Houston, R.C. "A Note on Two Coin Hoards Reported in Kao Ku," *The American Numismatic Society Museum Notes*, vol. 20, 1975, pp. 158–159.

Howard-Johnston, J. "The Two Great Powers in Late Antiquity: a Comparison," *The Byzantine and Early Islamic Near East*, vol. III, ed. A. Cameron, The Darwin Press, Inc., New Jersey, pp. 157–226.

Hoyland, R.G. *Arabia and the Arabs, From the Bronze Age to the Coming of Islam*, Routledge, London and New York, 2001.

Huff, D. "Archaeology IV. Sasanian," *Encyclopaedia Iranica*, vol. 2, 1989, pp. 329–334.

Huyse, Ph. "Noch einmal zu Parallelen zwischen Achaemeniden- und Sāsānideninschriften," *Archäologische Mitteilungen aus Iran*, vol. 23, 1990, pp. 177–183.

——. "Kerdīr and the first Sasanians," *Proceedings of the Third European Conference of Iranian Studies*, ed. N. Sims-Williams, Part 1, Dr. Ludwig Reichert Verlag, Wiesbaden, 1998, p. 109–120.

——. *Die dreisprachige Inschrift Šābuhrs I. an der Ka'ba-I Zardušt*, 2 vols., Corpus Inscriptionum Iranicarum, London, 2000.

Inostrantsev, K. *Motal'ātī darbare-ye Sāsānīān*, BTNK, Tehran, 1348.

Itō, G. "From the Dēnkard," *Monumentum H.S. Nyberg*, vol. I, E.J. Brill, Leiden, 1975, pp. 423–434.

de Jong, A. "Jeh the Primal Whore? Observations on Zoroastrian Misogyny," *Female Stereotypes in Religious Traditions*, eds. R. Kloppenborg and W.J. Hanegraaff, Studies in the History of Religions, vol. 66, Leiden, 1995, pp. 15–41.

——. "Women in Ritual in Medieval Zoroastrianism," *Ātaš-e Dorun (The Fire Within), J.A. Sourushian Memorial Volume*, ed. C. Cereti, 2003, Author House, pp. 147–161.

——. "Sub Specie Maiestatis: Reflections on Sasanian Court Rituals," *Zoroastrian Ritual in Context*, ed. M. Stausberg, Brill, Leiden, 2004, pp. 345–366.

Kanga, K.E. "King Faridun and a Few of His Amulets and Charms," *K.R. Cama Memorial Volume, Essays on Iranian Subjects in Honor of Mr. Kharshedji Rustamji Cama On the Occasion of his Seventieth Birthday*, ed. J.J. Modi, Bombay, Fort Printing Press, Bombay, 1900, pp. 141–145.

Kent, R. *Old Persian Grammar, Text, Lexicon*, American Oriental Society, New Haven, Connecticut, 1953.

Kervran, M. "Forteresses, entrepôts et commerce: une historie à suivre depuis les roissassanides jusqu' aux princes d'ormuz," *Itinéraires d'orient, hommages à claude cahen*, eds. R. Curiel and R. Gyselen, Res Orientales, vol. VI, 1994, pp. 325–350.

Kettenhofen, E. *Die römisch-persischen Kriege des 3. Jahrhunderts n. Chr. nach der Inscrift Šāpuhrs I. an der Ka'be-ye Zartošt (ŠKZ)*, Dr. Ludwig Reichert Verlag, Wiesbaden, 1982.

——. *Das Sāsānidenreich*, TAVO, Dr. Ludwig Reichert Verlag, Wiesbaden, 1993.

——. "Deportations. ii. In the Parthian and Sasanian Periods," *Encyclopaedia Iranica*, vol. VII, 1996, pp. 297–308.

Kister, M.J. "Al-Hīra, Some notes on its relations with Arabia," *Arabica*, vol. xi, 1967, pp. 143–169.

Knauth, W. *Das altiranische Füerstenideal Xenephon bis Ferdousi, nach d. antiken u. einheim, Quellen dargest*, Steiner, Wiesbaden, 1975.

Kreyenbroek, Ph. "The Zoroastrian Priesthood," *Transition Periods in Iranian History*, Actes du symposium de Fribourg-en-Brisgau (22–24 Mai 1985), Istituto Italiano per il Medio ed Estremo Oriente, pp. 151–166.

——. "On the Concept of Spiritual Authority in Zoroastrianism," *Jerusalem Studies in Arabic and Islam*, vol. 17, 1994, pp. 1–15.

Kröger, J. "Sasanian Iran and India: Questions of Interaction," *South Asian Archaeology*, ed. H. Härtel, 1979, pp. 441–448.

Labourt, J. *Le Christianisme dans l'empire perse*, Paris, 1904.

Laufer, B. *Sino-Iranica: Chinese Contributions to the History of Civilization in Ancient Iran, with Special Reference to the History of Cultivated Plants and Products*, Field Museum of Natural History, Publication 201, Anthropological Series, vol. 15, no. 3, Chicago, 1919.

Lerner, J. "Central Asians in Sixth-Century China: A Zoroastrian Funerary Rite," *Iranica Antiqua*, vol. 30, 1995, pp. 179–190.

Lieu, S.N.C. "Captives, Refugees, and Exiles: A Study of Cross-Frontier Civilian Movements and Contacts between Rome and Persia from Valerian to Jovian," *The Defense of the Roman and Byzantine East, Proceedings of a colloquium held at the University of Sheffield in April 1986*, ed. P. Freeman and D. Kennedy, part ii, British Institute of Archaeology at Ankara, Monograph no. 8, BAR International Series 297, 1986, pp. 473–508.

Livshits, V.A. "New Parthian Documents from South Turkemenistan," *Acta Antiqua Academiae Scientiarum Hungaricae*, vol. 25, 1977, pp. 157–185.

Lowick, N.M. *The Coins and Monumental Inscriptions*, The British Institute of Persian Studies, Siraf XV, 1985.

Lukonin, V.G. Lukonin, "Administrative division of Parthian and Sasanian Period," *The Cambridge History of Iran*, ed. E. Yarshater, Cambridge University Press, Cambridge, 1995, pp. 681–746.

——. *Tamddun-e Irān-e Sāsānī*, Translated from Russian into Persian by I. Reza, Scientific and Cultural Publication Company, Tehran, 1987.

MacKenzie, D.N. "Zoroastrian astrology in the Bundahišn," *Bulletin of the School of Oriental and African Studies*, vol. XXVII, part 3, 1964, pp. 511–529.

——. *The "Sūtra of the Causes and Effects of Actions" in Sogdian*, Oxford University Press, 1970.

——. "Shapur's Shooting," *The Bulletin of the School of Oriental and Africa Studies*, vol. 41, 1978, pp. 499–511.

——. "Mani's Šābuhragān I," *Bulletin of the School of Oriental and African Studies*, 1979, pp. 288–310.

——. "Mani's Šābuhragān II," *Bulletin of the School of Oriental and African Studies*, 1979, pp. 500–534.

——. *The Sasanian Rock Reliefs at Naqsh-i Rustam*, Iranische Denkmäler, 1989.

Macuch, M. "Barda and Bardadārī ii," *Encyclopaedia Iranica*, www.iranica.com

——. "Sasanidische Institutionen in früh-Islamischer Zeit," *Transition Periods in Iranian History*, L'Association pour l'avancement de études iraniennes, Paris, 1987, pp. 178–179.

——. "Charitable Foundations. i. In the Sasanian Period," *Encyclopaedia Iranica*, 1991, pp. 380–382.

——. "The Talmudic Expression "Servant of the Fire" in the Light of Pahlavi Legal Sources," *Jerusalem Studies in Arabic and Islam*, vol. 26, 2002, pp. 199–229.

Magistro, M. "Alcuni Aspetti della Glittica Sacro-Magica Sasanide: Il 'Cavaliere Nimbato,'" *Studia Iranica*, vol. 29, 2000, pp. 167–194.

Mahamedi, H. "Wall as a System of Frontier Defense during the Sasanid Period," *Mēnōg ī Xrad: The Spirit of Wisdom, Essays in Memory of Ahmad Tafazzolī*, ed. T. Daryaee and M. Omidsalar, Mazda Publishers, Costa Mesa, 2004, pp. 145–159.

Malayeri, M.M. *Farhang-e Iranī-ye Pēš az Islam wa Asar-e ān dar Tamaddun-e Islāmī wa Adabīyāt-e Arabī*, Tus Publishers, Tehran, 1374.

Malek, H.M. "The Coinage of the Sasanian King Kavād II (AD 628)," *The Numismatic Chronicle*, vol. 155, 1995, pp. 119–129.

——. and Sarkhos Curtis, V. "History and Coinage of the Sasanian Queen Bōrān (AD 629–631)," *The Numismatic Chronicle*, vol. 158, 1998, pp. 113–129.

Marquart, J. *Ērānšahr nach der Geographie des Ps. Moses Xorenacʿi*, Weidmannsche Buchhandlung, Berlin, 1901.

Marshak B.I. and Negmatov, N.N. "Sogdiana," *History of Civlizations of Central Asia*, vol. III, ed. B.A. Litvinsky *et al.*, UNESCO Publishing, Paris, 1996, pp. 235–258.

Mazdapur, K. "Chāštehā, Se Nahle-ye Feghhī dar Rūzegār-e Sāsānī," *Yād-e Bahār*, Tehran, 1376, pp. 383–412.

——. "Garmabe-ye bastani-ye Iran (Ancient Iranian Bathhouses)," *Farhang*, vol. 9, no. 3, 1996, pp. 1–11.

Melikian-Chirvani, A.S. "The Iranian bazm in Early Persian Sources," *Banquets d'Orient*, ed. R. Gyselen, Res Orientales IV, Bures-sur-Yvette, 1992, pp. 95–120.

de Menasce, J.P. de "La conqête de l'iranisme et la récupération des mages hellénisés," *Annuairel'École Partique de Hautes Études*, 1956–1957, pp. 3–12.

——. "Le protecteur des pauvres dans l'Iran sasanide," *Mélanges Henri Massé*, Tehran 1963, p. 283.

——. *Feux et fondations pieuses dans le droit sassanide*, Librairie C. Klincksieck, Paris, 1964.

——. "Textes pehlevis sur les Qanats," *Acta Orientalia*, vol. 30, 1966, reprint in *Études Iraniennes*, Studia Iranica Cahier, Paris, 1985, pp. 145–153.

Meskūb, Sh. *Sōg ī Sīyāwaš*, Khwārazmī Publishers, Tehran, 1374.

Minorsky, V. "Vīs u Rāmīn, a Parthian Romance," *Bulletin of the School of Oriental and African Studies*, vol. XI, 1946, pp. 741–763; XII, 1947, pp. 20–35; XVI, 1954, pp. 91–92.

Mochiri, M.I. "Garmikirmān: A Sasanian and Early Islamic Mint in Kirmān Province, *Numismatic Chronicle*, 145, 1985, pp. 109–122.

Molé, M. "Le Problème des sectes Zoroastriennes dans les livres Pehlevis," *Oriens*, vol. 13–14, 1960–1961, pp. 12–14.

Momigliano, A. "Persian Historiography, Greek Historiography, and Jewish Historiography," *The Classical Foundations of Modern Historiography*, University of California Press, Berkeley, Los Angeles, London, 1990.

Moorey, P.R.S. *Kish Excavations 1923–1933*, Oxford, 1978.

Mori, S. "The narrative structure of the Paikuli Inscription," *Orient*, vol. 30–31, 1995, pp. 182–193.

Morony, M. "Continuity and Change in the Administrative Geography of Late Sasanian and Early Islamic al-'Iraq," *IRAN, Journal of the British Institute of Persian Studies*, vol. XX, 1982, pp. 1–49.

——. *Iraq After the Muslim Conquest*, Princeton University Press, Princeton, New Jersey, 1984.

——. "Syria Under the Persians 610–629," *Proceedings of the Second Symposium on the History of Bilād al-Shām During the Early Islamic Period up to 40 AH/640 AD*, ed. M.A. Bakhit, Amman, 1987, pp. 87–95.

——. "Landholding in Seventh-Century Iraq: Late Sasanian and Early Islamic Patterns," *The Islamic Middle East, 700–1900: Studies in Economic and Social History*, ed. A.L. Udovitch, The Darwin Press, Princeton, New Jersey, 1981, pp. 135–176.

——."Mazdak," *The Encylcopaedia of Islam*, vol. vi, 1991, pp. 449–452.

——. "Sāsānids," *The Encycleopaedia of Islam*, 1998, pp. 70–83.

——. "Magic and Society in Late Sasanian Iraq," presented at a symposium on *Prayer, Magic, and the Stars in the Ancient and Late Antique World*, March 3–5, 2000 at the University of Washington, Seattle.

——. "Land Use and Settlement Patterns in Late Sasanian and Early Islamic Iraq," *The Byzantine and Early Islamic Near East, Land Use and Settlement Patterns*, eds. G.R.D. King and A. Cameron, vol. II, The Darwin Press, Princeton, New Jersey, 1994, pp. 221–229.

——. "Trade and Exchange: The Sasanian World to Islam," *The Late Antiquity and Early Islam Workshop, Trade and Exchange AD 565–770*, unpublished draft.

Munk, S. *Notice sur Rabbi Saadia Gaon et sa version arabe d'saïe et sur une version persane manuscrite de la Bibliothèque Royale*, Paris, 1834.

Naboodah, H.M. "The Commercial activity of Bahrain and Oman in the early Middle Ages," *Proceddings of the Seminar for Arabian Studies*, vol. 22, London, 1992, pp. 81–96.

Nai, H. *Studies in Chinese Archaeology*, The Institute of Arcaheological Academia Sinica, Peking, 1961.

——. "A Survery of Sasanian Silver Coins Found in China," *K'ao Ku 'Hsüeh Pao*, no. 1, 1974, pp. 91–110.

Naveh, J. and Shaked, Sh. *Amulets and Magic Bowls, Aramaic Incantations of Late Antiquity*, The Magnes Press, The Hebrew University, Jerusalem, 1998.

Nawabī, Y.M. *Opera Minora*, ed. M. Tavoossi, Navid Publications, Shiraz, 1998.

Neely, J.A. "Sasanian and Early Islamic Water-Control and Irrigations

Systems on the Deh Luran Plain, Iran," ed. T.E. Downing and M. Gibson, *Irrigation's Impact on Society*, University of Arizona Press, Tuscon, 1974, pp. 21–42.

Netzer, A. "Some Notes on the Characterization of Cyrus the Great in the Jewish and Judeo-Persian Writings," *Acta Iranica, Hommage Universel*, vol. II, E.J. Brill, Leiden, 1974, pp. 35–54.

Neusner, J. "How Much Iranian in Jewish Babylonia?," *Journal of the American Oriental Society*, vol. 95, no. 2, 1975, pp. 184–190.

——. "Jews in Iran," *The Cambridge History of Iran*, vol. 3(2), ed. E. Yarshater, Cambridge University Press, 1983, pp. 909–923.

Nikitin, A.B. "Middle Persian Ostraca from South Turkmenistan," *East and West*, vol. 42, no. 1, 1992, pp. 103–125.

Nyberg, S.H. *Religionen des Alten Iran*, Osnabrück, Otto Zeller, 1966.

Omrānī, N. *Šāpuragān*, Aštād Publishers, Tehran, 1379.

Ostrogorsky, G. *History of the Byzantine State*, Rutgers University Press, Revised Edition, New Brunswick, New Jersey, 1969.

Von der Osten, H.H. and Naumann, R. *Takht-I Suleiman*, Berlin, 1961.

Panaino, A. *La novella degli scacchi e della tavola reale. Un'antica fonte orientale sui due giochi da tavola piu diffuse nel mondo eurasiatico tra Tardoantico e Medioevo e sulla loro simbologia militare e astrologica*, Mimesis, Milan, 1999.

——. "The baγān of the Fratarakas: Gods or 'divine' Kings?," *Religious themes and texts of pre-Islamic Iran and Central Asia: Studies in honour of Professor Gherardo Gnoli on the occasion of his 65th birthday on 6 December 2002*, eds. C. Cereti, M. Maggi, and E. Provasi, Wiesbaden, 2002, pp. 283–306.

——. Panaino, A. "Astral Characters of Kingship in the Sasanian and Byzantine World," *La Persia e Bisanzio*, Accademia Nazionale dei Lincei, Roma, 2004, pp. 555–594.

Parhām, S. "Tārīkh-e khoan-e farš-bāfī-e fārs," (The ancient history of carpet weaving in Fārs), *AYANDEH*, vol. 7, no. 4, 1981, pp. 262–263.

Périkhanian, A. "Notes sur le lexique iranien et arménien," *Revue des Études Arméniennes*, Nouvelle série, Tome V, Paris, 1968, pp. 5–30.

Peters, F.E. *The Harvest of Hellenism, A History of the Near East from Alexander the Great to the Triumph of Christianity*, Barnes and Noble, New York, 1970 (reprint 1996).

Piacentini, V.F. "Ardashīr I Pāpakān and the wars against the Arabs: working hypothesis on the Sasanian hold on the Gulf," *Proceedings of the Seminar for Arabian Studies*, vol. 15, London, 1985, pp. 57–78.

——. *Merchants-Merchandise and Miliatry Power in the Persian Gulf (Sōriyān/Shahriyāj Sīrāf)*, Atti Della Academia Nazionale Dei Lincei, Roma, 1992.

——. "Madīna/Shahr, Qarya? Deh, Nāhiya/Rustāq The City as Political Administrative Institution: the Continuity of a Sasanian Model," *Jerusalem Studies in Arabic and Islam*, vol. 17, 1994, pp. 85–67.

Pigulevskaïa, N.V. "Economic Relations in Iran during the IV–VI Centuries AD," *Journal of the K.R. Cama Oriental Institute*, no. 38, 1956, pp. 60–81.

——. *Les villes de l'état iranien aux époques parthe et sassanide*, Paris, 1963.

Pirart, E. *Kayān Yasn, l'origine avestique des dynasties mythiques d'Iran*, Barcelona, Editorial Ausa, 1992.

Piras, A. "Mesopotamian Sacred Marriage and Pre-Islamic Iran," *Melammu Symposia IV*, eds. A. Panaino and A. Piras, Milano, 2004, pp. 249–259.

Potter, D.S. *The Roman Empire at Bay (AD 180–395)*, Routledge, London and New York, 2004.

Potts, D.T. "A Sasanian Lead Horse from North Eastern Arabia," *Iranica Antiqua*, vol. XXVIII, 1993, pp. 193–200.

Puhvel, J. *Comparative Mythology*, John Hopkins University Press.

Reider, C. "Legend Variations of the Coins of Ardashir the Great," *Oriental Numismatic Society*, no. 147, Winter 1996, pp. 10–11.

Rezā'ī Bāgh-Bīdī, "Sassanian Neologisms and Their Influence on Dari Persian," *Nāmeye farhangestān*, vol. 15, no. 3, pp. 145–158.

Rose, J. "Three Queens, Two Wives, and a Goddess: Roles and Images of Women in Sasanian Iran," *Women in the Medival Islamic World*, ed. G. Hambly, 1998, pp. 29–54.

Rostovtzeff, M. *Drua-Europos and its Art*, Clarendon Press, Oxford, 1938.

——. *Rome*, Translated from Russian by J.D. Duff, Oxford University Press, London, Oxford, New York, 1960.

Rubin, Z. "The Reforms of Khusrō Anūshirwān," in *The Byzantine and Early Islamic Near East, States, Resources and Armies*, vol. III, ed. A. Cameron, Princeton, 1995, pp. 227–296.

——. "The Roman Empire in the Res Gestae Divi Saporis," *Ancient Iran and the Mediterranean World*, ed. E. Dąbrowa, Electrum 2, Jagiellonian University Press, Kraków, 1998, pp. 177–186

——. "The Sasanid Monarchy," *The Cambridge Ancient History*, vol. 14, 2000, pp. 638–661.

Russell, J.R. "Advocacy of the Poor: The Maligned Sasanian Order," *Journal of the K.R. Cama Oriental Institute*, Bombay, 1986, pp. 74–142.

——. *Zoroastrianism in Armenia*, Harvard Iranian Series, Cambridge, Massachusets, 1987.

——. "Kartīr and Mānī: a shamanistic model of their conflict," *Iranica Varia: Papers in honor of Professor Ehsan Yarshater*, E.J. Brill, Leiden, 1990, pp. 180–193.

——. "On Mysticism and Esotericism among the Zoroastrians," *Iranian Studies*, vol. 26, nos. 1–2, 1993, pp. 73–94.

Sanjana, D.P. "The Alleged Practice of Consanguineous Marriages in Ancient Iran," *The Collected Works of the Late Dastur Darab Peshotan Sanjana*, British India Press, Bombay, 1932, pp. 462–499.

Sarkārāti, B. "Akhbār-e Tārīkhī dar Āthār ī Mānavī: Mānī wa Šāpūr," *Sāyehā-ye Šekār Šode*, Našr Qatre, Tehran, 1378, pp. 163–192.

Sarkhosh Curtis, V. and Malek, H.M. "History and Coinage of the Sasanian Queen Bōrān (AD 629–631)," *The Numismatic Chronicle*, vol. 158, 1998, p. 113–129.

——. "Minstrels in Ancient Iran," *The Art and Archaeology of Ancient Persia,*

New Light on the Parthian and Sasanian Empires, eds. V. Sarkhosh Curtis, *et al*, I.B.Tauris Publishers, London and New York, 1998, pp. 182–187.

Schafer, E.H. "Iranian Merchants in T'and Dynasty Tales," *University of California Publications in Semitic Philology*, vol. 11, 1951, pp. 403–422.

——. *The Golden Peaches of Samarkand, A Study of T'ang Exotics*, University of California Press, 1963.

Scharfe, H. "Sacred Kingship, Warlords, and Nobility," in *Ritual, State and History in South India, Essays in Honour of J.C. Heesterman*, ed. A.W. Van den Hoek, *et al.*, E.J. Brill, Leiden, New York, Köln, p. 309–322.

Schmidt, H.-P. "The Incorruptibility of the Sinner's Corpse," *Studien zur Indologie und Iranistik*, vol. 19, 1994, pp. 247–268.

Schmit, R. *Compendium Linguarum Iranicarum*, Dr. Ludwig Reichert Verlad, Wiesbaden, 1989.

Schippmann, K. *Grundzüge der Geschichte des sasanidischen Reiches*, Darmstadt, 1990.

Schwartz. M. *Studies in the texts of the Christian Sogdians*, Ph.D. dissertation of the University of California, Berkeley, California, 1967.

——. "*Sasm, Sesen, St. Sisinnios, Sesengen Barpharangés s, and . . . 'Semanglof,'" *Bulletin of the Asia Institute*, vol. 10, 1996, pp. 253–257.

——. "Sesen: a Durable East Mediterranean God in Iran," *Proceedings of the Third European Conference of Iranian Studies held in Cambridge, 11th to 15th September 1995*, Part 1, Old and Middle Iranian Studies, ed. N. Sims-Williams, Wiesbaden, 1998, Dr. Ludwig Reichert Verlag, pp. 9–13.

——. "Saugand Xurdan, 'To take an oath' not *'to drink sulpher'," *Études irano-aryennes offertes à Gilbert Lazard*, ed. C.-H. de Fouchécour and Ph. Gignoux, Paris, 1989, pp. 293–296.

——. "Kerdīr's Clairvoyants: Extra-Iranian and Gathic Perspectives," unpublished manuscript, 2006, pp. 1–12.

Sellheim, R. "Tāq-ī Bustān und Kaiser Julian (361–363)," *Oriens*, vol. 34, 1994, pp. 354–366.

Sellwood, D. "Minor States in Sourthern Iran," *The Cambridge History of Iran*, ed. E. Yarshater, vol. 3(1), pp. 299–321.

Senior, B. "Some new coins from Sind," *Oriental Numismatic Society*, no. 149, Summer 1996, pp. 6–7.

Shahbazi, A.Sh. "Narse's Relief at Naqš-i Rustam," *Archäologische Mitteilungen aus Iran*, vol. 16, 1983, pp. 255–268.

——. "Army," *Encyclopaedia Iranica*, vol. II, 1987, pp. 490–499.

——. "Studies in Sasanian Prosopography: III Barm-i Dilak: Symbolism of Offering Flowers," *The Art and Archaeology of Ancient Persia*, ed. V. Sarkhosh, *et al.*, I.B.Tauris, London, 1998, pp. 58–66.

——. "Early Sasanians' Claim to Achaemenid Heritage," *Nāme-ye Irān-e Bāstān, The International Journal of Ancient Iranian Studies*, vol. 1, no. 1, 2001, pp. 61–74.

Shaked, Sh. "Esoteric Trends in Zoroastrianism," *Proceedings of the Israel Academy of Sciences and Humanities*, vol. 3, 1969, pp. 175–222.

——. "Some Legal and Administrative Terms," *Monumentum H.S. Nyberg II*, Acta Iranica, E.J. Brill, Leiden, 1975, pp. 215–226.

——. "From Iran to Islam: Notes on Some Themes in Transmission," *Jerusalem Studies in Arabic and Islam*, vol. 4, 1984, pp. 31–67.

——. "First Man, First King, Notes on Semitic-Iranian Syncretism and Iranian Mythological Transformations," *Gilgul, Essays on Transformation, Revolution and Permanence in the History of Religions Dedicated to R.J. Zwi Werblowsky*, eds. Sh. Shaked, *et al.*, E.J. Brill, Leiden, 1987, pp. 238–256.

——. "Middle Persian Translations of the Bible," *Encyclopaedia Iranica*, vol. iv, Routledge and Kegan Paul, London and New York, 1990, pp. 206–207.

——. "Administrative Functions of Priests in the Sasanian Period," *Proceedings of the First European Conference of Iranian Studies*, 1990, pp. 261–273.

——. "The Myth of Zurvan: Cosmogony and Eschatology," *Messiah and Christos, Studies in the Jewish Origins of Christianity Presented to David Flusser on the Occasion of His Seventy-Fifth Birthday*, ed. I. Gruenwald, *et al.*, J.C.B. Mohr (Paul Siebeck), Tübingen, 1992, pp. 229–240.

——. "The Pahlavi Amulet and Sasanian Courts of Law," *Bulletin of the Asia Institute*, vol. 7, 1993, pp. 165–172.

——. *Dualism in Transformation: Varieties of Religion in Sasanian Iran,* Jordan Lectures in Comparative Religion, School of Oriental and African Studies, University of London, 1994.

—— and J. Naveh, *Amulets and Magic Bowls, Aramaic Incantations of Late Antiquity*, The Magnes Press, The Hebrew University, Jerusalem, 1998.

Shaki, M. "Drist-Dēnān," *Ma'ārif*, vol. 10, no. 1, 1372, pp. 28–52.

——. "Some Basic Tenets of the Eclectic Metaphysics of the Dēnkartd," *Archív Orientálni*, vol. 38, 1970, pp. 277–312.

——. "Sasanian Matrimonial Relations," *Arhív Orientalní*, vol. 39, 1971, pp. 322–345.

——. "The Concept of Obligated Successorship in the Mādiyān ī Hazār Dādestān," *Hommages et Opera Minor Monumentum H.S. Nyberg*, Acta Iranica, vol. ii, E.J. Brill, Leiden, 1975, pp. 256–263.

——. "The Social Doctrine of Mazdak in the Light of Middle Persian Evidence," *Archív Orientálni*, vol. 46, 1978, pp. 289–306.

——. "The Dēnkard Account of the History of the Zoroastrian Scriptures," *Archív Orientalní*, vol. 49, 1981, pp. 114–125.

——. "Dādwar, Dādwarīh," *Encyclopaedia Iranica*, vol. VI. 1984, p. 558.

——. "The Cosmologcial and Cosmological Teachings of Mazdak," *Papers in Honour of Professor Mary Boyce*, Acta Iranica 25, E.J. Brill, Leiden, 1985, pp. 527–543.

——. "Observations on the Ayādgār ī Zarērān," *Archiv Orientálni*, vol. 54, 1986, pp. 257–271.

——. "Pahlavica," *A Green Leaf: Papers in Honour of Prof. J. Asmussen*, Acta Iranica 28, Leiden, 1988, pp. 96–98.

——. "A Signal Catalogue of Sasanian Seals and Bullae," *Archív Orientální*, vol. 57, 1989, pp. 167–168.

——. "Sasan ke bud?," *Iranshenasi*, vol. 2, no. 1, Spring 1990, pp. 77–88.

——. "An Appraisal of Encyclopaedia Iranica, vols. II and III," *Archīv Orientálni*, vol. 59, 1991, pp. 406–409.

——. "The Filet of Nobility," Bulletin of the Asia Institute, Vol. 4, 1990, pp. 277–279.

——. "Dād," *Encyclopaedia Iranica*, vol. VI, 1994, pp. 544–545.

——. "Family Law," *Encyclopaedia Iranica*, vol. IX, Bibliotheca Persica, New York, 1999, pp. 184–189.

——. "Divorce," *Encyclopaedia Iranica*, vol. IX, Bibliotheca Persica, New York, 1999, pp. 444–445.

——. "Class System iii. Parthian and Sasanian Period," *Encyclopaedia Iranica*, 1999, pp. 652–658.

Shayegan, R. "The Evolution of the Concept of Xwadāy 'God'," *Acta Orientalia Academiae Scientiarum Hungaricae*, vol. 51, nos. 1–2, 1998, pp. 31–54.

Sims-Williams, N. "The Sogdian Fragments of the British Library," *The Indo-Iranian Journal*, vol. 18, 1976, pp. 43–82.

——. "Bactrian," *Compendium Linguarum Iranicarum*, ed. R. Schmitt, Dr. Ludwig Reichert Verlad, Wiesbaden, 1989, pp. 230–235.

——. "Sogdian," *Compendium Linguarum Iranicarum*, ed. R. Schmitt, Dr. Ludwig Reichert Verlad, Wiesbaden, 1989, pp. 173–192.

——. "Sogdian Translations of the Bible," *Encyclopaedia Iranica*, vol. iv, Routledge and Kegan Paul, New York and London, 1990, p. 207.

——. *Bactrian Documents, Legal and Economic Documents*, vol. I, Oxford University Press, 2000.

Skjærvø, P.O. and H. Humbach, *The Sassanian Inscription of Paikuli*, Wiesbaden, 1983.

——. "Kirdir's Vision: Translation and Analysis," *Archaeologische Mitteilungen aus Iran*, vol. 16, 1983, pp. 269–306.

——. "Thematic and linguistic parallels in the Achaemenian and Sassanian inscriptions," *Papers in Honour of Professor Mary Boyce*, Acta Iranica 25, E.J. Brill, Leiden, 1985, pp. 593–603.

——. "A Seal-Amulet of the Sasanian Era: Imagery and Typology, the Inscription, and Technical Comments," *Bulletin of the Asia Institute*, vol. 6, 1992, pp. 43–59.

——. "The Joy of the Cup: A Pre-Sasanian Middle Persian Inscription on a Silver Bowl," *Bulletin of the Asia Institute*, vol. 11, 1997, pp. 93–104.

——. "Iranian Elements in Manichaeism," *Au Carrefour des Religions: Mélanges offerts à Philippe Gignoux*, Res Orientales VII, 1995, pp. 263–284.

——. "Royalty in Early Iranian Literature," *Proceedings of the Third European Conference of Iranian Studies*, Part 1, Old and Middle Iranian Studies, ed. N. Sims-Williams, Dr. Ludwig Reichert Verlag, Wiesbaden, 1998, pp. 106–115.

Soudavar, A. *The Aura of the Kings: Legitimacy and Divine Sanction in Iranian Kingship*, Mazda Publishers, Costa Mesa, 2003.

Spuler, B. "Trade in the Eastern Islamic Countries in the Early Centuries," *Islam and the Trade in Asia*, 1970, pp. 11–20.

Sunderman, V. Sundermann, "Commendatio pauperum," *Altorientalische Forschungen*, IV, Akademie-Verlag, Berlin, 1976, pp. 179–191.

——. "Mittelpersisch," *Compendium Linguarum Iranicarum*, ed. R. Schmitt, Dr. Ludwig Reichert Verlad, Wiesbaden, 1989, pp. 138–164.

Le Strange, G. *The Lands of the Eastern Caliphate*, Barnes and Noble, New York, 1966.

Stratos, A.N. *Byzantium in the Seventh Century*, vol. I, Amsterdam, 1968.

Tafazzolī, A. "A List of Trades and Crafts in the Sassanian Period," *Archaeologische Mitteilungen aus Iran*, vol. 7, 1974, pp. 191–196.

——. *Tārīx-e Adabiyāt-e Irān Pēš az Isl*ām, Soxan Publishers, 1376.

——. "Un chapitre du Dēnkard sur les guerriers," *Au carrefour des religions: Mélanges offerts á Philippe Gignoux*, Res Orientales VII, Peeters, Leuven, 1995, pp. 297–302.

——. *Sasanian Society*, Ehsan Yarshater Distinguished Lecture Series, Bibliotheca Persica Press, New York, 2000.

Tavadia, J.C. *Die mittelpersiche Sprache und Literature der Zarathustrier*, Leipzig, 1956.

Thierry, F. "Sur les monnaies sassanides trouvées en chine," *Circulations des monnaies, des marchandises et des biens*, ed. R. Gyselen, Res Orientales, vol. V, Bures-sur-Yvette, 1993, pp. 89–140.

Utas, B. "Non-Religious Book Pahlavi Literature as a Source on the History of Central Asia," *Studies in the Sources on the History of Pre-Islamic Central Asia*, ed. J. Harmatta, Akadémiai Kiadó, Budapest, 1979, pp. 119–128.

——. "Chess I. The History of Chess in Persia," *Encyclopaedia Iranica*, ed. E. Yarshater, vol. V, 1992, p. 395.

Venetis, E. "The Sasanian Occupation of Egypt (7th Cent. AD) According to Some Pahlavi Papyri Abstracts," *Greco-Arabica*, vols. 9–10, 2004, pp. 403–412.

Weber, D. *Ostraca, Papyri und Pergamente*, Corpus Inscriptionum Iranicarum, Part III Pahlavi Inscriptions, London, 1992.

Wenke, R.J. "Western Iran in the Partho-Sasanian Period: The Imperial Transformation," ed. F. Hole, *The Archaeology of Western Iran, Settlement and Society from Prehistory to the Islamic Conquest*, Smithsonian Institution Press, Washington, D.C., and London, 1987, pp. 251–281.

West, E.W. "The Pahalvi Inscriptions at Kanheri," *Indian Antiquary*, 1880, pp. 265–268.

——. West, "The meaning of Khvētūk-das," *Pahlavi Texts*, Part II, Oxford University Press, 1882, pp. 389–430.

——. "Pahlavi Literature," *Grundriss der Iranischen Philologie*, II/2, pp. 75–129.

Whitehouse, D. "Chinese Stoneware from Siraf: The Earliest Finds," *South Asian Archaeology*, 1971, pp. 241–243.

Whitehouse, D. and Williamson, A. "Sasanian Maritime Trade," *Iran*, vol. XI, 1973, pp. 29–50.

——. "Maritime Trade in the Arabian Sea: The 9th and 10th Centuries AD," *South Asian Archaeology*, ed. M. Taddei, vol. 2, 1977, pp. 865–887.

Widengren, G. "The Establishment of the Sasanian dynasty in the light of new evidence," *La Persia nel Medioevo*, Academia Nazionale dei Lincei, Roma, 1971, pp. 711–782.

Wiesehöfer, J. "Ardašīr I," *Encyclopaedia Iranica*, ed. E. Yarshater, vol. II, 1987, pp. 371–376.

——. *Ancient Persia From 550 BC to 650 AD*, I.B.Tauris Publishers, London and New York, 1996, pp. 151–222.

Wilkinson, J.C. "Sūhār in the Early Islamic Period: The Written Evidence," *South Asian Archaeology*, 1973, ed. E. Taeddi, vol. 2, pp. 887–908.

——. "The Julanda of Oman," *The Journal of Oman Studies*, vol. I, 1975, pp. 97–108.

Williamson, A. "Persian Gulf Commerce in the Sassanian Period and the First Two Centuries of Islam," *Bāstān Chenāsī wa Honar-e Iran*," vol. 9–10, 1972, pp. 97–109.

Winter, E. and Dignas, B. *Rom und das Perserreich, Zwei Weltmächte zwischen Konfrontation und Koexistenz*, Berlin, 2001.

Wulff, H.E. *The Traditional Crafts of Persia*, The Massachusetts Institute of Technology, 1966.

Yarshater, E. "Mazdakism," *The Cambridge History of Iran*, vol. III (2), Cambridge, Massachusets, 1983, pp. 991–1024.

Zaehner, R.C. *Zurvan, A Zoroastrian Dilemma*, Biblio and Tannen, New York, 1955 (reprint 1972).

Index